Southern Exposure

A Solo Sea Kayaking Journey around New Zealand's South Island

CHRIS DUFF

FALCON®

GUILFORD, CONNECTICUT
HELENA, MONTANA

AN IMPRINT OF THE GLOBE PEQUOT PRESS

To all those who set off on journeys.

To those who see them off with love and await their return,
and to those who welcome them along the way.

May we all share in the journey.

Maps created by Rusty Nelson © The Globe Pequot Press
Text design by Casey Shain
Illustration on pp. 22–23 by Todd Telander.
All interior photos by the author.

Library of Congress Cataloging-in-Publication Data
Duff, Chris.
Southern exposure : a solo sea kayaking journey around New Zealand's South
    Island / Chris Duff.— 1st ed,
  p. cm.
ISBN 0-7627-2595-8
  1. Sea kayaking—New Zealand. 2. Duff, Chris—Journeys—New Zealand.
    I. Title.

GV776.91.A2D84 2003
796.1'224'0993—dc21

                             2002192712

Manufactured in the United States of America
First Edition/First Printing

Contents

Foreword

THE SOFT AUTUMN SUN WARMED THE BEACH IN FRONT OF US as we sat on a driftwood log looking over Puget Sound toward the peaks of the Cascade Mountains. Chris Duff talked of experiences he had had paddling distant coastlines, and I talked of having reached the time of life for pensive evaluation and the sharing of memories from long ago. The passion for kayaking upon open waters and beneath endless skies had brought us together many years ago, forming a relationship nourished by shared values that enhance our love for life. We talked of paddling stretches of ocean and of time, filled with an emptiness that required our focused determination. We spoke of situations where we had needed all our physical and mental faculties just to survive, to stay on course and to continue moving forward. We recalled times when the waves were full of sprinkled sunshine like scattered diamonds, and also of the radiance of the moon's glow on calm seas. And we spoke of the memories of people who shared a smile and opened their hearts to ours. Our talk was about the parallel journeys of paddling and that of life: how the moments of sitting side by side on a drift log bring to full realization the value of conscious living.

In comparison, we have both experienced the challenges and rewards of journeys: of loneliness and craving the companionship of another, and of aloneness, the reality at times, of total dependence on ourselves for survival. Sea kayaking is a paradigm of life's journey. Our futures lie beyond the horizon. And the path to self-discovery is moving toward, not away from that horizon. I believe Chris's book is about living life in that manner, of meeting the challenges of life: learning and sharing from others, and moving forward, believing in one's self and trusting in one's abilities.

I wish you well.

Werner Furrer Sr.
Founder of Werner Paddles

Acknowledgments

ONCE AGAIN I FIND MYSELF THINKING OF THE DOZENS of people who helped me not only with the writing of this book but also on the paddling journey. Both the journey and the book are products of cooperation and commitment without which neither would have succeeded. Without the sponsorship from companies like Werner Paddles, Nigel Dennis Kayaks, Kokatat, Cascade Designs, and SnapDragon, there would never have been a story to share in book form. Behind these company names are folks like Shelley and Bruce Furrer of Werner Paddles, who not only contributed the superb Molokai paddles but also covered much of the expense of the expedition. Thanks also to Nigel Dennis, who gave me an Explorer for the trip and whose boat I managed to almost break in half. Sorry about that, Nigel—it's still my favorite boat. Thanks also to the folks at Kokatat, who designed, cut, stitched, and sealed the incredibly durable products upon which my life depended. Thanks to Tom at Cascade Designs for arranging all the gear that I slept on, drank out of, used and abused for four and a half months. And thanks to Rich at SnapDragon for the bomb-proof spray deck and the back band that kept the seas out and me in the cockpit.

And how do I thank the people of New Zealand who never had anything to say but "Good on ye mate." I've had the joy of sharing my life with some wonderful people in my travels, and the Kiwis rank right up there with the very best folks I've met anywhere in the world. Thanks to Paddy Dillon, who brought me out of the torrential rains, drove me two hours into Dunedin for new tent poles, and fed me for two days while the gales ripped the east coast apart. And thanks to Innes and Helen McMillian, who took me in and showed me a bit of farming life. A big thank you to Tony Limburg, who met me with a cup of tea at the water's edge in Dunedin harbor with the perfect line, "I hope you take sugar in your tea." That's the kind of greeting a traveler needs at the end of a long slog into the wind. And Berni—thanks for sharing your secret of smoking fish, of your stories of world travel, and your spirit.

To Sam, Martha, and Gay—my shore crew and food cache team—I offer my thanks and a continued deep friendship that hopefully will include other journeys.

To the crew at Safeway, at Bonny's Bakery, and at the newspaper, thank you for your support. And to Mahde', thank you for your support and for the candle that you kept burning for my safe return.

Thank you to Al Zob, who not only designed but maintained the Web site for www.goals.com, which covered the trip. Without his work I would not have been able to share the trip with folks all over the world, nor would I have had their encouragement. Thank you to Lisa Redlin for the chapter icons as well as the initial work on the maps.

Perhaps the greatest thanks is to my family. I am blessed to have the support and love of parents and siblings who may not always understand my passions but have always given me the freedom to leave and the secure welcome of home when I return. It is a gift that few people in the world receive with such openness.

This book then is for all of you—and for all of the people along my route who extended a hand to the stranger who came ashore in the yellow kayak and stayed for just a short time. I thank all of you and share with you the entirety of the journey.

Introduction

As you go the way of life
You will see a great chasm.
Jump!
It is not as far as you think.
—Unknown

I HAVE A SELF-PROCLAIMED WEAKNESS FOR MAPS, especially maps of small countries surrounded by oceans, maps that can be folded out and knelt upon as I trace their convoluted coastlines with my finger, imagining a route along their shores and wondering who might live in the coves and behind the hooks of land that offer both access and protection from the sea. On these maps that I have studied and that have drawn me away from home and out onto the oceans of the world numerous times, I see a balance of exposure and the need for safe havens. I am by nature a curious person, one who loves to learn from people on their own travels and one who thirsts for the quiet of solitude. Maybe that's why island countries have their appeal; they offer the contrasts upon which I thrive—the land for the shelter and the human contact I seek and the open sea for its restless energy and its depths of infinite connection to the soul.

I didn't grow up with the sea at my doorstep and its smell on the winds surrounding my home. But after enlisting straight out of high school and working for seven years as a U.S. Navy diver, I discovered a love for the sea and its constantly shifting moods. The sea challenged and demanded something of me that nothing else had. It demanded that I be focused on the moment, aware that I was a visitor in a potentially hostile environment. In its watery seclusion I found a place where my slender build and introspective personality fit and where my confidence and self-awareness took off with the steady kick of black rubber fins.

The lessons of the sea came fast as a diver. I worked in its depths, gliding effortlessly with fins and aluminum tanks beneath ships bristling with Cold War tensions. I learned to swim against the sea's currents and to work blinded in waters where the visibility was zero and the water temperature in winter was cold enough to freeze the regulators upon which we depended. Steel flanges were bolted onto ships, wrenches were turned with the weight of bodies braced against steel hulls, and inspections were made with underwater video cameras of ships damaged by the Cold War cat-and-mouse games of the superpowers. At another duty station I wore the spun-copper helmet of yesteryear's diving technology and learned to walk on the bottom of the ocean. With lead-weighted shoes and the deliberate but slow movements of a spacewalker, I dragged salvage lines to a crumbled jet with pilot, copilot, and navigator still strapped to their loaded ejection seats. Nitrogen narcosis muddled the carefully laid plans discussed in detail 170 feet above the wreckage. In the currents and the stirred-up silt of the ocean bottom, my thoughts thickened like molasses in the below-freezing temperatures. Thoughts had to be sorted between the hiss of inhaled air and the gurgle of exhaled bubbles that slowly floated upward from the blackness of the sea floor. In this weightless, silent world, I learned to work and think through the confusion and disorientation that was part of diving.

Decades later, long after I had left the challenges of working beneath the sea, the lessons I learned and the ability to focus and stay "on task" when things went awry were still a part of me. In a foreign and potentially dangerous environment, I had learned the skills of discipline and self-control, which would serve me well in the years to come.

Perhaps it was a natural progression that my love for adventure and the sea, plus traveling and meeting people, should lead me on the path that now seems obvious—a choice of spending the last eighteen years of my life exploring various coastlines and cultures of the world. In the intervening years since leaving the navy, I had taken to a different kind of interaction with the sea—paddling a sea kayak—which allowed me to continue learning about this world that I had come to respect so deeply.

Two months after leaving the navy in 1983, a map of the United States and Canada, which I serendipitously found on my bookshelf, led me to purchase my first kayak and to begin an 8,000-mile trip around the eastern third of North America. I was at a crossroad in my life, leaving the order and routine of the military behind and suddenly having to choose who I was to become and what I was to do in my new life. The red-decked kayak, and an ebbing tide on the mile-wide Hudson River, started me on a journey that continues to this day—a journey of outward exploration and inner self-discovery.

When I started that first trip in the bitter cold air of a March morning, I knew very little about kayaking other than how to do an Eskimo roll. And of course I knew nothing of the challenges in the seasons ahead: violent winds and lightning storms, ice crystals forming on my life jacket, waves higher than any I could have imagined, intense heat, dehydration, and fear—which lead to the greatest threat of all—self-doubt. It would seem foolish to set off on such a journey, to purposefully paddle into a tide that would carry me away from family, home, security, and what passed for the norm in society. It may seem foolish, but my journey was in some ways no different than journeys that are begun every day with the same commitment, the same hopes, and the same thread of a dream. The risks and the unknowns are the price we pay anytime we choose to set off on a new path. How we face the changes and the currents we meet determine whether we turn back or continue down the chosen route. Hopefully a path is found that helps us see ourselves as unique individuals and helps us celebrate who we are in the world.

A year and a half after I followed the ebb tide down the Hudson, I paddled back upriver on a flooding tide. The journey had come full circle back to a place where new choices and new paths lay waiting. By the time I returned to the same beach from which I had departed, I had acquired not only the skills of a sea paddler—judgment, caution, and endurance—but also a deeper sense of who I was as an individual and how I wanted to spend my life. The journey had given me the time to observe and to reaffirm what I must have already known in my heart—that beneath the hurried pace of our modern times there was still the slow turning of the seasons and the tides where I had found a sense of belonging. The journey that had begun on a blustery cold March morning ended in the warmth of an Indian-summer September. I was home, and for a little while I was content to savor the trip and to settle back into the comfort of family and friends.

Two years after the completion of the first trip, the sea once again began its subtle calling. I had moved to upstate New York and proven to myself that I could make a living as a carpenter. I had enjoyed the challenge of learning the carpentry trade and had bought several dilapidated and abandoned houses, which I fixed up, sold, and then moved on to the next building project. I had money, a job, and enough time to paddle—but not on the sea. And the sea was what I missed.

For the last year and a half of my navy days, I had been stationed in Scotland and still had a map of Great Britain somewhere in the sea chest that held most of my memorabilia. In a restless moment of the spirit, I found the map, spread it out on the floor, and slowly began to think of the possibilities of another journey. The more I thought about it and reminisced about my first trip, the more attractive a trip around Great Britain became. The carpentry provided a living and allowed me to develop my creative side, but it couldn't compare with the adventure and challenges I had found in my sea-kayaking travels. The sea was a magnet drawing me back to its depths.

In another six months' time, I had finished the last house I was working on, rented it out, and left for England.

The British circumnavigation was entirely different from the American/ Canadian trip. It was less than half the distance but far more demanding, and a place where I learned what true sea kayaking was all about. I paddled through the weather and waters that Great Britain is infamous for: gale winds, fog, and tidal rips. The predictably troublesome seas taught me the more advanced lessons that my first trip had not. But beyond these new limits of sea heights and tidal strengths, there were other lessons I learned.

There is nothing better than local information when it comes to the sea. And there is no better source than the fishermen who make their living from the currents and tides through which they work their boats. They may have the same manuals and the general tidal and current information that any boater can acquire, but they also have something more—an innate understanding of the complexities of inshore waters, where the winds and the tides do not always follow a set standard. I was still looking for my place in the world, and while I was exploring the coast and the currents of the North Atlantic and the Irish Sea, I was also looking for bits of guidance for my own life. From the fishermen I met in the ports and out on the sea, I would ask the questions that got me around headlands or past points where the winds opposed the tides and turned the seas into impassable barriers. Then I would ask other questions: What was it like to work on the sea in all kinds of weather, day after day? What fueled the drive to cast off the lines and head out from the safety of the harbor? Was it work they enjoyed? And did they have dreams—plans for the future? I met a lot of fishermen, as well as land folks, who offered me help and guidance along the way, but one meeting in particular has remained with me to this day.

I was paddling in dense fog a mile off East Anglia in southeast England. The land, though I could not see it, was no more than a quarter mile to my right, and the water had an oily, flat sheen to it. Off to my left the sound of a boat's engine throbbed and occasionally died away—the wetness of fog muffling the engine noise like a blanket—disguising distance and direction. Minutes slid past as we moved in parallel lines of near blindness. And then suddenly there she was, appearing out of the fog like some ghost of the past, her graceful lines and her single mast amidships growing more defined as the fog thinned. She had no cabin or cuddy, and a boom swung over an open hold ready to receive the harvest of nets hauled over the side. At the stern was a stout old man, his lower body hidden by the high gunwales of the boat, his hand holding the curve of an oak tiller. He altered course and then eased off on the throttle as he motored alongside. He stood solid, dressed in dull-green foul-weather gear and wearing the traditional wool cap of a coastal fisherman. He held the bow of his boat on course, and without showing any surprise at finding me, asked where I was going. I told him and then asked where the nearest port in the fog was. Like fishermen all over the world, he didn't say very much at first. He just looked at my kayak fitted out for the sea and when he was ready, pointed in the direction I needed to go and told me roughly how far it was, information based more on intuition and experience than the compass that sat in its recessed fitting in front of me.

I knew in which direction the land was and I didn't really need to know where the harbor was. What I really wanted was something more of this solo, aged fisherman. He had come out of the fog like an apparition, and he seemed to know right where he was heading. His boat was simple and grace-ful. There weren't any radio antennas in the rigging and no compass in front of him. His auxiliary sail was canvas, and the lines of his boat were from a different era, an era out of which he seemed to have just sailed. In the lines of the fisherman's face, I saw both wisdom and knowledge, perhaps the things I was looking for myself. I didn't know how to ask of his life story and the lessons he had learned from the sea, but that was what I wanted.

I had no right to the brotherhood I sought, and the fisherman could choose to share what he knew, or he could choose not to. Perhaps it was the mood of the sea—no threat other than the fog the fisherman was comfort-able in—that allowed him to tell me his story. As we sat a generation apart but separated only by a few yards of wet mist, he told me he had been at sea since he was twelve days old—his mother bundling him in blankets and stowing him below while she helped her husband haul the nets. He was now well into his seventies. He asked me what I was doing, and I told him I was taking time to explore and to decide how it was that I wanted to spend my life. He nodded, a gesture I took as the acceptance I was hoping he would offer. That was all of the conversation we had—two men isolated by the fog yet united by the sea that held both lives in its hands.

I think perhaps we choose our teachers, some of whom do not realize, nor do we at the time, that they have a message to share. The fisherman had come out of the fog of a calm morning like a fisherman of old, offering what I did not and could not have known—the wisdom of decades of sailing the same waters year in and year out. We parted company as he slipped the single-cylinder engine into gear and slowly motored away. I have a picture of him standing at the tiller, holding his boat on a steady course, guided by some inner compass as he vanished into the thick of the fog.

I learned a great deal during the five and a half months I spent paddling around England, Wales, and Scotland, but maybe in hindsight the most valuable lesson was the one the fisherman taught me as he motored away from our mid-sea meeting: If you know where you've come from, and you know where you're going, the conditions you find yourself in don't matter—you just have to stay the course and trust in your intuition.

For ten years the memories and lessons of the British trip sat quietly within me while I sorted out my life and lived it as well as I knew how. I moved to the Pacific Northwest, worked carpentry jobs, took up white-water paddling, and continued to explore the sea, but not on extended voyages. And for ten years that was enough. Small trips were easier than the big ones I had done, and they left room for other passions.

But then something changed. I did a two-week sea-kayak trip with a friend and realized how much I missed the simplicity of the long journeys. The routine and the sense of accomplishment—the small victories of working with the weather and moving steadily down an unfamiliar coast—were both challenging and rewarding. I recalled living for months on end in a tent, of knowing exactly what I would eat every day at every meal and of finding freedom in the repetitive cycles upon which life on the sea depended. I had thought that long paddling journeys were something of my past and that I had tired of the strain of the exposure, but after my two-week paddling trip, I realized that wasn't true. The exposure was there, but so too was the love of the sea.

For the third time I felt the growing desire and excitement of planning another big trip. This time it was to a land I had glimpsed from the western shores of Scotland, a land half obscured in the layered memory of ten years and the sea haze that had hid all but the higher elevations seen across 20 miles of open sea. I think it was part mystery and part romance of the sea that led me to the next map pinned on my wall. The pattern was the same: the purchase of the map, its magnetic appeal every time I entered the room, and the innocence of dreaming that it invoked within me. I studied it for weeks, and when the excitement had grown too big to contain, I finally told my friends and family that I was heading off again, this time for Ireland.

In the spring of 1996, I set off from Dublin with my wall map encased in plastic on the front deck of yet another sea kayak. For the next three and a half months I explored not only the rugged coastline of this tiny wave battered island but also the ebb and flood of a genetic memory, which gave the trip a deeper significance. Through a series of meetings and walks through ancient ruins that were little more than sod-covered mounds, I found a truth that rang as clear as the message of the fisherman—that you have to know where you've come from or you can't know where you're going.

In the stones and the mist of Ireland, I discovered a message that spoke of my Celtic origins. I learned that my ancestors were warriors, music makers, and storytellers. And in a ruin overlooking the tides of Rathlin Sound in Northern Ireland, I felt the presence and the approval of my ancestors' gaze across the centuries of separation. If I had doubts as to my life's path, they were soothed in the cool mist of the ocean rising over the cliffs and wafting through the ancient embattlements that held the blood that ran through my veins.

I came back from that sea and soul journey, and for the first time I wrote of the things that one finds on ocean sojourns—of discoveries both outward and inward. And also for the first time, I realized that my love of words, coupled with the passion and intensity with which I have lived my life, was something I had inherited from my Irish ancestors. The art of storytelling, the love of people, the rhythm of music, and the mystery of legends are all part of my ancestry. Because of that sea journey, I now have a clearer understanding of who I am, of where I come from, and of where I am going.

Sometimes the paths of our lives are right there in front of us, yet we don't realize it until we look behind and see where we have already been. Sometimes it is our wake—the mark of our passage on the sea—that will tell us if we are still on course. I look over my shoulder at the miles of coastlines I have explored and the people I have been blessed to meet along my route. There haven't always been following seas to ease my journey, but it is the sea upon which I have chosen to travel, and it is the sea that has given me the freedom to tell that story.

Prologue

Once you have traveled, the voyage never ends,
but is played out over and over again in the quietest chambers.
The mind can never break off from the journey.
　　　　　　　　—Pat Conroy

IT IS ONLY IN WRITING THIS BOOK THAT I HAVE UNDERSTOOD the full impact of my journey around New Zealand's South Island. Unlike my other ocean travels, this trip afforded me little time to sit and reflect. There was always the presence and the enormity of the ocean and the challenges for which I could only hope I was prepared. Had I known what was going to be required of me, I wonder now if I would have set off. That's a difficult question to chase around in circles, and one for which I admit I do not have an answer.

I have struggled with the efforts to write this story and to relive what would have been much easier to leave on the more remote coasts of New Zealand's South Island. This book has given me the freedom to express the richness, the fears, the doubts, and the inner dialogue that are all part of a solo journey. I feel fortunate to have completed the circumnavigation and hopeful that in sharing the tale, others may understand and benefit, as I have, from the wonder of this journey which will forever be a part of me in a way that is deeper and more involved than simply paddling a kayak 1,700 miles.

Chapter 1

I hear and I forget
I see and I believe
I do and I understand
—*Confucius*

ON A WORLD MAP THE ISLANDS OF NEW ZEALAND appear cast off and insignificant sitting east and slightly below the Australian continent. Surrounded by the largest expanse of ocean in the world, the three primary islands—North, South, and tiny Stewart Island—lie in a northeast-southwest angle, as if the winds and the seas have set them adrift, pushing them farther into the isolation and emptiness of the South Pacific Ocean. In these southern latitudes known as the Roaring Forties, a continuous band of ocean encircles the earth with a westerly flow of winds and seas that create waves larger than any on the face of the planet—waves that are formed by storms to the west and southwest and build as they overtake smaller waves like a snowball rolling down a mountainside. These waves crash against the few scattered sub-Antarctic islands to the south of New Zealand, gathering volume and height until they approach the cliffs of the South Island, which rise sheer from the ocean floor.

Maori legends tell of the Polynesian navigator Kupe, who sailed from a land called Hawaiki around A.D. 950 in search of a new land to settle for his people. Kupe discovered the uninhabited islands and named them "Aotearoa," which means Land of the Long White Cloud. There is speculation that what he took for clouds may have been the snowcapped mountains and glaciers of the South Island. These 8,000- and 9,000-foot peaks wring out the moisture-laden marine air, dumping more than 200 inches of rain along the lower elevations of the west coast and creating snowfields and glaciers above tree line.

I don't remember exactly when the idea of paddling around New Zealand's

South Island first came to me. I think it was one of those vague dreams born of someone else's travel tales or photos. Somehow the idea took hold, more and more time was spent thinking of its possibility, and before long the momentum of the dream was carrying me away on its tides.

For a year prior to setting off for the South Island, I monitored the marine weather on an Internet Web site set up by the New Zealand Meteorological Service. Every morning before breakfast I would sign on and watch the digital image of the island take shape on the screen. Around the image were eight or nine stations that could be clicked on, and within seconds the wind speed, sea conditions, and the swell direction for that site would appear. I would log the information in a spiral notebook and move on to the next station. Within a half hour I had the complete weather synopsis for the day.

After a few months of this daily routine, I had begun to get a feel for the weather patterns and to understand how the low-pressure systems originating over the Tasman Sea affected the island. Hardly a day was recorded when there weren't gale-force and, in too many cases, storm-force winds somewhere around the country. The first time I saw a report for "storm force winds," I had to look up the meaning in a nautical almanac. The definition "Storm Force Winds: Winds in excess of 50 knots" was almost enough to put me off even thinking about the trip.

The other alarming factor in the reports was the swell heights. Swells of 3 and 4 meters were almost a daily occurrence along the south and west coasts. Unlike the winds, which seemed to moderate every few days as the low-pressure systems out of the south weakened, the swells hardly ever dropped below a minimum of 2 meters. If they did, it was only for a day or maybe two before the report was back up to 3, 4, or even 5 meters. I had paddled in 10- and 12-foot seas on my circumnavigation of Ireland, but the difference was that there had always been a safe place to land. It may have been 5 or 10 miles away but there was always a hook of land or an island that I could slip behind and get out of the big surf. Comparing coastline maps of both countries was like comparing apples and oranges. The long stretches of New Zealand beach were completely open to whatever the weather and the ocean swells threw at them, and in some places there were hundreds of miles—rather than 5 or 10 miles—between sheltered landings. What I needed was firsthand information from someone who not only knew the conditions but who also knew what a sea kayak could handle.

◆ ◆ ◆

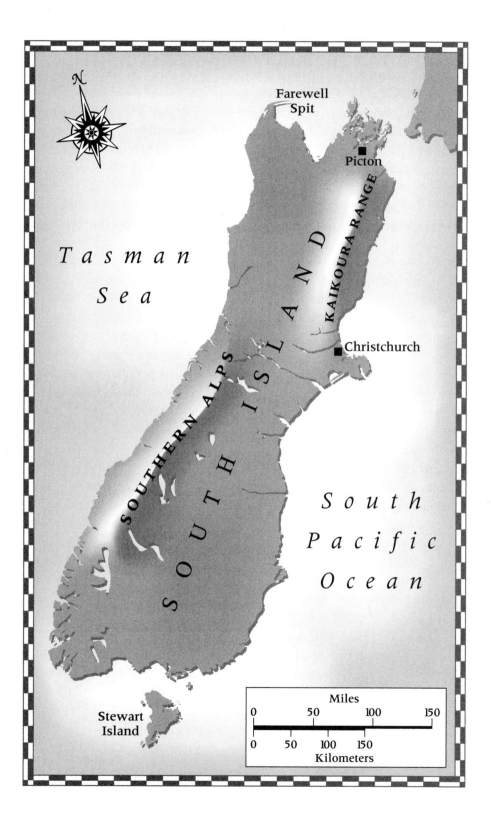

Paul Caffyn is one of those legendary people that all sports seem to breed. They are the ones who excel simply because of their ability to focus and to push beyond the limits that have previously been set. Practically anyone who has picked up a sea-kayak paddle has heard of Paul's epic paddling trips around Australia, both the North and South Islands of New Zealand, Great Britain, Japan, and a half dozen other extreme long-distance expeditions. While on a bike tour of New Zealand in 1994, I had phoned Paul and asked if I could stop by and talk to him about my idea to paddle around the island. He was quick to give me his address. Several days later I had arrived at his ocean-side cabin, which sits within a few yards of the sea cliffs north of Greymouth on the west coast. We spent the evening talking about kayaking: the trips we had both done, the advantage of certain kayak designs and rudder assemblies, and the possibility of a solo attempt at the South Island.

Paul had paddled around the island in 1978 with his friend Max, who accompanied him for the first 300 or 400 miles. Both he and Max had their share of capsizes and near misses, and on completing the Fiordland portion of the trip, Max had decided he had had enough. Despite the weather and sea conditions, Paul continued on and completed the circumnavigation with a shore crew helping him find places along the surf-bound coast to land safely. For almost twenty years Paul had the distinction of being the only person to have successfully paddled around the entire island.

As I sat at Paul's kitchen table looking out to the sea and listening to his stories of the South Island expedition, I tried to imagine a kayaker paddling beyond the lines of huge surf. To either side of his house, the waves rolled in over the reefs, crashed against the rocks, and left a mist hanging in the air between the sea and the steep, forested hills whose summits were obscured by clouds. As far as the eye could see, the coast was nothing but big surf rolling with explosive, broken energy. The rugged, unspoiled coastline intrigued me, but did I have the skills and the stamina to dare think of paddling it?

I slept in the loft over Paul's garage that night listening to the constant rumble of the waves. For a long time I lay awake, imagining what it would be like to hear that rhythmical folding and crashing for months at a time. After a while my mind adjusted to the incessant pounding, and I eventually fell into a restful sleep.

The next morning I said good-bye to Paul as I climbed back onto my bike and continued north along the coast. That first meeting with Paul had been brief, but I had the feeling that I had connected with someone who knew the sea as I did. If my idea to paddle around the island ever came closer to reality, I was sure Paul would offer whatever help he could.

Six years after that first meeting, I called Paul from my home in Washington State and told him I was ready to attempt a solo paddle around the island. We exchanged e-mail addresses, and over the next six months he kept me posted on the weather predictions for the upcoming summer, gave me addresses for the charts and maps I would need, supplied me with names and addresses of paddlers around the island, and generally offered whatever help he could in my planning.

Paul told me that in February of 1995, Kazutomi Yoshida, a Japanese kayak instructor, had departed from Nelson on a solo attempt to paddle the island. His trip had been plagued with southerly winds on the east coast, which pinned him down for days at a time. High seas and winds along the exposed and unpopulated south coast had forced him ashore, and while waiting for better weather he had depleted his stock of food for the critical Fiordland leg of the trip. Kazutomi retraced his route back to a village, where he restocked his boat and then set off again for the west coast. With a break in the weather, he made it around Puysegur Point, the beginning of the west coast, but again ran into severe weather and sea conditions off Breaksea Sound. A fishing boat reported finding him in poor condition and pulled him and his boat out of the sea. With more than half of the trip completed, Kazutomi made the difficult but wise decision to discontinue the trip while he was still in the relative safety of the west-coast fiords.

In October 1996 a second attempt to solo the island was made by Brian Roberts of Colorado. Brian left the village of Picton in the northeast corner of the island and paddled clockwise down the east coast. Favorable north winds pushed him southward, then abruptly swung to the south and halted all progress very close to where Kazutomi had been wind bound for several days. When the winds abated, Brian continued along the south coast and rounded Puysegur Point in near calm conditions. According to Brian's journal the trip up the west coast was fairly straightforward with the exception of some northerly gales, which forced him ashore for several days at a time. Eighty-six days after leaving Picton and after getting knocked over once and having to swim his boat to shore, he paddled back into Picton, completing the first solo circumnavigation of the island.

The fact that the first solo circumnavigation had already been completed didn't alter my decision to attempt my own circumnavigation. The idea had appealed to me from the beginning not because of the record of being the first, but rather for the experience itself. I wanted to see the penguins, the dolphins, and the albatrosses that lived along this band of uninterrupted ocean circling a tiny piece of earth. I had paddled the oceans of the Northern Hemisphere, and now I wanted to paddle these southern waters—to ride the waves of the Tasman Sea and the South Pacific Ocean. The more I learned of Paul's trip, Kazutomi's attempt, and Brian's successful solo of the island, the more certain I became that this was a coastline I wanted to explore. The weather and the seas would obviously have the final say in whether or not I made it completely around, and there was no guarantee I would succeed, but maybe that was the challenge—to pit the skills that I had acquired over the last eighteen years of paddling against the waters of the Roaring Forties.

Success is something that is easier for the psyche to understand than apparent failure. Paul and Brian's trips were obviously successful, and I could draw both knowledge and inspiration from them. It wasn't the past successes that I focused on, however, but rather Kazutomi's attempt. As I prepared for my trip, I kept wondering what kind of an individual he was and what had been his motivation for attempting the South Island. I wanted to know how he had maintained the "edge" that is so critical and at what point that edge had begun to dull with fatigue or even self-doubt. More important I wanted to know how he had prepared for the reality of what he faced every day of his trip. Every question I asked of Kazutomi's failed attempt I also asked of myself. At the core of the questioning was whether I could paddle around the island if I was thrown the same, or worse, weather and sea conditions. Kazutomi had been lucky that the fishermen had found him. I hoped that given the same conditions, I would have the wisdom to pull out before I reached a point where a rescue was necessary.

From past expeditions I knew the intensity and narrow focus that these endeavors breed. With each mile, day, week, and eventually month that the trip progresses, the momentum of the journey builds, and it is easy to become blinded by the goal of completing the trip. Failure, however, is just as possible, and maybe even more probable the further one is worn down by the intense physical and mental demands of the sea. The key is having the judgment and wisdom to quit if that is what is required. As I set about preparing for the trip I knew that success or failure in terms of completing the trip would be decided on a day-to-day and, in some cases, a moment-by-moment basis.

As the mental preparation for the trip proceeded, so too did the logistics of the trip. The paddling and camping equipment that piled up on the living-room floor was very different from the gear I had relied on for my other kayak trips. I remembered my first trip in 1983 and how I had slept on my life jacket rather than a regular sleeping pad for the 8,000-mile journey. The stove had been a secondhand mountaineering stove that flared up and singed the hair on my knuckles every time I lit the pooled fuel to prime it. In those days I didn't have the money for, or the knowledge of, half the warm clothing that would have been a darn sight better than the gray cotton sweatpants and matching long-sleeve shirt that comprised my "camp clothing." I looked at the pile of nylon bags, Gore-Tex paddling jacket and dry suit, the synthetic underwear, the wind resistant outer garments, the low-profile tent with its high-tensile-strength poles, the underwater camera, the carbon-graphite paddles, and on and on and on. The gear was the best available anywhere and spoke of how seriously I was considering the risks of this trip.

Half buried by all the other gear in the living room was a hand-held VHF radio that was more symbolic of how I felt toward this trip than any of the other high-tech gear. By taking the black radio, with its rubberized knobs and short whip antennae, I was admitting to myself and to my family and friends that there was a possibility I might have to use it for an emergency rescue. I had purchased one for the Irish trip and then at the last minute had returned it. This time the radio would not be sent back. Two and a half months into the trip I would be thankful that I had made the decision to take it along.

There was one other piece of equipment that was very different from the one I had on the past three major trips I had taken. The boat. For thirteen years I had paddled a Nordkap, a fast, seaworthy boat, which has probably been used on more major expeditions than any other kayak design in the world. It felt strange to be planning a trip without the familiar lines of the Nordkap and the knowledge of how it would handle the seas. On the Irish trip I had developed chronic sciatica and I could no longer sit in my old boat for more than a few hours. I had switched to another British boat, a Romany Explorer built by Nigel Dennis of Wales. The boat had more rocker in the hull than most sea kayaks, which made it maneuverable in big surf, plus there was slightly more storage space for gear. The biggest advantage was that it didn't aggravate my sciatic nerve. I knew there would be days when I would have to run lines of potentially hazardous surf after eight hours of paddling and then jump out and pull the boat up a beach.

Several weeks before the actual departure date of November 30, 1999, I had all the gear organized, the boat was en route to New Zealand via ship, and I finally had time to train.

Paddling an empty boat is nothing like paddling a boat loaded with a hundred pounds of gear. An empty boat is skittish even when the waves are small, and it doesn't track as steadily as a loaded boat. Any time the winds kicked up I would rush down to my favorite put-in on Ediz Hook—a long neck of land that separates the protected harbor of Port Angeles, Washington, from the open waters of the Straits of Juan De Fuca—shoulder the boat off the truck, and go out and play for a couple of hours. I would look for waves to surf on, paddling with the following seas and letting the waves surf the boat offshore. It wasn't so much the physical training I was looking for as the body memory and the familiarity of connecting the boat, the paddle, and myself to the sea.

Even when the water was almost flat, there was value in just putting the hours in visualizing and feeling the different muscle groups pulling together and working as a whole. I would concentrate on posture, on sitting upright and shifting the torque of each paddle stroke from my arms, back, and stomach muscles, down to my thighs and calves, and finally onto the pads of my feet. I could feel the pressure on my fingers holding the shaft firmly but not tightly, pulling through the stroke, lifting the blade clear of the water at my hips, and then opening my hand so that the shaft rested in the notch between thumb and forefinger and pushing with a relaxed grip as the opposite hand took the strain of the next stroke. I pictured muscle fibers, red and stringy, overlaying one another in complex bands wrapped in elastic sheaths that stretched and flexed. My mind became the muscles, became the energy, blocked out everything but what the paddle and the boat telegraphed to me. The sea, hull, paddle blades, the physical me, and the mental me merged into one. There was no thought of balancing the boat or of gripping the paddle shaft; there was only the fluidity of motion. The mind relaxed into a half state of meditation while the body worked in a rhythm of matched synchronicity. The gears that connected the physical, emotional, spiritual, and the psychological worlds were slipping into interlocking rings of motion.

Paddling on flat, calm, protected water was nothing like the conditions I would find on the Tasman Sea or the South Pacific, but that wasn't the point. What I was doing was very slowly building an intricate base, a body memory that would continue functioning regardless of what happened. There was no denying that the trip was going to be a league above anything I had attempted before. I had the skills, the physical strength, and the conditioning to do the trip, but I needed something more—something deeper, more resilient and flexible. I have had terrifying experiences on the sea when the winds and the waves were completely overwhelming—where there was no horizon either literally or figuratively—and only the absolute loneliness of realizing how insignificant I was. In that environment understanding one's mind can be the difference between life and death. The first acid of panic begins burning holes in any defensive plan, and something has to surface; some inner calm has to be brought forth in equal measure to counter the loss of focus. Just as the Eskimo roll brings the boat back from a capsize, the inner focus has to roll the mind back to a place of survival, back to a point where one can rely on the skills that are still there but may be temporarily blocked by fear. The work of paddling on smooth water and establishing the body/mind memory was the silk thread that would tie the other elements of paddling together. It would be the thread upon which my life would depend.

Throughout all the planning and training, there were times when the trip felt too big and filled with too many obstacles: the predictably unstable weather, the waves that rolled in from the expanse of the Roaring Forties, the exposure of the west coast, and the lack of radio communications in places where the mountains would block any transmissions. The surf along the unpopulated and exposed west coast was also a big factor. Questions kept surfacing as if probing for weaknesses in my plan: Could I carry enough food for the long stretches between resupply points? What if the surf was huge and there was no place to land? And what would happen if I got hurt coming through the surf and was stranded on a remote beach? These questions didn't have any firm or reassuring answers. When the questions and the unknowns threatened to overwhelm me, I would mentally shift to three factors I was confident in: my physical abilities, the clarity of the goal, and the faith I had in the gear that would support me. Beyond these three certainties were the winds, the seas, and the surf, all of which I had no control over. I needed to stay focused on those things I could control and then deal with the other variables when they arose. It was a matter of simply staying in the present and not letting the "what-ifs" derail me mentally.

I arrived in New Zealand two days before my boat arrived by ship from the East Coast of the United States. I had arranged with Kevin Beaumont, a New Zealander who was moving back to New Zealand, and his American wife, Dawn, to have my boat included in the shipment of their household goods from the United States to New Zealand.

Kevin and Dawn live in Te Anau in the southwest corner of the island, a twelve-hour drive from where I wanted to start the trip. After flying into Auckland on the North Island, I caught another flight into Queenstown, three hours from Te Anau. After meeting with Kevin and Dawn, we drove another two hours to the freight center, where their container sat in a gated compound. I pulled my shiny yellow kayak from the confines of the shipping container and set it aside; then we loaded their household belongings onto a truck and headed back to Te Anau. Two days later, after helping Kevin and Dawn move into their rental home, the kayak was strapped to the top of Dawn's car, and we headed north. Dawn had to catch a business flight from Christchurch to Johannesburg, South Africa. We would drive the eight hours to Christchurch, where I could rent a car, and then drive west to meet up briefly with Paul Caffyn, who was loaning me some charts for the trip. From there I would head for the village of Picton in the very northeast corner of the island.

By the time I arrived in Picton on December 5, all I wanted to do was find a place to sleep. I had been on the go for the last seventy-two hours; flying through too many time zones to keep up with, moving beds, couches, and framed pictures, and then driving for hours on end through the night along narrow country roads. Through the blur of fatigue and the curve of macadam winding north through farmland and woods, I would forget which side of the road I was supposed to be on. Driving on the left in a foreign country had little significance when the only things to worry about were the rabbits and opossums that darted away from the yellow beam of light that disturbed their nocturnal life. When I approached a village or an intersection, I would switch on the windshield wipers that were set in the place where the turn signal would have been in my eighteen-year-old Toyota pickup 7,000 miles away. Both my brain and body were numb from too little sleep and too many changes in the last three days. I found a quiet beach across the small harbor from the village of Picton, got rid of the rental car, and flopped down on the grass beside the boat for a nap in the warm sun.

The starting point of any circumnavigation—any path in life—is more than simply a physical place of beginning. It is a place of unknowing, of committing to something that is completely open-ended with the full spectrum of success as well as potential failure. It is also a place of transition, moving from the planning to the actual doing. After months of preparing, planning, questioning, and imagining, there is finally the reality and the relief of the physical. The boat is pulled to the water's edge, where the bow sits resting on the firm sands while the stern floats easily on the water. As each piece of gear is removed from the duffel bags and carefully packed in one of the three compartments, the boat slowly settles deeper in the water and takes on the weight not only of the equipment but also the weight of all the months of preparation. Each piece of gear has its assigned place, and there is a simple finality and commitment to its placement—an order and a purpose that appeals.

Picton was the perfect place from which to start the trip. It was 20 miles from the open sea and well protected from the gales that swept through Cook Strait, which separated the North Island from the South Island. It was still early in the tourist season, and except for an older couple having a picnic lunch on the grass above the beach, I had the shoreline to myself while I quietly and methodically loaded the boat. From the experience of past trips, I knew where each piece of equipment went in the three compartments. The sleeping bag and pad, the clothes, journal, various charts, and the daypack all were packed in the front compartment. The tent, stove, fuel, radio, and cook kit fit snugly in the hatch behind the cockpit. In the back compartment stuffed toward the very end of the boat where larger items wouldn't fit were the first-aid kit, repair kit, film, extra stove fuel, and the dry suit rolled as tightly as I could get it. The three colored bags that were left went in last, up close to the cockpit where their weight would affect the boat the least. In these bags was the other "fuel" that I would need. In the green breakfast bag was the muesli with powdered milk, bagels, peanut butter, and honey—a mixture heavy on carbohydrates, upon which my body ran so well. In the blue lunch sack was much the same: bagels, peanut butter, honey, dried fruit, and for some fat, a thick roll of salami. A bunch of energy and candy bars filled the corners of the bag that barely fit through the round rear hatch. The last bag was the red dinner bag, red for stop and rest. Dinners would be the same ones I had eaten on countless nights of previous trips: pasta with a dehydrated sauce, a little chunk of the lunch salami, and some freeze-dried peas or beans. The food was far from gourmet, but with a little fresh fish sautéed in olive oil, the hunger that would come from eight hours of paddling would take care of the repetitious nature of what mostly filled the back compartment.

By the time everything was loaded, the sun had disappeared behind a bank of heavy clouds that promised rain. December in New Zealand was like our April back home—the weather unsettled and the winds blustery and unpredictable. I slipped both break-down paddles into the cockpit, turned the boat upside down, and walked back into the village to get a few more candy bars and fruit and to look for some advice on the local waters.

Once the shopping was finished, I found the commercial fishing pier and walked down the floating docks where some fishermen were working on the stern of one of the boats. They were sorting out fishing tackle, thick rods with

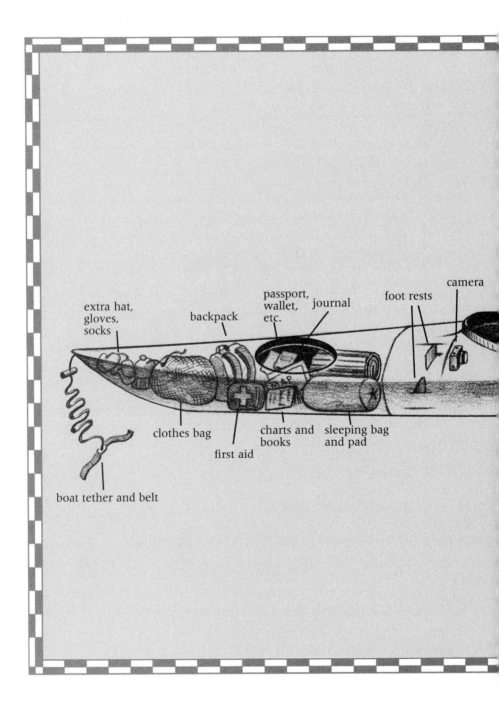

extra hat,
gloves,
socks

backpack

passport,
wallet,
etc.

journal

foot rests

camera

boat tether and belt

clothes bag

first aid

charts and
books

sleeping bag
and pad

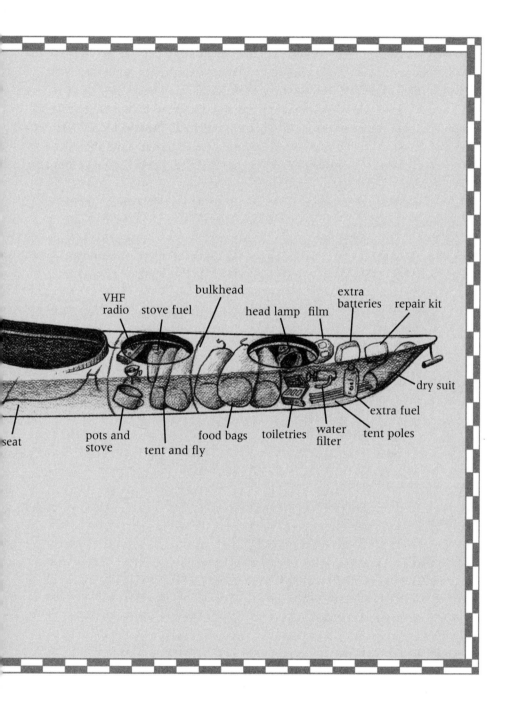

VHF radio — stove fuel — bulkhead — head lamp — film — extra batteries — repair kit — dry suit — extra fuel — tent poles — water filter — toiletries — food bags — tent and fly — pots and stove — seat

big reels of translucent monofilament and heavy snap swivels on the ends of the line. A blood-streaked bucket of fish heads, mouths agape and marble glazed eyes staring upward, sat near the engine covering that served as a workstation. An older man with an unshaven stubble and white hair was giving orders on where to stow the gear from the day's work. He was obviously the captain. He was dressed in jeans and black, calf-high rubber boots. A ball cap sat high on his head, the visor pushed out of the way for the work he was doing in the shadow of the pilothouse. He moved from the pilothouse, around the waist-high engine cover on the rear deck, and was fumbling through some engine parts when I walked up.

"Morning," I called out as he sat the bucket of parts heavily on the deck and kicked it with his toe until it was out of the way between a couple of bulkhead supports. The skipper either didn't hear me or was just too busy with his troubles to reply. He mumbled something to himself, shuffled forward, and disappeared into the wheelhouse. One of the other guys handling the rods looked up, nodded, and returned my greeting.

I always feel a little out of place talking with fishermen. They've got a tough job working in all kinds of weather and sea conditions. When they come back into port, there's always gear that has to be stowed, equipment that needs to be repaired, and fuel and food brought on board for the next sailing. The sea is hard on people as well as equipment; the only rest fishermen seem to get is when they are away from their boats. They are generally hardworking and hard-living people who don't waste much time with polite chitchat. If you have something to say, you had best just get on with saying it.

"I'm looking for some advice on the weather and the tides on the outside and was wondering if you could help me."

The fellow dumping the fish heads from the bucket into large, clear plastic bags looked up and didn't say anything. The other guy with the rods in his hand stopped and asked, "Where ye goin'?"

I wished he hadn't asked that question so soon. I hadn't even put my foot in the water to see how cold it was, and now I had to tell him I was going to attempt to paddle a sea kayak around South Island. Maybe I could be a little vague and still get the information I needed before leaving the shelter of the harbor.

"Well, I'm heading south and was just wondering if you think this weather will hold for a few days."

"How far south are ye goin'?"

"Oh, down toward Christchurch for starters," I replied.

"Well, unless you got an awful fast boat, yer not goin' to get very far. I think we got a weather fax this morning—sou'easter is supposed to come through tomorrow."

The fellow turned as the skipper reappeared from the wheelhouse and said, "This guy's looking for a weather forecast. Wasn't there something 'bout a southerly coming through?"

The skipper looked as though he was having a bad day with some mechanical problem that had just gotten the best of him. I must have lucked out and showed up just as he needed a break. He tossed a greasy towel with ragged edges on the engine cover and said: "Yeah, there's a fax inside; come aboard and have a look at it."

The boat rocked slightly as I stepped from the dock to the boat railing and down onto the blood-streaked rear deck. I followed the skipper into the low-ceilinged wheelhouse and carefully ducked under the radar screen that hung just to the left of the skipper's swivel chair and the boat's wheel. Two radios were mounted beside the radar screen and dangled loops of coiled cables leading to the mikes clipped to the sides of each one. As the boat gently rocked in response to the men working out on the aft deck, the radio cables swung in a hypnotic arc right at eye level. I tried to imagine what this cabin would feel like in a heavy cross-sea with rain and sea spray flying against the thick plate windows.

The skipper rifled through a bunch of papers on the ledge below the windows and found one that was curled from coming out of a fax machine. It showed a digitally produced image of South Island with the contour lines of a low-pressure system moving up the east coast. The concentric lines were closer on the northern edge of the pressure ridge than on the southern edge.

"Looks like it's going to be a southerly. She'll probably blow hard for a couple days, then swing 'round to the nor'east." He tossed the paper back on the ledge and continued looking for something else in the pile of papers, radio manuals, and old coffee stained newspapers. "What size boat are ye in?"

Well, there was no being vague about that question. From the sounds of it, the winds might be pretty serious, so I thought it was time to just admit what I was setting off to do. The skipper's question was one I would be answering a lot, so I figured I might as well hear what my answer sounded like out loud.

"I'm paddling a kayak. It's about 18 feet—what's that, 6 meters or so? And I'm going to try to paddle it around the island. But I wanted to get some information about the weather before I set off." It all came out a bit faster than I wanted and sounded like something I had just dreamt up last week.

For the first time the skipper actually looked at me.

"Yer in a kayak?"

"Yeah."

"And yer going to paddle it around the South Island?"

I looked right back at him, smiled, and said, "Ah yeah."

There was a slight pause, long enough to make me regret ever walking down the floating docks to this weathered-looking boat. He squinted his eyes as if he was trying to figure something out, then asked in a gravely puzzled voice, "Why?"

Why? Why not? How did I tell this guy who has to go out on the ocean to make a dollar that I just want to poke along the coastline and see what there was to see? I like the feel of the waves. I like looking at rock formations carved by thousands of years of wave action. I like camping and cooking simple meals beside my tent. I like feeling the sun and the wind and the power and the sensuous feel of ocean swells driving the boat forward. And I like meeting people, especially people who love the sea.

I wasn't so sure this grizzled old man wanted to hear all of that, so I just said, "I just want to see your country and do it at a nice slow pace."

It sounded like a dumb thing to say to a crusty fisherman.

There was another pause and the same squinted stare.

"Well, if that's all ye want to do, then why don't ye just take the train. It's a lot faster."

If the guy hadn't been so deadpan serious I would have laughed out loud. But one thing you don't do is laugh at a boat skipper while you're standing in his wheelhouse.

"Another fellow—Japanese I think—tried that a few years ago. Had to be rescued somewhere off the west coast. Lucky he got that far, I guess."

"Yeah, I heard about him." Then to get back to the weather issue, I asked, "What do you think the winds will do with this system moving in?"

He looked at me as if I was some kind of an idiot. "It'll blow like hell, that's what it'll do," he practically shouted. "Right outta' the south, and if yer out in it, good luck. If yer gonna paddle around the whole South Island in a damn kayak, you better learn something quick. Keep an eye on the clouds. The southerlies on this coast come up fast . . . in twenty minutes the winds'll go from nothing to 30 knots. You see a line of black clouds on the horizon and you better get you and your kayak to shore *fast*."

The skipper was getting a bit worked up. Maybe it was time to thank him and gracefully get off his boat. I had one more question though before I left.

"Do you know what channel the marine weather is transmitted on?" I asked.

"You got VHF or AM/FM?"

"VHF."

"Well that's one thing yer doing right. Channel 68 at 5:30, 7:30, 1:30, and again at 5:30 in the evening."

"Well, thanks for the advice. I'll probably just head out Tory Channel and wait for the northeast winds before going on the outside."

As I turned to leave, he asked in a concerned voice, "You ever do anything like this before?"

I thought for a second before replying, "Not quite like this I don't think. Anyway—thanks for the help."

As I walked aft and then stepped up on the dock, I heard the skipper tell the fellow with the rods, "Train'd be a lot safer."

After my first night of sleeping beside the packed boat, I had awakened early, eaten the same breakfast that would sustain me for the next 130 days, and then shoved the weight of the boat into the sea for the first time. As I straddled the boat in shallow water and then dropped into the seat, I realized that although I had been training in the same model of boat back home, this was the first time I had actually sat in this new boat. Instead of the thoroughbred feel of an empty boat used in training and on day trips, there was now the solid feel of a boat loaded for an expedition. The glistening gel-coat deck stretching out in front of me and pointing down Queen Charlotte Sound was my new home and the perspective from which I would see New Zealand's South Island. I reached forward with the first paddle stroke of the trip, dug into the cool, clear depths and very slowly pulled the boat up to its cruising speed. Like a freight train straining against its load, the boat responded sluggishly at first and then more easily as its inertia lent itself to the task of getting underway. The pull on the paddles lightened as the boat's speed increased and the sandy bottom dropped off into deeper water. The trip had begun.

Three days after pushing off from the quiet of Picton harbor, I was sitting 18 miles away in a stockman's cabin near the mouth of Tory Sound. A southeast gale shrieked its way from some polar-based storm and pushed its green-black waves across the narrow opening to the sea. Occasionally the gale found its way past the cliffs and into the more protected waters of the sound. The winds raced across the inner waters and hit the land with gusts that tore through the pine trees and then slammed into the tiny one-room cabin. I sat on the bunk writing in my journal as the cabin walls creaked and popped, and the chimney pipe rattled so loudly I thought it was being ripped from the roof. Only 18 miles from the start, and already I was pinned down.

I had paddled into Whekenui Bay two days earlier, when the winds stopped me from venturing into the open Pacific. As I came into the bay, a 40-foot crayfishing or lobster boat was off-loading a couple of boxes of groceries to a woman standing on an old wooden pier. She strapped the boxes on the front of a four-wheel drive ATV, then turned and waved as the boat eased away from the pilings. Two toddlers, with blond hair streaming out from under wool hats and with cheeks as red as tomatoes, sat strapped into a makeshift wooden box over the rear wheels. As the boat's diesels rumbled across the bay, I glided to within hailing distance of the woman. I introduced myself and asked if there was anywhere I could fill a water bag and if it was OK to camp on the beach near the pier. The woman asked where I was going. After I explained, she invited me up to the house that sat a few hundred yards above the beach and looked out over the mouth of the sound. I pulled the boat up amid some driftwood, then followed the puttering four-wheeler up a dirt track splattered with cow manure and sheep droppings. The track curved through a stand of huge gnarled pines and came to a beautiful old home fenced off from the surrounding hills dotted with sheep and cattle. By the time I reached the house, another older woman was helping to unload the children and groceries. As the kids toddled off across the lawn, I was formally introduced to Betty, the grandmother of the children, and to Antonia, their mother. Antonia explained what I was trying to do and that I had stopped at the pier to ask for water and a place to camp. Betty held out a hand covered in dry dirt from the garden and cheerfully said, "Well I was just going to make some tea for the kids and Antonia. Why don't you join us?" Then, turning back to Antonia she said, "Why doesn't he stay in the cabin? The gas is on, and there's hot water for a shower."

Before I knew what was going on, everything was decided for me. Betty picked up one of the children, Sahra, and headed for the house. Her twin brother, Jacob, wanted to walk alone. "Come on then, let's go. We'll get something to eat. Then Chris can get his things and move them into the cabin." I was left at the gate a bit baffled at this sudden hospitality. All I had wanted was a place to camp and some fresh water. There didn't seem to be anything I could do about the decisions that had just been made. Not that I was complaining, mind you. Any reprieve from the cold winds and the drizzle that was just beginning was welcome.

Over a plate of tomato-and-cheese sandwiches and steaming cups of tea, I was instantly made to feel like a member of the family. While the winds hurled the rain against the windows and bent the pine trees in sweeping arches, the children were put down for their afternoon nap, and Betty and Antonia told me about their life on an isolated sheep station.

Antonia had met her husband, Mike, while she was traveling in the United States. They had worked as abalone divers in California for years, then had moved back to New Zealand and bought the 900-acre sheep station overlooking Whekenui Bay. Up until the 1960s, the station had been the home of the Perano family, who operated powerful whale-chasing boats out of the sheltered bay. From the heights of the nearly vertical hills behind the house, the whales would be spotted coming through Cook Strait. Spotters would signal the boat operators, who would race to intercept the whales as they passed close to the mouth of Tory Sound.

The only remaining relics of the whaling days were the pier and the low, sprawling building down near the water, which now served as a sheep-shearing shed. Twice a week mail came out from Picton on a boat that also delivered visitors to the island. Antonia explained that she and Mike had plans to build an abalone, or paua, farm on the foreshore of the bay. Fresh water would be pumped into tanks on the land where the young paua would be carefully watched over as they matured. While Mike worked part of the year in California as a diver, Antonia kept an eye on the 400 sheep and 100 head of cattle that grazed the steep-sided hills of the station.

Across the half-mile-wide bay was another sheep station, owned by Joe and Heather Heberly. A dirt track clung to the side of the hill above the bay, disappearing into the ravines and gullies and eventually linking the two farms. The only motorized vehicles were the four-wheel-drive ATVs that New Zealanders call "motor bikes." The "bikes" are used for everything from visits between the farms, mustering—moving the sheep from one paddock to the next with the help of sheep dogs—and checking the miles of fence line that keep the stock from wandering off the station. The squat, powerful machines are the workhorses of the modern New Zealand sheep stations.

The boat I had seen earlier in the day had been Joe Heberly's. He had been returning from a run into Picton and before heading over to his dock had stopped by with the weekly groceries. The two families lived isolated from the outside world and were dependent on each other for the day-to-day realities of island living. It may be as simple as a borrowed cup of sugar that prompts a visit or the shriek of storm-force winds that rip through the narrow opening of Tory Sound. Either way the families were there for each other as well as for the fishermen who ventured out into Cook Strait.

Antonia disappeared into the living room and returned with a couple of books written by Heather. After almost thirty years of living on the edge of the strait, Heather had begun writing down some of the adventures of her family's farming and fishing life. Between stories of rescuing calving cows from floods and gathering the sheep from the far reaches of the station for shearing, there was the tale of a boat explosion that almost took the life of one of her sons, as well as numerous accounts of Joe heading out in the middle of the night in search of boats that had sent out Maydays. For more than three decades, she and Joe had answered the Maydays of countless boaters who had come to grief on the waters of Cook Strait. When Joe left the safety of Whekenui Bay, Heather monitored the radio and waited for the outcome of the searches. The southerly gale that drove the rains against the windows of the farmhouse made reading the rescue accounts very real. From a window in the front room, I could see the bay covered in whitecaps and could only imagine what the "outside" must look like in the 30-knot winds. Some of the rescues that Heather wrote of were successful, the fisherman or yacht eventually being towed past the rocks at the entrance of the sound and into the shelter of the bay. Other searches continued until some piece of floating debris was found, or the remains of the boat were spotted driven onto the rocks below the cliffs. All too often the search boats returned with nearly empty fuel tanks and nothing but bone-deep weariness to show for the hours spent beating into the winds and seas.

Later that night I lay listening in the dark while the winds tried to rip the corrugated roof off the stockman's cabin. Sleep wouldn't come. I closed my eyes for a while, then opened them to the same blackness. It wasn't only the noise of the wind that made sleep impossible; it was also the inner noise and worry of my mind. Three days into a 1,700-mile kayak trip and already I had heard and read too many stories of these stormy waters. The question of the Picton fisherman haunted me, "Ye ever do anything like this before?"

I closed my eyes and thought about my answer—"Not quite like this, I don't think."

Chapter 2

SOLITUDE AND GALES

What is the only thing that passes across
the face of the sun yet leaves no shadow?

The Wind.

—Arabic riddle

THE MORNING I LEFT WHEKENUI BAY, Antonia baked a dozen lemon-poppy muffins for me, piled the kids on the four-wheeler, and drove down to the pier to see me off. The winds had shifted to the northwest, knocking down the previous day's 6-foot southerly swell and sweeping the sky clear of any clouds. The worries of gales and 20-mile sections of cliff-bound shores were lessened with the warmth of the sun and my eagerness to be off. Antonia handed me the paper plate with its golden mound of muffins wrapped in clear plastic—the first of many gifts I was to receive along my route. I carefully packed the muffins in the middle hatch, then double-checked the seals on all three hatches. After three days of waiting for the winds to calm and getting to know Antonia, Betty, and the children, the moment of departure was mixed with feelings of excitement as well as regret in leaving new friends. West Head, and the real start of the journey on the open Pacific, lay just a mile across Tory Sound. We exchanged addresses and said our good-byes, and as I sat fitting the spray deck around the cockpit rim, the ebbing tide began pulling me away from the pier.

By the time I reached West Head, the winds of the last few days had settled down to 15 knots out of the northwest. Four- and five-footers rebounded off the cliffs and made the approach to open water a rough and wet ride. The bow rose sharply on the random, close-packed waves, and dropped just as quickly into the troughs. I had zipped up the dry suit just before entering the rough water, and although an occasional breaker swept over the boat from bow to stern, briefly burying the yellow deck, hatch covers, and compass, I stayed dry and warm as the boat rose out of the broken water and continued on. Once around the headland and far enough offshore to avoid the refraction of the waves, I turned the boat on a southward heading and settled into the more rhythmic rise and fall of the swells. The winds that had been kicking up whitecaps and blowing noisily on the left side of my face were now at my back. I sprinted onto the backs of the waves in front of me and then eased up as the following waves caught the stern and surfed the boat southward. After hearing so much about this coastline—its treacherous currents, the miles of cliffs, and the gales that can make the coast a death trap—I could hardly believe my luck. I had an ebb tide, a following sea, and a relatively gentle and warm wind escorting me along. A half mile to my right the coastal cliffs rose dramatically above jagged rocks that had fallen from the heights. Arid and bare of any vegetation, the ravines and headlands looked more like southern California than how I had imagined New Zealand to look. Between the sheer cliffs and the steep hillsides of closely cropped brown grass, there were occasional small pockets of rocky beaches that would be exposed at low tide.

As I paddled along trying to catch as many of the surfing waves as I could and enjoying the rush of finally being underway, I was suddenly aware of how relaxed I was. All the months spent watching the weather and wind reports, hearing stories of the southerly gales, and then being pinned down by the winds had built up a tremendous amount of anxiety. The rough water of West Head had finally given me something physical with which to deal. Once I was into the work of moving the boat through the rebounding waves and feeling how it responded to the pull of the paddle, I could get out of my head and balance the psychological weight of the trip with the reality of paddling. The transition from the broken rebounding waves of the headland to the free-running swells of the open water was similar to the psychological release I felt within. The open sea horizon to my left and the line of cliffs to my right defined the obvious: the direction and the simple goal of the journey. Now I could shake out the reins, clear my head, and get on with what lay in front of me.

Cape Campbell, the first prominent point along the east coast, juts out into the Pacific and trips the blue swells into lines of murky, sand-laden breaking waves. As I approached the point, I could see the lighthouse set back from the windswept dunes and, off shore, the discolored waters that marked the shallows running a mile straight out from the light. Rather than paddle all the way around the outside of the breakers, I decided to try and sneak in close where the 5- and 6-foot waves ran through a channel of deeper water that wasn't breaking. With the ebbing tide and the increasing wind at

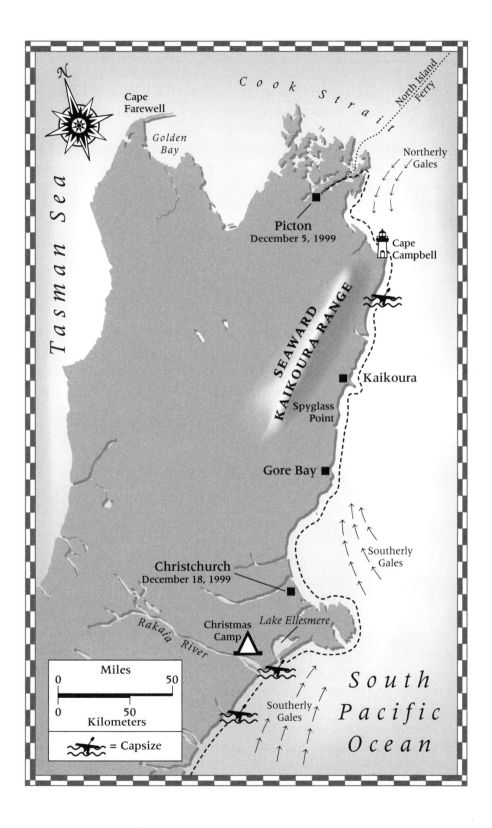

N

Cook Strait

North Island Ferry

Cape Farewell

Golden Bay

Tasman Sea

Northerly Gales

Picton
December 5, 1999

Cape Campbell

SEAWARD KAIKOURA RANGE

Kaikoura

Spyglass Point

Gore Bay

Christchurch
December 18, 1999

Southerly Gales

Christmas Camp

Lake Ellesmere

Rakaia River

South Pacific Ocean

Southerly Gales

Miles
0   50

0   50
Kilometers

= Capsize

my back, I was moving through the swells at almost 6 knots, reaching and pulling with the paddle and feeling the sea through the blades and through the hull of the boat. I was "spinning the paddles"—a physical place where my mind and my body were coordinated and running on high without any undue threat. It was a perfect balance of adrenaline and calculated risk. Nothing else existed but the simple reality of the moment: the purity of the winds, the seas, and the paddle driving the boat southward. On a cloudy day the noise of the wind, the breaking seas, and the tide race would have been intimidating, but with the sun shining warm on my face and sparkling on the white broken water, I was as happy as any sailor on the ocean could be. When the following seas picked the stern up and raced it straight down the waves, I would lean back, hold the paddle clear of the water, and let the boat run. By shifting my weight from side to side, I could use the edges of the boat to turn in the same way a skier uses the edges of the skis to turn in deep powder. If the boat started to veer too far off to one side and I couldn't turn it with a lean, I would drop the paddle into a stern rudder, and in an instant I was back on course, flying along on the first miles of the trip.

Each wave has its own shape and steepness, which either carries the boat along in a nice, smooth, controlled surf or breaks in a hissing rumble of white water that piles onto the rear deck and seems to swallow the boat in its spent energy. As I came even with the lighthouse, I glanced back, as I often do, to see how the next wave was shaping up and what kind of a ride I could prepare for. What I saw made me forget about surfing and had me grabbing for the camera, which was under the forward bungee cords. While I had been keeping the boat running fast and true through the waves, the streamlined shadow of a six-foot shark—a third the length of my boat—had been silently cruising 10 feet behind my stern. I let the boat veer off the wave and decelerate in the next trough while I tried to balance the boat and adjust the f-stop of the camera. As soon as the shark realized I had seen him, he slipped into deeper water and was instantly gone. He must have been hunting in the tidal race, taking advantage of the current to pick off prey in the murky waters. Maybe it was just simple curiosity, or maybe he was sizing up the shape of the boat and thinking it was similar to that of a seal surfing through the waters. Apparently the hunter of the seas didn't like being stalked, even if it was only for a photo.

Within an hour of rounding Cape Campbell and leaving the shark somewhere below the breaking waves, the predicted north winds kicked into high gear. The paddling became a wild ride of not only trying to surf the waves but also of just trying to stay upright. The powerful gusts were coming from behind and at a slight angle off the land—a warm, dry wind that grabbed at the high blade and almost knocked me over with its strength. After another two hours of hanging onto the twisting paddle shaft and leaning into the winds and breakers that constantly overtook the boat, I was nearing my reserves. With a team of strong paddlers, it might have been possible to stay with the winds and get another 10 miles or so down the coast, but paddling alone means paddling conservatively. I wasn't at my limit, but I was pushing my body hard, too hard for this early in the trip.

The constant twisting of the paddle shaft had raised ugly blood blisters on my hands, and my shoulders were aching from the unfamiliar strain of working the loaded boat through the waves. Despite the months of paddling and training I had done prior to the trip, I was still nowhere near my peak paddling condition. It was tempting to push on and get the miles in while the north winds blew in my favor, but I was still in my "breaking in" period of paddling. The last thing I needed was a torn muscle or ligament from over-use. Twenty miles in high winds and moderate seas was enough for one day. It would be several more weeks before my muscles could take the strain of seven or eight hours of constant paddling in high winds.

Considering how stiff I was from the day's paddling, I made a decent landing through the small surf, jumped out of the cockpit, and ran forward for the grab loop just before another set rolled in. After five or six trips up and down the cobbled beach, I had the boat and the assorted bags of gear piled behind the first dune, just above the cobbles. I could feel the fine grit of sand between my toes; my shoulder, back, and stomach muscles had that wonderful feeling of healthy strain; and a growling rumble in my stomach spoke of good hunger, a hunger that had been well earned.

On the edge of the cobbles where the land began to rise with a purpose from the sea, the winds had formed a random pattern of dunes rolling like ground waves toward the higher hills farther inland. Beach legumes and grasses grew amid vague lines of flotsam: Half-buried logs and crisply dried mattings of tangled seaweed marked where storm waves had probed the dunes with the long fingers of the sea. On the lee side of the dunes, where the grasses crept onto the shoulders and established a foothold in the slow avalanche of sand crystals, single blades of grass stood encircled by perfectly inscribed arcs, the calligraphy of wind and grass tips.

Within moments of landing and walking into the calm of the dunes, my world of breaking seas and winds that threatened to tear the paddle from my hands was abruptly forgotten. In the shelter of the dunes, I peeled off my dry top, kicked off my sandals, and stood on a rounded, flat stone that perfectly matched the instep of both feet. The transition from marine to land mammal was completed as the wind and the warm sun dried my skin. Behind me I could hear the surf piling up on the gravel and sand, but for now I could forget the concerns of the sea and just soak in the radiant warmth of the afternoon sun. The rewards of traveling on the sea are very simple: a good day running with the winds and the waves and a wind-free camp in the evening in which to sit and write.

By the time I had the tent set up and the stove roaring away under a pot of water, it was time for the evening forecast. I tuned the radio to channel 68 and sat in the tent doorway listening as the announcer began the nightly reports. A general weather synopsis for the entire island was given first, followed by wind and swell reports from the nine automated stations around the island. The last part of the report gave actual wind speeds and barometric pressures from a variety of stations around the island. "All stations. All stations. This is Maritime Radio, Maritime Radio. Maritime weather bulletin for New Zealand coastal waters issued 1500 on 13 December 1999 with a further outlook for the following one two hours! A ridge of high pressure from Greymouth to Cook moves slowly northeast while a low pressure moves in from the south Tasman Sea."

The reporter then began reading wind and swell conditions for the nine sites around the island beginning with Cook Strait. "Cook—Gale force winds northeast easing overnight. North swell 2 meters easing. The twelve-hour outlook: A low pressure will extend over the region by midday on 14 December. Strong southerly gales are expected with southeast swells 2 meters and rising."

The reports then continued counterclockwise around the island: Abel Tasman, Greymouth, Milford, Puysegur, Foveaux, Chalmers, Rangitata, and finally Conway. After the report was read, a computerized voice came over the radio and gave specific wind speeds and barometric pressures from a dozen different sites beginning at Cape Campbell. "Cape Campbell: North northeast 32, barometric pressure one zero zero nine and falling rapidly."

Thirty-two knots. No wonder I was tired! Five hours of paddling in gale-force winds had just about wiped me out, but at least now I knew what the boat and I could handle when the winds did kick up.

The last part of the marine forecast was a little disturbing: barometric pressure 1009 and falling rapidly. That meant high winds out of the south, the southerly gales about which I had been repeatedly warned. These

December winds were a little higher than usual but not far off the average. I turned the radio off and placed it in a net pocket of the tent close to the head of the sleeping bag. I could only hope that the winds of the last week would gradually fall off as more high-pressure systems established themselves over the island. What I didn't know, of course, was that the winds would be my near constant companion for the duration of the journey.

A general rule of the sea is that after you get done patting yourself on the back for a job well done, the sea usually turns around and puts you back in your rightful place of humility. Two days after paddling in the 30-knot winds and feeling as though I had done a pretty fair job of it, I came through some relatively small surf and did just about every possible thing wrong. This time the sea was kind; I walked away from the botched landing with nothing but my pride injured.

I was low on water and had debated whether to stop in Kekerengu to fill the water bag or to just keep paddling while the winds were calm. For the first time in three days, the winds were almost nonexistent. A low, 3-foot swell rolled in from behind, gently lifting the stern, then passing harmlessly southward. Ten miles inland the Seaward Kaikoura mountain range rose above the greenery of the coastline in a dazzling brilliance of new snow that had blanketed the range the previous night. The low-pressure system that the maritime forecast had predicted had brought heavy snow in the mountains, followed by a high pressure that cleared the skies of any clouds and raised the air temperature to a comfortable sixty-five degrees. It was a perfect day to be offshore and enjoying the rhythm of smooth-water paddling—the reach, plant, and pull of the blades slipping into the emerald-green water and moving the boat effortlessly across the ocean. I would close my eyes for a few minutes and keep paddling, feeling the swells beneath the boat and the warmth of the sun on my face. Occasionally I would glance over at the surf rolling onto the beach with a formidable rumble and think, "I really don't want to run the surf line. I'm warm, dry, and happy out here." The last thing I wanted to do was to break the rhythm of deep-water paddling and deal with the swells as they peaked and crashed onto the sands. If only I didn't need the water. But . . . I turned the boat toward the beach and started in.

From a hundred yards off the beach, the surf didn't look very big—3-footers with the occasional 4-footer breaking a little farther out. If I timed it right, I could probably get ashore without even getting wet. I thought about the dry top that I had taken off earlier and stuffed between my legs in the cockpit. Normally I would have had it on and maybe even have strapped the helmet on if I thought the surf was big enough. But surely I could surf this little stuff and not bother with either the top or the helmet.

I rode the first wave to within 20 yards of the beach before I realized I had underestimated the speed of the waves and the steepness of the beach. The waves were rolling in fast and dumping sharply within 3 feet of the steep sand and gravel. I had also timed the set wrong and wasn't close enough to the wave in front of me to maximize the time before the following wave would catch me. If I didn't land quickly and get clear of the boat, the wave behind me would catch the boat in its break and throw it sideways up the beach.

As the bow slid onto the sands, I reached for the grab loop of the spray deck. By pushing forward and pulling up at the same time, I could pop the spray deck free of the cockpit and instantly jump clear of the boat.

As soon as I pulled the grab loop, the deck popped off the front edge of the rim. I could hear the wave behind me starting to break, and instead of quickly running my hands around the back of the rim and checking to see if the deck was fully clear, I tried to jump straight out of the boat. The spray deck caught under the rear lip of the rim and held me in the cockpit. By the time I sat back down, ran my hands around the rim and freed the deck, the breaking wave was practically on the boat.

A cubic yard of water weighs almost a ton, and even a relatively small wave travels at almost 10 miles an hour. With that kind of force, it doesn't take much of a mistake to really get pounded into the sand.

Just as I had cleared the spray deck from the rim and jumped out of the boat, the breaking wave hit the stern and swung the boat sideways, launching it directly at me. There wasn't any time to turn or sprint away from the boat, half buried in the broken wave. More out of instinct than anything else, I jumped over the back of the boat as it shot toward me. In midair I caught my foot on the leading edge of the back deck and hit the water on the far side, shoulder first. By the time I got my feet under me and came back to the surface, the boat was washed up onto the beach with the cockpit filled with a slurry of sand and water. The camera lay beside the boat, buried in the sand but still attached to the boat with its double tether. My dreamy world of gentle swells and warm sunshine now consisted of being soaked and a bit shaken by almost getting hit by the boat.

There wasn't anything graceful about the landing, but at least I hadn't gotten hurt. My first mistake was misjudging the surf. The second mistake, which could have left me with two broken legs, was jumping out of the boat on the down-wave side of the boat. I should have jumped out on the opposite side and just let the wave carry the boat harmlessly to the beach. As I emptied the boat and then dragged it to higher ground, I berated myself for treating the small surf with such little respect. I could have ended the trip right there, banged up with two years of planning and training out the window just from doing something as simple as not paying attention. The sea doesn't tolerate that kind of lax attitude. This time the waves were small and the consequences minor: a dunking in the surf and a boat filled with sand and water. The camera and the dry top needed a good rinsing, but other than that I had gotten off easy.

The many thousands of miles I had paddled on previous trips had given me a great deal of experience and confidence, but at the same time, there was the danger of complacency, becoming too comfortable in conditions that were moderate and not seeing the potential danger. On calm days especially after several high-energy, windy days, it was easy to let the defenses down and just relax. Coming off the high of a demanding day was important; the body and mind need the down time to release the adrenaline and the healthy tension. The difficult part is finding the balance between relaxing and staying alert, allowing the system to unwind and recharge the energy reserves and, at the same time, continue to stay alert to potential threats of the sea. It is this near-constant state of awareness—of not being able to totally shut down and turn off the alarms—that eventually takes a psychological and physical toll. The surf incident at Kekerengu was a valuable reminder of something I knew well: Never turn your back on the sea. It doesn't matter that the day is calm and the winds are not whipping the seas into breaking waves; the potential for danger is always there. It was a lesson better reminded of earlier in the trip and one that would stay with me for the next four months.

The challenge and the beauty of ocean paddling is that no two days are alike. You wake in the predawn light, unzip the tent, and the sea greets you with anything from a roar of boisterous energy to the gentlest wave receding over the colored stones of a gravel beach. The winds and waves, or the lack of them, set the pace and the mood of the day.

Days of wild winds and breaking waves leave little time for daydreaming and wandering mentally. The winds and, consequently, the waves, demand that the paddler stay alert. The day is spent anticipating the unexpected: gauging the speed and angle of the waves as each one approaches the boat, monitoring the ever-changing subtleties of wind directions and speed, being aware of the energy spent controlling the boat and how much longer one can maintain the pace, and continually, though subconsciously, being aware of how narrow the edge is between the high of running with the sea and the consequences if something were suddenly to go wrong. The high-energy days are the ones that are remembered simply because of the intensity with which the day is lived.

The reality of ocean paddling is that there are also days when the seas are nearly calm and there is little to occupy, entertain, or challenge the mind. On these days the first hour is spent watching the shoreline, gauging the speed of travel by lining up distant hills one in front of the other and noting how fast they change relative position. A buoy might be spotted a quarter mile away, and a detour is made to see if there is any telltale sign of current assisting or slowing the rate of travel. Either way it doesn't matter. When the winds are calm, one paddles whether the tide is running in favor or not. To wait for a favorable tide is to invite the winds—winds that seldom seem to blow in the desired direction. If the buoy indicates a head current, the course is shifted closer to land. Sometimes there is an eddy or a countercurrent in closer to shore; sometimes there isn't. It's a factor of how straight the coast is and how strong the tidal current. When there's no escaping the current, it's a matter of spinning the blades faster—of picking up the tempo, digging deeper into the reserves for the necessary push, and then finding a pace that can be held until the tide changes or progress is made down the coast, where there is rest. It is a matter of settling into the task, accepting the monotony and the strain of fighting a current and knowing that this too is part of ocean paddling. It is about going inside, letting the mind wander while the body stays dutifully at the task, propelling the boat toward hopefully slack water. Eventually the calm days settle into hours of watching the bow wake, feeling the body working, tolerating the musings and wanderings of the mind, and being thankful the wind is not howling.

On these windless days, rare though they are, even the gulls seem to lack their usual bountiful energy. Instead of soaring and reeling on updrafts of air, they sit on their own reflections and only take to the air when the boat's course threatens them. Without the winds the gulls also seem to be less vocal, as if they can't be bothered either to protest the intrusion or muster the energy with which they seem to always announce their presence. They open folded wings, lift off the water's surface in silence, and disappear in low flight toward some unmarked point of another ocean landing. With the absence of the gulls, and only the occasional jellyfish undulating below the surface, previously overlooked details come into sharp focus, and there is time for the luxury of introspection.

Calm days are usually slightly overcast with the horizon line softened and shortened by sea haze. The world feels closer and more intimate. After days or weeks of running with or fighting against the winds, the senses strain to define the sudden silence and the calm. The smallest of sensory ripples go unnoticed for minutes at a time before you realize the soft brush of shirt fabric beneath the spray skirt tube is the sound your ear has been focusing on for the last five minutes. You listen and hear the subtle difference in sound the left stroke has compared with the right. Maybe one arm brushes closer to the body. You pay closer attention because that is what happens in silence. You watch how the position of the arm affects the entry of the paddle blade on one side of the boat; perhaps the blade isn't slicing as cleanly or as vertically into the water. The almost imperceptible brush of cloth against neoprene is left in the wake of a new focus, that of the placement of the paddle. Now it is the eye that becomes aware of the smallest detail.

The blade position is corrected and for the first few strokes feels slightly awkward. The eye registers the new position and trains the shoulder, forearm, wrist, and fingers to carefully slice the blade into the sea at just the right angle. The eye is the final measure of pass or fail. With each stroke the point of entry is studied and the next stroke is freshly aligned. The finer the attention to the angle and the silent slice and burying of the blade into the sea, the greater the effort there is in seeking perfection. A slight improvement leads to closer examination, an examination that is part philosophical, part physical, and part poetic—purity in its most elemental and innocent form. The goal becomes the complete moment of simple and concise attention. Nothing else exists but the reach, plant, and pull of a solo paddler out on the sea.

What value can lie in the perfection of a single stroke that is over in less than three seconds? What value is there is any pursuit of perfection?

Not until the symmetry is balanced and the entry not only looks clean but flows and feels as smooth as hot honey does the conscious eye relax its attention, leaving the mind to wander to other realms.

The oily, smooth surface of a calm sea is a canvas upon which the paddler briefly leaves his mark of passage. The boat wants to glide not so much on the water but almost above it, where the soft haze masks the blurred transition of sea and air. Across this liquid plane of emptiness, the boat carves its signature.

Windless days are also when the questions begin, the simplest of which is: Why? Why am I out here paddling endlessly forward with nothing but a vague target of coastline somewhere above the yellow tip of the bow? There is no drama or tension to weld the moment into a story that will be told months later. There are no textures or changing shapes. There is nothing to hold the eye for more than a few seconds on an ocean that is as flat and as blue as the overhead sky. The miles slip behind, and the goal up ahead grows slightly more defined—but only slightly.

The question of why still remains. And the answer doesn't make a lot of sense unless one believes there is value both in the emptiness of the moment, as well as its richness. I am there because if I am not, then I am going to miss whatever happens on the sea when no eye observes it. I am also there for not only what happens on the sea but also for what happens inside when I have grown comfortable or, at least, have accepted the silence and the questions that come with deep solitude. Similar to moments of sitting meditation, thoughts and images drift in like morning mist, the quiet hollows of the mind filling briefly with the touch of family, friends, and home. It is all part of the journey, and the day is just as it should be, a day of calm and rest that allows the mind and body to run free and to find a pace that is dictated not by the strength of the sea but by the healthy wanderings of the heart and mind. The calm days are treasured because they are not only rare but they are also short-lived. And in that calm there is the time for rest before the next gale.

On December 13, I was 10 miles south of Kaikoura, heading for Spyglass Point and hoping to make it under the protection of the bluffs before the forecast southerly gale hit. Straight in front of the boat and rolling in from the south was a gray-black band of clouds that seemed to grow by the minute, stealing more and more of the light and blue from the sky. The forecast had called for gale-force southerlies—40 knots—for the next two days. I was within 2 miles of Spyglass Point, its rocky, low headland jutting out into the Pacific and forming a slight hook that would offer protection from the winds and seas. Already I could feel the energy in the air, the electric charge of tension before the storm. Up high the gulls were tearing along on the edge of the first blasts of wind. Wheeling and soaring they flashed by, climbed, then dove to within a few yards of the suddenly blackened waters. A few hundred yards in front of the boat the wind touched down in short blasts, leaving its signature of steep little wavelets. The wind and wavelets hit the boat at the same time, the wind grabbing at the high paddle and flattening the fabric of the paddle jacket against my chest. Three or four seconds later, the air was still, and the water once again smooth and oily looking. A hundred yards ahead and slightly off to my left—farther out to sea—another scaly area ripped across the sea's surface and then was gone as quickly as it had appeared. These cat's-paws, the quickly developing band of black clouds, and the erratic flight of the gulls were all classic signs of the approaching frontal system. It was time to get to land, find a place to pitch the tent, and wait out the winds.

Just as I was about to turn the boat toward a break in the low chalky bluffs, a flash of movement against the near horizon caught my eye. A half mile away a shaft of sunlight lit up an area of the sea like a stage bathed in light. Maybe it was simply the sun dancing and reflecting on the waves that had caught my eye. I rested the paddle across the cockpit and watched the sunlit patch. Even from a distance, the water looked odd. The waves were choppy and confused, yet the surrounding sea was colorless and relatively calm. A second later there it was again, something leaping clear of the sea, silently arching into the sky and catching the sun on shining skin, then crisply slicing away again.

Dolphins!

What had appeared to be a tide-rip of disturbed water were actually thirty or forty dolphins playing or feeding and churning the sea into a confusion of reflected waves. As I sat watching, a dolphin arched into the air, leaping 10 feet clear of the water, then crashing down sideways with a great glistening splash. Seconds later two more dolphins leapt into the air, arched, then nosed cleanly back into the sea. From a distance all I could hear was the occasional muffled explosion as one of the dolphins landed sideways, throwing a wall of water out to the side. Whatever was going on I wanted to get closer for a better look. If I could get over to the dolphins and back to the protection of the cliffs in the next half hour, I might beat the thickening clouds that marked the approaching front.

I turned the boat away from the cliffs and was sprinting out toward the pod when suddenly three dolphins surfaced 10 feet from my right paddle blade. Puff-f, Puff-f, Puff-f. The glistening arched backs sliced into the air and then just as suddenly vanished. As I sat with the paddle frozen in midair, a flash almost straight under the boat caught my eye. The dolphins were still with me, cutting left to right beneath the bow and then back again. One of them was swimming upside down, the lighter side of his belly catching the fading light through the sea. Suddenly more and more darting shapes and shadows joined the three at the bow. Sharp exhalations and quick inhalations had me spinning my head around to catch a glimpse of one, two, now four, and another pair coming up for air just to the right of the boat. A dorsal fin, sharp as a scythe, knifed across the water and then was gone. Two ghostly torpedoes of light gray converged on the bow, one from the left, one from the right. They sliced by each other, a foot under the bow, then broke the surface with twin exhalations.

The original pod was now less than a quarter mile in front of me—a mayhem of dorsal fins, backs, tails slapping, and other dolphins leaping in the air. One dolphin cleared the water a few hundred yards ahead of me, shooting gracefully into the air, rolling over on its back, then crashing into the sea. In its brief flight I could clearly see its muscled body—the arch of its back defined by the scimitar of dorsal fin, its thick powerful girth, and the shocking size of something so powerful yet so beautifully graceful. The classic extended snout and smiling face identified them as bottle-nosed dolphins, the ones often caged in pens and forced to perform for cheering audiences.

The closer I got to the main pod, the more dolphins joined in my escort. I was completely surrounded by them—both sides, straight underneath, front and back as well as in the air. These animals were so fast, so utterly in control and so powerful. I was right in the middle of them, caught up in the pod's energy but knowing that I could not even begin to match their strength or agility in the sea. It was obvious that there was a dynamic—a cohesiveness— to the pod. They had overtaken me, chosen to surround me and to play with what appeared to be a wild abandonment. What I was so conscious of, because of seeing these 10-foot, 500-pound mammals leaping into the air, was that I was a plaything in their minds. My ignorance of their world was enough cause for me to wonder that if I did something wrong within the pod, could their play suddenly turn into aggression?

I was sprinting in an effort to keep up with them, trying to match their energy and watching their shadows below me as they swam for a few seconds, inches from the sweep of the paddle blades. I couldn't see their eyes through the refraction of my bow wake and the bulge of water that they pushed in front and above them, but I could see when they turned sideways, and I knew they were looking up at this yellow sliver of a boat with the rapid cadence of black blades slicing inches from their heads. They kept coming closer, more frequently sliding into this parallel course of mine. While I spent all of my reserves and strained every muscle from my fingers to my toes, they cruised in ease until bored, then shot away with a thrash of a tail, only to be replaced by the next one that must have been waiting its turn. As if for fun, they would then cut the wave in front of the boat, break the surface, and exhale and inhale with a rapid *puh-whoo*. Another few seconds of swimming just below the surface, then back up for another quick breath. They were master marathoners, and I was a novice sprinter trying to compete in the same game of endurance and speed. What an absolute thrill to be in that all-surrounding energy, to be swept along with something so beautiful, so natural, and so incomprehensibly intelligent. After fifteen minutes I was spent, too exhausted to continue the game that they so clearly were enjoying. I finally had to give up, to let them continue without me and join up with the main pod that was moving farther out to sea. I dropped the paddle, grabbed the camera, and took a few parting shots as the last of the dolphins swept past. Ahead there were still dolphins clearing the waves in leaps of play and excess energy. I was content—no, more than content—to watch them go and to know in the pounding of my heart that I had just been privileged to have been included in their play. In that moment of watching them go, of being left behind, I was filled with a sense of wonder, excitement, and exhaustion. It had been a brief ten minutes of intense interaction, ten minutes that I would relive a hundred times in cherished memory.

By the time I paddled back behind the protection of Spyglass Point, the bank of clouds had blotted out the sun's light and warmth, and the offshore waters were covered in whitecaps. I landed at the break in the chalk bluffs that I had spotted earlier, timing my landing as a swell rolled gently over the lower rocks and left the bow teetering just long enough for me to jump out and pull the boat higher. The beach—if a jumble of chalk rocks all perfectly rounded and polished by the surf could be called a beach—was no more than 50 yards wide and two boat lengths deep. A wall of white cliff rose 50 feet straight up at the back of the beach, ending where the land was slightly less vertical and allowing a heavy covering of windswept, knotted grass to grow. The bluff continued higher, slowly leaning back into itself for another 200 or 300 feet before hiding the summit. With the tip of Spyglass Point extending out a half mile from this crescent of white stones, I would be sheltered from anything coming out of the south, southeast, or southwest. It wasn't an idyllic camp, but it was a safe one.

The rains were only minutes away as I emptied the boat of most of the gear and carried it to the top of the steep beach. Most of the higher rocks and stones were small as a result of the storms that continually throw the smaller rocks higher, settling them into a tightly packed jumble where each is intricately locked in place. By tossing aside a few of the larger stones and rearranging some others, in a few minutes I had a fairly level spot for my camp.

I set the tent up just as the first fat drops of rain splattered down. I slid the sleeping pad under the tent to protect the tent floor from the stones, crawled in, and surveyed my temporary home. There were a few odd bumps and lumps under the sleeping bag, but all in all it wasn't too bad. The tent opening looked out toward the point where I could watch the approaching gale, and the boat was high and dry, well above any surge the gale might kick up. The one thing I was assured of was drainage. The forecast was for high winds and rain. At least with the tent set up on the rocks, there wasn't any chance of getting wet—a small concession to the minimal comfort of the camp. All I had to do now was sit and wait.

For two days there wasn't much to do but sleep, eat, write in my journal, and sleep some more. The cliff at the back of the beach was slick with the rains and probably too steep to climb even if the rocks had been dry. On either side of my camp, perched above the now rhythmic dumping of the surf, were colonies of fur seals draped like woolly brown caps on the boulders just above the surf. They lay perfectly molded to the contours of the rocks, oblivious to the contortions of their bodies and the threat of the surf just feet below them. The first few times I left the tent to retrieve more food or clothing from the boat, they would turn their heads in a sleepy roll, watch as I went about my business, then lazily roll back into sleep. Clearly I wasn't a threat to their napping—naps that lasted for the better part of the two days.

Four or five times a day—mostly for a distraction from the boredom of sitting and waiting—I listened to the marine weather on the VHF, only to hear the same report: southerly gales 30 to 40 knots, southeasterly swell 2½ to 3 meters. Looking out the tent opening I could watch the seas beyond the point rolling northward, great volumes of endless black swells with their tops breaking in lines of white streamers. The swells wrapped around Spyglass Point and rolled higher up the white cobbles below my camp. Several times during the second night I woke to the rumble of the rising tide. I unzipped the tent and shone my headlamp out onto the rocks, watching the height of a wave as it spent itself amidst the boulders down low and the smaller rocks higher up. At the height of the tide, the swells washed to within 3 feet of the tent, throwing spray against the tent fly. I watched the waves until I was sure they weren't climbing any higher, then retreated with a wet head back into the warmth and relative comfort of the bag. Nestled into the folds of the bag and not ready to slip back into sleep, I wondered where the dolphins had gone. Did they seek the shelter of a cove somewhere along the coast as I had? Surely they wouldn't battle the breaking seas if they didn't have to. I wanted to think of them circling and milling about in the lee of the land somewhere, waiting as I was for the gales to subside. When my mind could no longer hold the memory of the dolphins, or the concern for the surf, I must have finally let go mentally and fallen asleep.

An hour after dawn I woke with shoulders and back stiff from sleeping on the rocks for three nights in a row. I unzipped the tent and looked out on a sky that was rapidly breaking up; the gale had finally blown itself out, the low pressure moving off shore and being replaced by the high that had been forecast.

Although the winds had shifted to the north with a stiff 15 knots, the southerly swell continued to roll in for three more days. Eight- to ten-footers lifted and lowered the boat in a gentle, continuous roller-coaster ride. The northerly winds slowly built the following seas to 3-footers that picked up the stern and surfed the boat up and over the oncoming swells. The ride was a glorious race down one side of the swell and up the next. After three days of sitting, it was exhilarating to be moving again, to be working with the sea instead of watching it from a distance.

The run from Spyglass Point to Gore Bay was almost 25 miles with no safe landings in between. With calm seas there would have been several places to land and stretch beneath the chalk bluffs but not when the surf was running as big as it was. As with most of the east coast, the ocean floor here was relatively deep to within 20 yards of the beach. The swells maintained their full power until they hit the gravel or exploded against the faces of the bluffs. I stayed a half mile offshore, content to ride the waves and use the power of the following seas to cover the exposed coastline. The constant din of the surf was all the warning I needed not to wander any closer to the land.

After five hours of paddling, the high bluffs gave way to forested ravines, backed by rolling, open meadows. Just as the following winds began to pick up and the seas started to break on a more regular basis, the expanse of Gore Bay appeared, with its line of holiday houses curving around the mile-long beach. Even from a distance of 3 miles I could see the multiple lines of surf starting 300 yards out from the sand. The lines meant that here, at least, was a shoaling sea bottom. The power of the surf would be gradually broken down at each surf line. I knew there weren't any sheltered landings for the next 20 miles or more when the surf was running as it was. The only choice was to attempt another surf landing here at Gore Bay and hope to thread my way through the lines of breakers. If I could get past the first breaker without getting dumped, I would have it made.

Chapter 3

The simpler you make things,
the richer the experience becomes.
—Steve House

WHEN ONE TRAVELS AT 4 MILES AN HOUR, there is plenty of time to watch what is ahead and come up with a plan. As long as the paddler stays in deep water and the winds aren't shrieking overhead, nothing happens very suddenly. There is time to think. Time to assess the conditions, weigh the risks, and formulate a plan. As I came up on the beach at Gore Bay, I studied the lines of surf and watched how steep and fast they were hitting the outer bar. The confusion of the big southerly swell and the local 3-foot northerly wind waves had broken the lines of surf into irregular patterns that would be impossible to read once inside the surf zone. Without some idea of a safe route, the five lines of breaking surf meant the potential of getting knocked over five times. I needed better odds than that.

The cliffs at the southern end of the beach extended farther offshore than the crescent of sand. As I slowly drew closer, I could see the southerly swells breaking over a reef that reached out beyond the cliffs. The reef break would bend the waves around the cliff point, where there was a risk of getting washed onto the rocks, but where there also appeared to be a narrow channel close to the rocks that wasn't breaking. I paddled the length of the beach, passing the line of houses that looked so safe and snug tucked under the hill, then sat and watched the reef break for ten minutes. If there was ever a place to test the maneuverability of the boat, it was here. I pulled the hatch cover off immediately behind the seat and quickly stuffed my hat, sunglasses, and the camera into the last remaining space. The helmet was snapped on, and the life jacket was zipped up with the side straps snug around my ribs. I shoved the water bag forward of the foot pegs and snapped the spray deck back in place. The boat was now ready—nothing on the deck except the spare paddles and the compass and nothing to slow me down or entangle me when I eventually had to jump clear of the boat.

Gore Bay was the largest surf I had to deal with so far on the trip, a proving ground for not only my paddling skill, but more importantly, for my ability to remain focused. Despite having paddled more than 15,000 miles and having surfed for years as a recreational sport, big surf still intimidates me. I have miscalculated sets, committed myself to the surf zone, and looked back to see huge breakers cascading down on me. An awful feeling of complete helplessness set in, knowing there is no way out except through the back of these waves, if they let me go. Because I've made those mistakes and have been in that position of looking at a wall of white water, I not only have a great deal of respect and fear for the surf, but I also know how to survive in it when it crumbles over me. If I had my choice, I would land only on beaches where I could step cleanly out of the boat without ever having to run another line of surf, but that isn't possible. My passion is the sea, to explore not only its subtleties but also its extremes. The surf is part of that exploration—how to work with it, survive it, and learn from it.

The Gore Bay landing was one of those potentially dangerous landings where I seemed to hit each line of surf at precisely the right moment and in the exact place where I needed to. From the time I sat looking at the reef break until I was safely on the beach, less than five minutes passed. In those five minutes I was completely engrossed in what I had to do. No other world existed other than the immediate surf, the boat, and me. I was aware of my position in the lines of surf: gauging the shallows and the channels of water by the color of the breakers and moving the boat laterally within the lines of surf and away from the brown, churning water that indicated the sandbars. Within those white rumbling lines, I stalled the boat several times, waited until I could see a channel of deep water—waited until I had a plan—then pushed the boat hard, pressing the charge that is so important when the opportunity is so narrow. I was focused, tense but flexible—the perfect combination that keeps one keenly aware but not frozen with sensory overload. The boat handled the lines of surf brilliantly, surfing down the face of the waves and outrunning the larger of the swells until I was well inside the outer break. By leaning the boat hard on its edge, I could turn it when I had to and maneuver it without slowing the hull speed down. Whether it was luck, skill, or the design of the boat I didn't know, and perhaps it didn't matter. The important thing was that with the right approach and patience I had run the 10-foot surf without so much as getting my helmet wet. Before I knew it the bow was driven onto the packed sand by the last wave. I jumped out, grabbed the bow loop, and pulled it up beyond the reach of the tide.

People have repeatedly asked why I choose to paddle long trips alone. Some have argued that I would be safer with a partner. The landing at Gore Bay was a perfect example of how little another person can help in difficult conditions. There is probably no other sport where the individual is so completely alone as in rough-water sea kayaking. Unlike mountain climbing there are no harnesses or ropes that connect one to another. The very elements that make climbing safe—contact and physical support—are the entanglements of danger for the paddler. The ability to assess a dangerous condition, to know one's abilities within that situation, and to move freely and quickly through or away from the danger are what make kayaking safe. Beyond a certain degree of winds and waves, every paddler, even in a group, is essentially on his or her own. There isn't room or time to look around and check on someone else. The paddler is part of an environment that is constantly in motion, and that brief moment of hesitation—of trying to find a paddling partner in the noisy chaos of breaking seas—shifts the focus and increases the risk of a mistake or of simply losing the mental edge of critical timing. The only safety net is the one that is within: the assessment skills that one develops and the mental discipline to focus and to react.

After six hours of surfing the following seas and guiding the boat through the waves, I stood looking out over the lines of surf and thinking how sudden the transition is from open-water paddling to standing on solid ground. What a strange feeling to not be moving—not balancing or shifting my weight, not spinning the blades and feeling the boat surge forward on the face of a wave. The beach beneath my feet felt so solid even as tiny waves washed over my ankles. The threat of surf was suddenly gone, the breakers looking almost benign from the safety and perspective of the land. I was still pumped with the adrenaline that had gotten me through the surf as I dragged the boat higher into the dunes and started pulling the camp gear out of the back compartment. I wanted to set the tent up, get something to eat, then sit and write in my journal—sit and write in the company of the sea.

I had just opened the journal when a young girl, maybe ten years old, left the hard-packed sand to come over and look at the boat that was edged into the dunes. Her friend, a boy of the same age, was too busy playing in the surf to bother hiking up through the soft sands. The girl looked at the boat and asked, "What kind of a boat is that?"

"It's called a sea kayak." I answered.

"Where do you sit?" she asked.

"I sit in the middle there where the big hole is."

She leaned over the cockpit and looked inside where the foot pegs were bolted to the sides of the boat.

"It's really small. Where are ye going with it?" she asked.

"Oh, I'm trying to paddle it around the South Island."

"Around New Zealand?"

"Well, not around the whole country, just the South Island," I explained.

Then very matter of factly she said, "You should do the North Island too."

The North Island? I wasn't so sure I was going to get around the South Island, much less anything else. Her statement caught me completely off guard. "Umm, I think I'll just try to do the South Island first."

"Are you American?" she asked.

After several days of not speaking with anyone, I felt as though this cute little ambassador from Gore Bay was grilling me. I knew from past travels that kids are the first ones to approach a stranger and then disappear with the treasure of information to share with parents or friends.

"Yup. I'm from the United States, but I've been to your country before, and I really like it here."

"That's good. Well, I have to go find my friend. Bye."

"OK, see you later."

And with that she was gone, running down the slope of sand to where her friend was still playing.

Kids have such a great way about them. They live in the present and don't seem intimidated by what they don't understand. She had looked a little disappointed when I told her I wasn't planning on paddling around the North Island. Why would someone want to paddle only the South Island when there was the North Island too? I'm sure it didn't make any sense to her at all.

An hour later I had another visitor, the young girl's mother.

The woman walked up from the same direction her daughter had come from and called out as she approached, "I hope Tahouya didn't bother you. She told me there was a weird boat and this American camped down here on the beach. I thought I'd come over and say hello." She held out her hand. "My name is Edwina. We just live up the road a few k's. Are you really paddling around the island?"

A "few k's" was short for 3 kilometers. I assured her that her daughter's curiosity was no problem. "Oh, no she wasn't any bother at all. She was just curious. And yes, I am. At least I'm trying to paddle around the island. This surf is making it a bit of a job, but so far it's been really beautiful."

We sat in the sand and talked about the ocean for a few minutes. Edwina expressed some disbelief about my trip and asked about camping and how the seas had been so far. I told her a little about the trip and how a friend back home had designed a Web site that school kids all over the world could use to follow the trip. Edwina was a seventh-grade teacher and was excited about looking at the site and perhaps using it in her classroom. The conversation then turned to the local waters, and she warned me that it was a good thing I hadn't gone around the point and tried to land on the next beach.

"We live right above Manuka Beach, and it can be really nasty—big dumping surf, no place to pull out, and a strong current. You did well to land here next to the cliffs."

And then almost as an afterthought she said, "You must be tired of camping. If you'd like a shower and a hot meal, you can come home with us and meet the rest of the family."

The Kiwis are known worldwide for their hospitality, and Edwina's openness and warmth were typical of how I remembered my first visit to New Zealand. A hot shower and something other than pasta and rice sounded like a great way to finish off the day. I had more writing I wanted to do, and Edwina had the kids to watch before they wandered farther down the beach. We made a plan to meet later that afternoon and left each other to our tasks.

At five o'clock I walked up the narrow beach road, the blacktop feathering out to a strip of soft golden sands on either side, then lush green grass. Edwina sat chatting with another woman, the outer wheels of both cars resting on the sands and completely blocking the road. "No worries," as they say in New Zealand. There wasn't any traffic on the dead-end road, and if there was, I was certain they would know who it was anyway, and the conversation would just get a little busier. As I walked up, I caught the end of an apology from Edwina to the other woman, something about a pig getting out and digging up the other woman's "spuds," her sweet potatoes. The apology was waved off as I opened the car door and slid into the seat. A minute later a U-turn was made, and we were on our way.

Edwina drove me along the high coast road, which twisted like good country roads do, a ribbon that flowed over short hills and into ravines, then back up to open meadows with patches of native bush in between. Down one peaceful, windy road and up another, we eventually turned down a dirt road and into a driveway bordered with high native bush. We walked around the side of the house and out back, where there was a shed with a partially built aluminum boat under construction. Ian, Edwina's husband, was grinding away at a weld while her father, Paddy, looked on. Though Ian was dressed in coveralls that clearly showed the grime of many days' work on his latest aluminum skiff, Paddy was dressed like a happy gnome. He wore the traditional black calf-high boots of a fisherman, baggy pants tucked into the tops, and a bright pair of suspenders on either side of his jolly belly. He appeared to be a happy-go-lucky, gutsy, laughing old man. A green floppy hat tied under his chin with a piece of cord topped him off beautifully. Ian was a quiet worker, concentrating on the job of grinding and fitting a seat mount to the boat. Whether Paddy was helping or just watching, I wasn't sure. Being a carpenter, I know what it is like to work with my hands and the pleasure that comes from doing a job well. I also know when I am intruding into someone's workspace and time.

As soon as the introductions were made, a plan for dinner was set, and Edwina, Paddy, and I got out of Ian's way. Paddy made it clear to Edwina that he and I had a job to do before dinner. "We'll just go on up to my batch and get some of those beans for tea. We'll be back in two shakes of a lamb's tail."

We headed for the little car filled with fishing rods, a bait bucket, and the things that fishermen always take with them: an extra sweater, rubber hip boots, a box of tackle, a thermos, and a lunch box of sorts—all tossed on the passenger seat. I of course headed for the wrong side of the car, mumbled an apology as I almost bumped into Paddy and eventually got seated beside all his gear. As he backed out the driveway and headed down the dirt road, he laughed his hearty belly laugh at all the gear in the car and said, "I love my fishing, I do. I fish from 5:30 in the morning till 5:30 at night. I don't do it halfway, I don't. Right down there at the river mouth near the beach. I'll be down there in the morning, yes I will."

Paddy seemed to have more interests than most people half his age. He told me that he lived in Christchurch with his wife but came down to Gore Bay every chance he got to work on the "batch," to fish, and do his gardening.

"I was a chippy for years, I was. That's what we call a carpenter here. I worked hard, but I'm seventy-four now and I'm busier than I ever was. I just bought a computer. 'Tis a marvelous thing, it is." Then with a gleeful giggle he said, "I'm on the Internet, I am, and even have me a code."

We pulled into a grass driveway and left the car, with Paddy leading the way to a sheep fence hitched across the path to a small, one-story house, his "batch," a unique name for the small seasonal houses that New Zealanders have for their holidays. The house sat fenced off in the middle of a field, surrounded by grazing sheep and overlooking Gore Bay and the ocean below. Paddy loosened the fence, let me pass, then hitched the fence in place again. "I had my lemon trees looking so good, and all the flowers, too, but the damn sheep got into them all. I could 'ave cried when I saw it. They ate nearly everything."

The sheep had indeed gotten into everything—the garden of flowers, spuds, and beans trampled under the split hooves of the very sheep that looked at us from the far side of the fence as if we were intruding on their turf.

"Ah, never mind. We'll pick what they missed and have a few beans with our tea."

Paddy didn't seem the kind to stay mad for long. And how can you stay mad at something as numb-brained as a sheep? We got a bucket full of sweet beans, made sure the fence was securely closed, and headed back for dinner.

After weeks of sitting on driftwood, cooking over a single-burner mountaineering stove, and eating a pretty bland diet of rice spruced up with some kind of soup mix, the dinner that Edwina placed on the table was like a banquet. There was crisp lettuce with diced eggs and tomatoes. There were also buttered spuds, hot bread, a fish casserole, and hot tea. Rather than balancing a stainless-steel pot on my knees and drinking from a water bottle, I was almost giddy with the normalcy of real plates, glasses, and cloth napkins. It was fun to let these minutes register for what they were, a treat and a novelty that I was enjoying in the company of my new Kiwi friends.

Ian, Edwina, and Paddy drove me back to the beach later that evening and looked at all the gear: the boat, the carbon paddles, the mountaineering tent, and the compact stove that assembled in seconds and became my kitchen. I passed the gear around, showed them how the tube of the stove fit into the fuel bottle, handed them the compact waterproof VHF, and watched their eyes when they lifted the feather-light paddle. I showed them the diving camera tethered to the front-deck lines and the spare paddles strapped beneath the bungee cords on the rear deck, and then rolled the boat over on the sands and ran my hand over the semihard chines and explained how when I leaned the boat, they helped me to maneuver in heavy seas.

As I passed the various pieces of equipment around, I realized how much of it I took for granted. I knew it was the best gear in the world, and I looked after it because my life depended on it, but I never really looked at it. Sometimes the obvious—like the dishes and the silverware that I had commented on during dinner—becomes so comfortable that we lose sight of their function in our lives. Not until I stood there in the half-light, handing each piece around and explaining its function, was I reminded how precious every item was to me.

While the surf pounded the reef and rolled onto the sands, we stood in the fading light as I shared with them my world of ocean kayaking. The physical journey all came down to what they could see spread out on the sands—carbon, fiberglass, Gore-Tex, neoprene—the hardware upon which I depended. The other part of the journey, the psychological side and the skills needed on the open water, they could not see, and neither could anyone else. This hidden portion of the journey is the side that is difficult for me to share because I am talking about myself. I have to speak of skills and psychological discipline. I have to stand there and tell someone I do not know that I have these abilities and that I believe in myself when everything around me has turned literally and figuratively upside down. How do I tell them that when I sit in my boat I can feel the weight of this gear now spread out before them, feel it like an emotional anchor that settles the boat deeper in the water, giving me a feeling of solidity and security. How do I tell them that I take on the weight mentally and know that it is positive, that there is nothing extra or superfluous onboard, that the heavy weight of the boat registers as tent, fuel, film, and journals, as water filter, first-aid kit, and warm dry fleece and that this knowing is both physical and psychological, that it is heavy but that in that weight there is comfort?

I know what the boat and all of the gear are capable of. I know also what I am capable of and, more important, where my limits lie. Sometimes I am conscious that I have trained for and can function in a world that is foreign to others. I am overly conscious of my voice when I speak of my comfort level in that world of big seas. I think I am sounding like an elitist, and I don't like that. When people see my focus and the high-tech gear that I have carefully chosen, and I tell them I am afraid of the sea, I want them to believe me. I worry, especially when people know of my past sea journeys, that they see the miles and the experience and they do not hear the words when I talk of the terror I have felt. I wonder if they think I am just trying to sound self-effacing. I wonder if they know as I show them the gear and tell them of the journey, that I am just as awestruck as they are, and that as I speak, I am listening to my words with wonder, with disbelief, and with humility. They do not know that I am superstitious, that I am more comfortable talking of gear because I am afraid I may jinx my luck if I speak of my own skills.

And if I tell them of my fear, do they block the whole ocean experience under the dark cloak of that statement and wonder why it is that I do what I do? It would take more words and more intimacy than I can give if I tried to explain all of this to each individual or group that I meet along the way. I let them see the obvious, and I answer the easy questions. When I am alone in the tent or when I am out on the sea again, I think about my words and wonder, did I say too much? In my words was there any hint of boasting or of "mastering" the sea? I think what these people will remember of our meeting if my boat or body is found washed ashore.

I am not fatalistic. I am realistic. That realism births the questions and keeps me safe. I hope.

The fear that I speak of causes me to train, to observe, to study with the vigilant eye of the novice the clouds and the waves, as well as the inner emotions and the outer spoken word. Fear is a good thing. And to know that awful terror of helplessness is also good, if for no other reason than it reminds one of the terrible consequence when one doesn't respect in equal measure the wonderful freedom and the awful callousness of the ocean. Fear of dying on the sea is not something one has to experience more than once. It is a branded scar that remains tender every time the sea begins to show its natural and wild tendencies. It is that feeling when the most basic part of the brain fires off the flight-or-fight reaction. Which will it be? And by the time the brain sends the message, is it too late? And what will be the outcome?

So why go? What are all these thoughts in the tent, in the dark of night when the absence of light is like sitting in the belly of a drum with your doubts, fears, and worries ricocheting off the drum skin and keeping sleep at bay with its relentless, booming questions? If it is all that scary, then why make the choice to be there? Get out. Go home.

Go home? And miss what I know is there amid the moments of fear? No . . . let me be quiet and think this out.

I will listen to the fear and let it be part of the whole. I will not throw a heavy blanket over the fear and pretend that it is not there, bury it so thoroughly in overconfidence that its voice is not heard until it is screeching its vengeance and release. But neither will I let the winds of my emotions fan the embers of fear into consuming flame. I will let the fear inside every day. Hold it as I hold the joy and the wild song of that joy. Both must be part of the journey. Side by side and held with the same light hand on the reins. Feel them both; let one temper the other. Sprinkle the wild fire of joy with water so that it doesn't consume reason. Sing to the fear so that it has company; become familiar with it, then make it my friend. Recognize the tone and timbre of its voice so that neither it nor I will betray the other when the moment of truth speaks. All of these thoughts and flickerings of emotions lie intertwined with the gear that my life depends upon. Without one the other is useless. And occasionally when the marriage of the physical and the psychological occurs, the blending is an awareness of how integral and wonderful life is when it is lived simply.

After Ian, Edwina, and Paddy had left, I put all the gear back in its proper place in the boat and crawled into the shelter of the tent. The thin nylon did nothing to block the noise of the surf, but it reduced my world to a smaller space, allowing me to focus on the little things inside the arched poles. The radio was placed in the upper mesh pocket above my head. The headlamp and toothbrush went into the pocket near the floor of the tent, and the fleece jacket and pants were rolled into a pillow. I wriggled into the sleeping bag and zipped it up to my chin. It was cold. Too cold for the summer-weight bag with the seam near the bottom that was starting to split from years of lying curled in its limited warmth. A heavier bag would be warmer but would take more space. I pulled the balaclava over my ears and thought of the boat just outside the tent opening—it was upside down with everything inside and ready to go in the morning.

My trio of Kiwi friends were back at first light as the last of the camp disappeared into the 10-inch hatches of the boat. Edwina had a weather fax in her hand: southerly winds dying out, with a northerly building by late morning. I didn't like the 10 knots of southerly that were still blowing. Ten knots? What is 10 knots? Nothing. Unless the forecast is wrong and the 10 knots goes to 20. Or 30. I tell them I may leave later in the morning, and we say our goodbyes, the hard part of making friends.

At ten o'clock Paddy walked out of the dunes again, announcing his arrival with his belly laugh and happy heart, "I was thinking you might be settin' out, and I wanted to come down to see you off." As I finished with the last preparations—checking the camera tethers, the rear bungees holding the paddles, the fit of all three hatches—Paddy talked and I listened.

"I had my little trailer in for its inspection this morning. It's a good little trailer, it is. The fellow said it needed the wheel bearings repacked. He told me if I went and did the work right away, he would give me the sticker before the work was done. So that's what I've been doing all morning. If someone says he trusts me, then I must do the trustworthy thing."

We carried the boat to the line where the last wave skimmed onto the sands and melted in, rather than receded back out to sea. We shook hands again, his fingernails blackened by grease, my hands calloused by the pull of the paddle.

"I wish I was going with you, I do. Oh, if I was younger, I'd be right there like a big hound dog, I would. Now you be careful and call me when you get to Christchurch. I'm in the book."

Paddy gave me a good push when a wave reached up the sand and floated the keel off the beach. I didn't look back until I was through the last line of waves. Seawater was dripping off the top of the helmet and stinging my eyes as a wave lifted me high enough to see him standing with the dunes at his back. I held the paddle on end and waved it back and forth. He lifted both hands high over his head in a farewell salute. Paddy's feet were planted on the sands, but his heart was out on the waves with me.

Chapter 4

My best friend is the man who in
wishing me well wishes it for my sake.
—*Aristotle*

AT 5:30 I GROGGILY OPENED MY EYES, unzipped the sleeping bag enough to reach for the VHF radio, and thumbed the top right switch to the "on" position. The forecaster was already into his general synopsis of the weather pattern: "A low pressure system extending from Puysegur to Conway will move north by mid-morning. Winds out of the northwest early morning, changing to southerly gale force 30 knots by late morning."

Gale force southerlies? Not again. I didn't even bother listening to the rest of the report. I had heard enough.

It was December 24, and it looked as though my Christmas present was coming straight up from the Antarctic. If I stayed where I was, I would get blown off the gravel long before the winds hit 30 knots. I was 20 miles into a stretch of 90 miles of steep beach with no sheltered landings. I had already been through three southerlies that certainly lived up to the warnings I had heard from everyone along my route. The last thing I wanted was to try and sit out another gale, especially on this exposed beach.

I pulled my map from its clear plastic case beside the sleeping bag and measured the miles from my camp to the mouth of the Rakaia River. Twenty miles. If I hurried, and if the weather forecast was right, I might have enough time to get up the river before the gales hit. There was nothing between the river mouth and where I sat but miles of the same endless gravel that the sea had pushed like a bulldozer out of the depths. Behind the beach was a bog land that eventually led to the shores of Lake Ellesmere, a brackish lake that extended as far as I could see in all directions. This racing between weather fronts was becoming all too familiar, and a little too stressful. I made a quick breakfast of powdered milk and granola, a peanut butter and honey bagel for "the road" and started breaking down camp. In an hour I was through the surf and heading for the Rakaia.

Forecasting the weather must be one of the most thankless tasks in the world. Everyone recalls the countless times when the forecast is wrong, but no one remembers when the meteorologists nail the weather "spot on." The forecast for December 24 was one that I would remember for a long time.

For the first three hours of the day I paddled as fast as I could without burning out. As I spun the paddle, I kept a nervous eye on the southern horizon, where the blue skies gave way to thickening dark clouds. They didn't seem to be moving very fast, but they certainly indicated the front edge of the predicted southerly. The winds were true to the forecast, 10 knots out of the north, which helped me along at not quite a surfing pace but faster than I could paddle on flat water. By 10:30 the north winds had dropped to barely a breeze that I could feel on the back of my neck. The near-sprint pace that I had set earlier had taken much of my energy, but at least I was within sight of the river's mouth. Five minutes later, as if the weather gods could see me approaching the Rakaia, the southerly winds kicked in.

I could see the waters farther offshore getting whipped by the blasts that were steadily working their way toward me. The few rays of sun that had pierced the earlier clouds were now just a memory. The water reflected the blackness of the sky with an opaque sheen that seemed to suck any existing light into its depths. The mouth of the river was less than 100 yards away. On both sides of the river mouth were eight or ten fishermen, several of them already turning away in a fast walk back to the line of four-wheelers silhouetted against the skyline. I surfed a small wave into the river current and managed to land just as a fisherman waded into the small surf and grabbed the bow.

Three or four days earlier I had been in Christchurch, where the newspaper had done a front-page story on my attempt to paddle around the island. The fisherman had obviously seen the article.

"You wouldn't be the fella that was in *The Press* the other day, would you?"

The approaching front was the only thing on my mind as I leapt clear of the boat and ran forward to relieve the fisherman of the bow. It took a few seconds to make sense of what he was asking.

"Oh yeah, they did a story on the trip when I was in Christchurch."

A warning blast of wind sent some dried seaweed flying out of sight over the top of the gravel beach above us. A pair of ATVs sputtered to life on the berm as two fishermen swung their legs over the machines and abandoned the river mouth to the increasing winds.

The fisherman who had waded into the surf held out his hand in congratulations. "Good on ye, mate. I wouldn't want to do what you're doing, but I think it's great that you're giving it a go. This southerly is goin' to blow a stinker. You gonna be all right out here?"

I looked at the seas that had suddenly gone berserk: white water leaping and flying in confusion as the northerly seas were hit by the winds that almost knocked the two of us off our feet. The fellow was standing less than 5 feet away, and we had to yell to make ourselves heard above the surf and wind.

"Yeah, I'll be OK. I'll drag the boat on the far side of the berm, wait to see if this blows itself out in an hour then head upriver and see what tomorrow brings."

"All right then, but let me help ye get her up outta the wind."

I gave the bow toggle back to this stranger and waded deeper into the surf to grab the stern. The carry up the steep cobble and gravel beach was like walking on marbles, each step sinking into the gray polished stones and making the 50-yard carry feel like a half mile. We finally set the boat on the lee side of the berm, and with our backs to the winds that were filling the air with fine sand and wood debris, I thanked him again for his help.

"Ye sure yer goin' to be all right out here?" he shouted.

"Yeah. I'll be fine. Thanks for the help with the boat. That's the worst part of the trip, just getting it above the high-water mark."

We shook hands again; then I watched as he loaded his fishing gear on his "bike" and headed down the beach.

The last four-wheeler at the river mouth motored up as I was pulling on my wind pants and looking for my gloves and balaclava. A short, solid fellow sat straddling the machine as it lurched over the stones and lashed the air with the fishing rods held in short plastic pipes on the rear bumper. This wild-looking guy, with the long, flowing, white beard and hair that no hat could restrain, was dressed in oilskins and looked every bit the classic fisherman. He didn't even bother to say hello but instead brought the bike to a stop next to the boat and bellowed over the screech of the wind. "Ye better get the #*! off this gravel spit. The waves'll come right over the top of this son-of-a !#* and you'll be a goner." The fellow had an American accent and wasn't afraid of telling me exactly what his thoughts were. As a last offer to either lighten his load or to make my passage to the afterlife a bit easier, he yelled, "Ye want a beer?"

He pulled a can of beer from the back compartment on the bike and held it out as if I had already agreed to the offer. I had my back half turned towards him in an effort to shield my face from the stinging wind and flying debris. With the blasts of wind throwing me off balance, I must have looked as if I had already had my share of beer or whatever else apparently made me unable to stand upright. I accepted his offer because it would have taken too much time and talk to decline it. I thanked him and then watched as he too motored off.

With the last of the fishermen and their bikes gone from view, I now had the dubious honor of being the only one left at what must normally be a very good fishing spot. I also had a can of beer that I didn't really want. Across the river where previous floods had deposited layers of mud and silt, the air was brown with clouds of swirling sand, leaves, and flying weeds. The sea was covered in steep wind waves that had scoured the shallows, churning the blue waters of morning into an uninviting brown slurry of sand and broken waves. I thought of the forecaster and thanked the nameless voice I had heard on the radio that morning. The forecast had predicted the arrival of the gale and the wind shift almost to the minute. If I had been caught short of the river's mouth, there wouldn't have been any place to hide from what was going to be a real hummer of a storm. I took one last look at the sea and recalled the fisherman's advice about getting the "!#* off the gravel spit." It was time to run and hide, to find a place to hole up until the front passed.

Two hours later I was tucked under the whipping limbs of a stand of willow trees 250 yards upriver from the surf. Flax plants and a tangled growth of head-high bush provided a perfect place to wait out the storm. The river murmured and whooshed by 20 feet from the tent opening while overhead the willows bent and swayed with the onrush of the winds. I was warm and dry in my fleece camp clothes, toes to neck in fuzzy warmth that was a welcome change from Gore-Tex and neoprene. A thick, luxurious matting of grass puffed up the bottom of the tent like a featherbed that I lay back in and listened to the sounds of this camp. Beneath the roar of the distant surf and the equally powerful rush of the wind ripping through the willow tops, I could hear the first tapping of rain on the tent fly and the music of songbirds in the nearby bush. Considering the option of camping out on the exposed beach, this was going to be a lovely place to spend Christmas Eve, surrounded by the power and the noise of nature yet safely sheltered and patiently waiting for the gale to blow itself out.

If it wasn't for the people I met along the east coast, I doubt if my spirits would have sustained me through the nearly continuous southerly gales that raked the coast through December. Time and again I was invited into the lives of perfect strangers who had either read the Christchurch newspaper article or who simply befriended me on the beach or in the villages while I waited for the winds to calm. Not only was their hospitality warm and comforting, but also their sense of adventure and spirit was encouraging.

Brian Wilson and John Grater of Christchurch had originally called The *Christchurch Press*. I had met Brian and John in their kayaks just outside the surf, and we had immediately struck up a friendship. They in turn had called John Kirk Anderson at *The Press* who showed up with a van packed with photography and kayaking equipment. Throughout my travels by sea kayak, I had been interviewed dozens of times but never by a reporter who donned a wet suit and helmet, then swam into the surf with a waterproof camera to get an action shot of me attempting to land in one piece. I don't know who spent more time getting knocked over in the rumbling surf, the cameraman or the kayaker.

I had mentioned to John, who was not only the wet-suited photographer but also the reporter for the paper, that a friend in Port Angeles had designed a Web page for my trip. I explained how I sent my friend, Al Zob, e-mail messages from libraries along the way or whenever I had access to a computer. John had included the Web address in the article, and, as a result, hundreds of New Zealanders were following the trip as I progressed along the coast.

Two days after the Christmas gale, I met a family who were camping in their converted tour bus on the same 90-mile stretch of gravel beach. Wendie Blain and Alan Marsden waved me ashore, told me how they had read the article and had hoped to see me paddling past their camp. They invited me into the old converted bus with its stained-glass window, couch, and dining table—all the comforts of home—and fed me a thick ham sandwich, tea, and the traditional New Zealand Christmas cake, fruitcake with thick, white icing that had enough calories to fuel me for the next 20 miles. A retired neighbor, Russell, who lived in one of the few permanent homes tucked into the bush beside the surf, rode up on his four-wheeler as we were finishing up "tea."

"I saw the kayak there on the beach and thought you might be the fella paddling around the island. I've been watching for the past week, hoping to catch sight of you. Good on ye mate for what yer doin'."

Russell then told us he had read in the paper about a white-tipped shark—the Kiwi name for a great white—that had been sighted off the Kaikoura coast. It had been spotted cruising near shore and probably feeding off the fur-seal colonies in the area. "Have you heard about NZ-7?" he asked.

"NZED-7? No," I answered. "What's that?"

Russell explained that NZ-7—the z pronounced as ZED—was a 7-meter great white shark that had been coming down to the South Island for the past five or six years. The shark apparently fed in the same waters that the local surfers used, and they had given him this unusual name.

Seven meters? That was more than 3 feet longer than my boat. I had seen a photo of an 18-footer caught in Australia. What had stunned me was not the length but the tremendous girth of the shark, which must have been 8 or 10 feet around at it widest. I thought of the 6-foot blue shark I had seen near Cape Campbell. It had appeared so streamlined and sleek, beautiful and frightening in how easily it had been following me. I couldn't, and didn't want to, imagine what a 21-foot shark would look like beside my boat.

The conversation then turned back to my trip. Everyone wanted to know how the trip had been so far, where I had camped the night before, and where I was heading for the next camp. This instant acceptance, concern, and enthusiasm that I had felt in everyone I had met kept me going. Like all the other kayak trips I had done, I could see in people's eyes some hint of envy or adventure. They all wanted to somehow be a part of the journey, to lend a hand in any way they could—by grabbing the bow in the surf, by the offer of food or a hot shower, or a ride into the nearest town for any food or repair item I needed. The farther I went along the coast, the deeper I became attached to these wonderfully hospitable folks. Each time the winds knocked the "stuffing out of me," it seemed there was always somebody there to pick me up emotionally. "You'll be right mate" was the common way of saying that everything would work out and that I was going to make it.

These unplanned meetings, some as brief as a few hours, others as long as the winds kept me ashore, gave me the balance that I needed along the way, the balance between the intense solitude of the sea and the rich exchange of the New Zealanders' lives that gave the trip such variety.

Chapter 5

Whatever you do will be insignificant,
but it is very important that you do it.
—*Mahatma Gandhi*

FORTY KNOTS OUT OF THE SOUTH. I SIT WITHIN A *shuddering frame of stretched nylon and flexing aluminum. Wind-driven rain lashes the drum-skin shelter and almost obliterates the roar of wind and surf. Gone is the rhythm of wave sets breaking with distinct choruses, one followed by the next. Now there is only the constant bass rumble of countless panicked waves driven beyond rhythm and thrown in confusion upon the reef and rocks. Beside the ocean, streaked with white rollers, I sit and watch. No birds take to flight. There is no chatter of tern or whistle of oystercatcher. All seem to await the outcome of the gale.*

No stranger to this stage set with reef and crashing sea, I also wait, aware that time, expectations, or concerns are nothing more than the coarse sands and tiny bits of broken shells from which my tent threatens to take flight. Hours tick by—day to dusk, dusk to the dark of night—and still the rage bellows. There is no reprieve, no escape from its onslaught. Dreams are filled with and interrupted by compressive downdrafts that flatten one side of the tent, pushing its wetness against the sleeping bag and waking me to the worry and weight of poles that cannot stand the onslaught for long. Will night ever end?

Dawn edges in on the backs of massive ocean breakers born of the last thirty-six hours of storm. The sets have returned, have sorted themselves in ranks of terrible and awe-inspiring power. Endless walls of blackened faces topped with avalanches of foaming white. Deadly beauty admired from the safety of shore.

The winds had gone elsewhere, leaving a crumpled heap of sand-covered nylon, bent and broken tent poles, and rainwater that soaked into my clothing as well as my spirit, dampening my will to continue. During the gale I had little to do but sit and listen to the storm from which I could not hide. Within the meager shelter of the tent, I was part of the storm. When sleep would not come, I had unfolded the back of a chart and penned those lines that spoke of my weariness between the blasts of wind and amid the drops of condensation that shook from the ceiling of the tent. When the gale eventually began to weaken, I rolled everything into a ball of wet nylon, hauled the boat a little higher against the crumbling shale and sand bluff, and sought higher ground to dry out and regroup.

The winds and waves were not typical, so said the shop owners and the people I met along the coast roads when there was nothing to do but walk rather than paddle. Summer was steadily passing like the fine white sands in an hourglass that I wanted to turn over and start anew. The solstice had passed, and now, though I couldn't measure it, I knew the days would gradually shorten.

I looked at the soaked tent, snapped tent poles, and sodden sleeping bag. My gear was taking a beating in the near-daily battle of winds—my gear as well as my spirits.

The first month of paddling had not in any way developed into the kind of trip I thought it would. With little more than the first 500 miles behind me, I had already gotten knocked over three times in the surf, smashing the helmet that had been strapped to the rear deck on one of the landings and compressing my right eardrum by getting thrown over in another. Now with the tent covered in wet sand and two snapped tent poles, it was hard to think of the 1,200 miles that lay ahead.

Quitting would have been easy; at least the first part would have been. It would have been so easy to walk away from the thunder of the surf that never allowed a quiet thought. I could have sold the gear that was too bulky to ship home, packed what was left and been away in a matter of days. I could have walked off the plane, back into all that was familiar and comfortable in a life that wasn't anywhere near as threatening or uncertain. Friends and family would have welcomed me home with the same love and acceptance as they had sent me off with. But I knew that as soon as the comfort of home wore off, I would have again felt the restlessness that had started the dream in the first place, the dream of exploring an unknown and seldom-visited coastline. The unfinished journey would never have slipped quietly away but would have called out as certainly as the original beckoning had. By even considering quitting, even writing the word on the pages of my journal, I feared that I was permitting it to take a foothold, one that would lead to the next foothold, and the next, and the next, until defeat would come not from the winds or the sea or the relentless surf but from within, from the desire for things to be as I wanted them to be and not as they naturally were. The South Pacific and the Tasman Sea could not be expected to cooperate with the mere desires of man. They were simply wild and unpredictable, something I reminded myself of as I trudged up the low bluff and found a place out of the wind to sort and dry my gear.

And so it was that I watched the sea and I waited. And while I waited, I balanced the trip on a set of imagined scales. On one side were the stresses of the surf, the wind, and the damp cold that slipped through the layers of clothing and stole away some of the magic of the adventure of the journey. On the other side of the scales were the memories of dolphins, of rainbows, and of quiet camps set in dune grass, where purple daisies with brilliant yellow centers watched over a pot of boiling water. When I thought of the trip as a whole rather than getting self-absorbed with its immediate discomforts, the scales came back into balance and then tipped steadily toward the positive side.

I believe that all things in life are cyclical. The shifting of emotions, weather, winds, and tides are part of the natural flow. The highs come in, with their sunshine and clear skies, and for a while everything seems idyllic. The goal is easy not only to define but also to keep in sight on the horizon. Nothing in the nature of man or the natural world, however, remains static. As comforting and solid as the highs are, they aren't meant to be permanent. The winds shift, bringing with them clouds, often rain, and the chill of an approaching front. The roller-coaster ride of weather, comfort, and emotions is part of any long journey.

On this South Island journey, the sea was no different in its cycles. When the sun disappeared and took with it the brilliance of reflected sun on waves, the ocean suddenly felt less friendly. As the winds increased to gale force, the troughs deepened and shone with an ominous blackness that matched, then surpassed, the chill of the southerly winds. At the height of the gale, when there was no escaping the roar of the wind or the earth-shaking concussions of wave on gravel or rock, it was almost beyond imagining that the sea could ever be calmed again. The gulls and terns stood on the land facing into the winds, their heads tucked into feathered shoulders as they watched the sea from well above the crushing, debris-filled fury. They seemed to want the company of their own species as they stood or sat in groups staring out at the sea.

Crabs and starfish were torn from the intertidal shallows, thrown and dashed onto the rocks, then washed higher as the tide rose and continued its relentless claim of any life left below the highest reach of its waves. The plentitude of the ocean—or maybe it is just the unfortunate fate of that which lives within the turmoil of the surf—was culled. The cycle of life and death was apparent in the patience of the gulls and terns and in the spent forms lying amid the highest rocks. The seabirds would have a feast when they returned to the rocky shore.

Maybe it was faith, believing in something that seemed impossible, that allowed optimism to hold fast while the waves piled seaweed torn from the ocean floor upon the rocks and reefs. As the low pressure system that ushered in the gale moved northward, so too, albeit much slower, would the sea calm. The chaos of local wind-generated waves would quickly lie down as the winds blew themselves out. The sea has a longer memory than the winds, however, and it would take days before the big rollers settled down.

One day after the gale subsided, the clouds broke and the sun pierced the gloom and cold of my camp. Steam rose off the rocks as I spread the gear out to dry, repaired the poles, and watched the gulls and terns take to the skies again. The winds were now out of the north, and the cycle of high to low and back to high meant that it was time to paddle, the following winds and seas lending an urgency to get on the water.

After sitting for three days and waiting for the safety of the north winds, the first pull of the paddle felt full and smooth, like the feeling a kite has when it first lifts into a breeze. There was energy beneath the boat that day, energy that was going in my direction instead of against me. Five, then ten strokes, and the boat neared its cruising speed. Another ten minutes and the stiffness from sleeping on the ground was gone. It wasn't long before the fresh wind and light waves had loosened me up and I was settled into the pace of the day.

Within two hours the seas were running 4 feet from dead astern. I was 50 miles south of Dunedin, shaking off the doubts and fatigue from the gale. The clearing of blue sky to the south had spread, and the water now had turned a brilliant deep blue green. The northerly winds and waves had knocked the 8-foot swell down to 6, and the boat was surfing, plowing and rising onto the face of the southerly swells and then sliding down the far side. There, for the first time on this sea journey, the wind and the waves seemed united in their efforts to assist me. The land to my right gently fell farther away as I crossed a shallow bay. The details of ravines and stands of trees were lost to land shadows and piercing reflected ocean light. I was 5 miles offshore, enthralled and flowing with the purity of the open ocean.

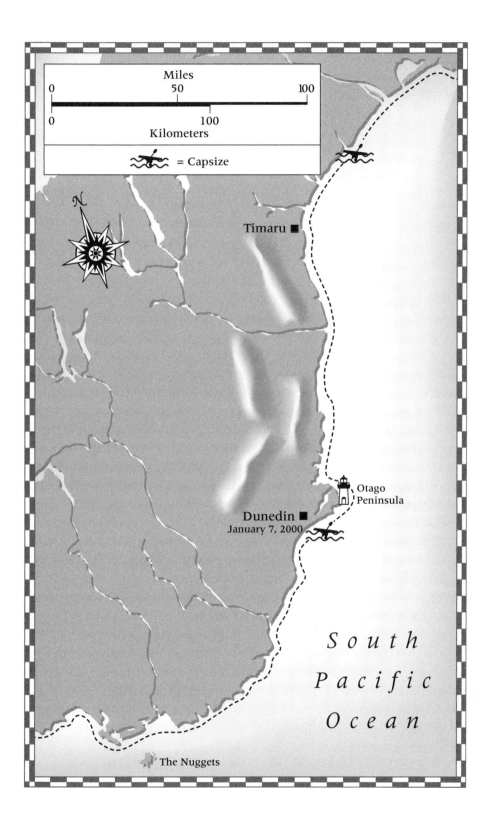

Miles
0   50   100

0   100
Kilometers

~~~ = Capsize

N

Timaru ■

Otago
Peninsula

Dunedin ■
January 7, 2000   ~~~

South

Pacific

Ocean

The Nuggets

Sooty shearwaters, or mutton birds as they are called in New Zealand, tore past from behind, tipping their wings like fighter jets to get a closer look, then veering off to either side as if I were a threat to them. Throughout the day they ripped past in endless numbers. I had no idea where they were going but was thrilled to have their company, to know that I was part of this southerly race with the wind.

Five hours of paddling slid by, and now the northerly waves were running as large as the southerlies of early morning. Six- to eight-footers overpowered anything left of the southerly swell. On the face of these waves, the boat took off like a sled on an icy hill, accelerating down the steep-watery slopes. Twin arcs of glistening water shot out to either side of the bow as the stern was lifted sharply, shoving the bow into the wave in front. For a little while longer, the strength of the wind and the size of the waves were perfect. I was matching their combined energy and was on a wonderful high, pouring myself into this stream of energy.

On the face of a surfing wave, I looked back as I trailed a stern rudder, holding the boat on its surfing course. Behind me was a world of blue-green seas, with streaks of white that marked where a wave was breaking or where another was already reforming. It was easy to pick out the waves that were going to break. They were the ones with the nearly translucent crests and with faces that were impossibly steep and mirror shiny. These rogues, these wild ones that seemed to lead the pack, had a kinetic, perfect beauty. They moved faster and were more erratic, driving and pitching themselves forward until their tops hissed and rattled like a disturbed snake warning of its strike. When the wave broke, the explosion of white destruction was both beautiful and terrifying. The fluid symmetry and graceful arc of the wave was instantly transformed into a blinding white avalanche that ran its course with a deep, throaty roar. In front, behind, and to either side of these lines of 50-yard-wide breakers, the sea ran the color of blue seemingly created and reserved specifically for the depths of the ocean.

If the sun were not so startling in its brilliance, I would have been terrified by the scale of everything around me and the fact that I was so far from land. Much the same way as the gale of two days previous had so completely held me shorebound in its grip, now the seas held and raced me onward in front of their deep-water breakers. If I thought of the distance from land, the depth of the sea beneath me, or the size of the waves, my stomach would knot up in fear and my breathing would immediately shorten. It was like driving at 70 miles an hour in heavy traffic and thinking what would happen if a tire blew out. Suddenly fear washes over you like a fever. Muscles tighten and movements lose their smooth fluid coordination. The situation has not changed, but the tension is suddenly twice what it was seconds earlier only because of the perceived danger. I had to let the distance, depth, and wave height slowly recede from my mind. I couldn't push it forcefully away but rather let it have its say and then wait for my mind to come to grips with this new awareness. I took a few deep breaths to help me relax and to find the harmony I needed in the big water. I had to stay focused, alert with just the right amount of tension, but also very fluid. Three or four minutes later I was centered again and refocused. The fear was not entirely gone; it was always there just beneath the surface, but it was the fear that provided the balance and the tension needed to perform the dance—a dance that required balance of mind, body, and boat.

In the course of the five hours of surfing, sliding back into the troughs and watching the waves slowly build and constantly over take the boat, the inevitable finally happened. A breaker caught me off guard.

The wave announced its arrival with the same raspy roar I had been listening to all day, except this time it was already upon me. The stern rose sharply, and I quickly dropped the paddle into a stern brace and waited for the rush of rumbling white water. The temptation was to look back, but it was better to lock onto the bow visually and to feel the wave with the trailing paddle. My eye needed something solid to hang onto, a reference point that would tell me where the boat was in relation to the angle of the wave.

The breaker buried the boat from astern, washing over the cockpit and covering the forward half of the boat. The wave rumbled over the boat, shifting it violently to one side before racing onward. The boat shook itself free of the sea washing over the deck and then seemed to slide backward into the following trough. In seconds, before there was time to think what had happened, it was over. From the backside of the trough, the wave looked huge, taking the view of the horizon with it as it rolled away. Now I knew the feeling of being consumed by what I have been watching all day—this unfolding of power that until now I had been able to outmaneuver.

It was a rite of passage, this breaker that caught me off guard, threatened me with its power, then let me go free. It was a reminder—as if I needed yet another—that the sea was allowing me to pass. I was playing and at times working with all of my skill on its surface while it had merely begun to show its strength. If there was someone beside me in another kayak, we might have called out to each other as we passed crest to trough, or at least found security in the glimpse of the other's flash of wetted paddles. Without the presence of another, the solitude of the sea was greater. There was no other kayak, no other boat, not even the contrail of a passing jet 30,000 feet overhead. There were only the waves and the gulls and the shearwaters tearing along on the wind's currents. The senses took in all that was surging and rolling, and somehow they found a rhythm amid the apparent mayhem. I could not match the power that the waves had, but I could find the mental and physical balance needed to use the ocean's energy.

After eighteen years of ocean paddling, I wanted to believe that the sea must recognize the cadence of my stroke. I knew the sea, and I wanted it to know me. But in my superstition I could also believe that the sea might have been tired of my visits and my quests, that maybe it knew me too well and was waiting to teach me a lesson if I was pushing the limits of its patience. It was foolish to assign human characteristics to the sea. It was foolish, but I did it anyway. Cultures that live exposed to the whims and wonders of nature tend to be superstitious. Kayakers are no exception. And solo kayakers are the worst of the lot. I didn't want to tempt fate, God, or King Neptune, so I was careful in how I thought of these waves. I talked to them, praised them for their beauty, and at other times sat in total awe, not speaking a word, believing that whatever power created them or created the storms that birthed these huge rollers knew that I was not proud or arrogant. I was the visitor, the one that was watching and learning from the sea.

Twice more the waves overtook me in their collapsing rush. Each time there was the frozen feeling of quickened heartbeats and the realization that it was too late to do anything but hang on. The waves hit the stern first, twisting the boat off course a millisecond before sweeping forward and burying the deck. The boat lurched from one side then the other as the waves had their way. It was useless to fight the hydraulics that coiled and collided beneath the hull. It was better to just ride it out, stay upright with a low brace that acted like an outrigger to the 22-inch-wide boat that was somewhere beneath the broken wave. Each time the result was the same: the rush of anxiety and fear, followed by the thrill and exhilaration of rising out of the white avalanche and watching the deck of the boat glistening brilliant yellow as the sea poured off its contours.

Eventually the high energy of the open sea was too much for me. I did not want to break the rhythm of running with the winds and waves, but after eight hours and forty miles of paddling I knew I was near my limit. I paddled past Chrystalls Beach and headed for the Tokomairiro River. I started in but at the last minute decided the feel of the surf wasn't right. The thrill of running with the big seas all day was now replaced with the fear of having to run the surf. A mile or two south of the river a set of huge waves broke farther out than the others and crested just yards off my left side. The first one peaked, broke, and slammed the bow toward the beach. I turned the boat as quickly as I could and narrowly escaped the next two waves, sprinting over the crests, getting airborne for a second, then slamming down on the seaward side of the waves. After working all day in the big seas, the last thing I was looking for was an adrenaline rush that would wring the last of any strength from my arms and body. I needed to find a little sheltered cove or hook of land that would make landing through the 6- to 8-footers possible.

I finally came ashore near the mouth of the Wangoloa River, picking the wave sets just right—letting the big ones roll in and patiently waiting for the lull that would eventually let me land safely. I timed a small set of waves, watched as the wave in front of me broke and crumbled over the shallows, then sprinted in over the broken waters. It was a perfect way to end the day.

Later, in the doorway of the tent, I wrote of the day, filled my stomach with simple and satisfying food, and looked out on the rolling sea. The glaring light was gone, replaced with a softer glow of evening, the last of the sun's rays slipping below the land. Tomorrow it would edge over the horizon again and warm my dune camp. In the meantime I looked forward to a well-earned sleep.

Sometime in the middle of the night, I awoke from being cold. I uncurled from a fetal warmth position and looked out through the open tent doorway to a sky that sparkled and shone with the brilliance of thousands of diamonds. A wide band of lights, so clear and crisp, arched overhead from horizon to horizon. I got up to check the boat and to stare in chilly wonder at a sky that I had never seen so clear. The stars seemed closer, more distinct, and far more numerous in this country, where there was so little heavy industry or light pollution to dilute the night. The air cleared my sleepy head as I leaned back and tried to see all of the Milky Way at once. I got lost in constellations that weren't familiar to my northerner's eye and forgot about trying to see it as a whole, and instead was drawn deeper into its depths. To either side of the band of lights were two areas, small but distinct areas devoid of any stars. I thought maybe they were clouds but watched carefully and saw that they were indeed places simply empty of lights. I had looked at the Milky Way for years, yet I'd never seen these "holes" of starless sky.

No wind stirred the dune grasses around the tent nor touched my face with its breeze. There were no bird songs or gulls screeching. No shooting stars. No movement in the dark of the night. There was only the sound of the surf through the blackness and the mystery of the lights overhead. I stood in the comfort of the darkness and tried to recall the last twelve hours—of spending the day offshore racing with the northern waves, of all the miles that slid past the hull of my boat, and of where the day had begun, at a camp far up the coast but not unlike this one where I was now camped. The little sleep I'd had and the cloak of the night confused me. It was hard to think of blinding sunlight, breaking waves, and balancing a kayak when I could barely see the curved outline of my tent, even harder to imagine the miles covered since the previous night's camp. I was struck with the simple reality of where I stood on the earth and of what had brought me here, awakened by the cold and searching for the Southern Cross in the multitudes of stars bannered across the sky. I wanted to shout happily to myself, "Look at where you are, Chris. Look at this night." I didn't shout anything. I only whispered on an exhaled breath, "Wow."

As I stood in the darkness, I thought about life and how or what we make of it. I thought of growing old and wondered if I would remember that night. Would I think back and be happy with my choice of how I spent the days of my life? I thought I would. That was the reason for these trips, these journeys. Sometimes it took the cold awakening and the dark brilliance of a night to clear the head and to realize what time was all about. It was about living, about being aware.

Only when I felt the first shiver run down the middle of my back did I leave the company of the stars and retreat into the lingering warmth of the sleeping bag. I pulled a fleece shirt from the bundle that served as a pillow, pulled it on over the layers that I already wore, and tried to settle back toward sleep. I shifted the raincoat over the top of the bag for more insulation and tried not to compress the sides of the narrow bag by curling into too tight a ball. I tried to will my body to be warm, but it didn't work. I was tired and wanted the comfort and rest of sleep. Five minutes after I lay down, the first chill crawled up my side and brought me out of the haze of sleep. I shifted and wiggled and pulled the paddle jacket on top of the rain jacket, then settled in again. When sleep came, it was not a restful sleep.

All too soon my inner alarm clock told me it was close to 5:30 and time to listen to the marine forecast. I was stiff from curling against the night's chill, but already I could see the sides of the tent brighten with the clear sky that would bring the sun. Waking at 5:00 to tune the radio was a ritual of each morning. So far I had moved through three radio ranges, each one fading slowly, then disappearing completely for a day or so before I was able to pick up the next station. I listened each morning to the same message: the wind and barometer readings for the nine locations around the island. The reports were repetitious but so was much of the trip. The repetition formed the structure of the journey.

When I first listened to the forecasts, the locations, the wind speeds, and directions came through the tiny VHF speaker in a tinny-sounding voice. I had trouble keeping up with the rapid-fire locations and conditions. A month later the thin monotone of the reporter's voice still fired nonstop, but I had learned to better decipher the low-pressure readings and the various wind speeds and directions. I blocked out the reports to the north and those too far up the west coast to be concerned with and concentrated on the regions immediately to the south of my position, the direction from which the weather would come.

What I was listening for was the report for Puysegur Point. I had no idea what this headland looked like except for how it appeared on my map—an almost insignificant headland that marked the beginning of the west coast and divided the South Pacific Ocean from the Tasman Sea. The headlands to the north looked more impressive and forbidding, but Puysegur was the one that had the wind reputation—and the one with the remote automatic weather station. The point split the weather coming up from the south, and the automatic monitoring station helped predict the southerly gales and storms that affected the south coast. The closer I had gotten to it, the more the point had taken on near-mythical proportions. It alone stood in the way of where I wanted to go—west and eventually north. It was as if there was a deity living on its headland that could whip the winds into storm force and send them whichever way it pleased.

I couldn't afford to miss the 5:30 report because the next one wasn't until 7:30. If the report was favorable, I wanted to be on the water no later than 7:00 A.M. because the winds usually picked up later in the mornings. Waking up at 5:00 A.M. was getting harder to do after more than a month of hard paddling. The closer I got to the south coast, and eventually to the west coast, the more important these forecasts would become. All along the east coast I had been listening to reports of higher winds in the south. Now I was on the doorstep of that south coast and more and more dependent on favorable winds.

The morning's forecast called for light winds out of the southwest. If a deity had been controlling the winds, maybe it had a different plan than the one it had been using since early spring. This was the fourth or fifth straight day without gale-force winds. When I needed it the most, maybe the winds would be in my favor.

Nugget Point was like a crooked finger of ridges and knuckles that dropped in stages from the grass- and bush-covered ridge along the skyline. The point seemed to have taken the brunt of the winds and the sea spray, the clumps of vegetation getting thinner and sparser the farther out the eye explored its gnarled joints. On the final ledge of this bony finger, a lighthouse stood stark white with its gleaming windows reflecting the sun's glare. The lighthouse, dwarfed by the cliffs it sat upon and by the endless expanse of sky it was silhouetted against, looked fragile, seemingly glued to its rocky station with nothing to shield it from the full exposure of its perch. Below and a quarter mile straight out to sea, five or six towering stacks rose out of the swells. The line of sea stacks were the remains of the ridge above upon which the lighthouse sat. Some of the stacks were crowded close together with just a narrow slice of sky separating the vertical walls. Another had a hole carved through its base large enough to easily paddle through if the surge were not so thick. The swell was low without the speed and power of three days earlier, but there was still plenty of volume left in it.

I sat beside one of the pillars of rock with an archway eroded out of its center. The swell flooded through one side, surging and gurgling up the inner walls. The water level climbed with the thickness of the swell, then rapidly drained as the swell moved on toward the headland. I had been holding the bow into the waves and watching the flood and recession of the sea through the arch. Now as the swell passed, the walls streamed with a silvery river of water pouring off the hidden ledges and crevices. Limpets and chitons clung to the black, streaming rock in their tiny armadillolike shells. Starfish hung by orange arms spread wide and searching for the next mussel or chiton to pry loose and devour.

A back surge tried to suck the boat into this vortex of swirling sun-dappled sea and shiny rock walls. I back-paddled and held the boat against the slow pull of the back current. Another swell gently rolled through the arch, reversing the flow of water. This time I didn't fight the wave but let the slope of water wash me backward away from the stack.

With hardly a breath of wind, it was easy to sit back in the cockpit and feel lazy. I slid my feet off the foot pegs and lay straight back, my head touching the rear deck. I closed my eyes and felt the stretch in my lower back and in my stomach. The sun was warm on my face and neck, and for the first time in many days, I couldn't feel or hear the wind. As I lay there slowly drifting around the point, I could feel the sun shift from one side of my face to the other as the boat gently spun in the current.

When Paul Caffyn paddled around the South Island in 1978 he took a shortcut through The Nuggets, these same jagged rocks below the Nugget Lighthouse. The shortcut almost cost Paul his life when a huge wave capsized him and pulled him out of his boat. He was somehow able to get himself back in the boat despite the rebounding and confused seas and eventually took refuge in one of the sheltered bays to the south of Nugget Point.

The difference in the sea conditions between Paul's experience and mine could not have been greater and was typical of the changing face of the sea. I had worried for weeks about how I was to get around the notorious point, with its needlelike offshore sentries. In hindsight the worrying had been a waste of energy. Nugget Point had loomed large on my map not only because it marked the beginning of the south coast and the large southern seas but mostly because of Paul's near miss beneath its cliffs. Thoughts of Paul getting torn out of his boat and fighting for his life amid those rocks left me with a haunted feeling. I wanted to flee before the winds turned this serenity and beauty into a raging chaos of refracted waves and breaking seas. I also wanted to just sit there and soak in the warmth and beauty.

Each journey, whether it is a mountain expedition, a desert crossing, or a sea venture, is always a gamble of weather. It helps to know that others have shared the challenges and the joys of similar journeys and to also know that in this brotherhood there is an acceptance and the needed approval upon which we humans depend. As I had been moving along this coast—and at other times just sitting and watching the seas from camp—I had thought of Paul, Brian, and Kazutomi. There was a camaraderie and a strength to be drawn upon in the knowledge that they had paddled these same waters. Each of them in his own way had given me fuel to continue. I thought of Paul in particular and wondered how he kept going without the benefit of at least knowing that it had been done before. Paul had the advantage of a shore crew; I had the advantage of his and Brian's success, as well as Kazutomi's attempt. The one unpredictable factor each of us had to deal with was the sea. At that turning point, the beginning of the south coast, I could not help but wonder if the winds and the seas would allow me to progress much farther. For the past week the winds had been calm, but I didn't trust them.

As difficult as the east coast had been, there had always been a village or a road within a day's hike that I could get to in case of injury or simply running out of food or water. I was quickly moving away from that security. From Nugget Point westward for 75 miles to the fishing village of Bluff, there were only a few dirt roads that twisted through the bush and emerged along the coast. Bluff would be the last place to stock the boat with food and to make the critical decision of whether to continue on to Puysegur Point or to call the trip off. The weather would determine that decision.

The south coast was the start of the most challenging part of the circumnavigation and also where I needed the weather to be on my side. It was still early in the year, and though the locals were saying this was the worst summer they could recall, I wanted to believe the weather had to improve. My mind slipped from the present, from the cool water numbing the soft tissues between my fingers as I dangled them beside the boat, to the warmth of the sun on my face and to the concern of what was ahead. Long journeys are all about finding the balance between enjoying the moment and being drawn onward by the adventure of the unknown. I was sitting, as I had so many times on previous journeys, looking over my shoulder at where I had been, then turning and looking across the bow at what was farther down the coast. I liked pivotal points on kayak trips, places where the coast took a definite change in direction, a change that couldn't be ignored and one where I was reminded to pause and to savor where I had been. In the calm of The Nuggets, a place that had represented such stress and fear, I sat and was aware of how happy I was just in being there. I was a lucky man to sit in that narrow sea kayak on such calm seas and to have known the years of paddling that had brought me there. Whatever was ahead, whether it was calm or storm, I was happy to have had this moment and the satisfaction of having gotten as far as I had.

Chapter 6

EXPEDITION MOMENTUM

And I thought over again my small adventures
As with a shore wind I drifted out in my kayak
And thought I was in danger,
My fears, those small ones that I thought so big
For all the vital things I had to get and to reach,
And yet there is only One Great Thing,
The only thing:
To live to see in huts and on journeys
The great day that dawns,
And the light that fills the world.

—*Translated from Inuit by Knud Rasmussen*

AFTER WEEKS OF PADDLING BELOW LOW BLUFFS and along steep gravel beaches, the sudden change in the shore topography of the south coast was stunning. The headland of Nugget Point was just the beginning of a line of cliffs that soared out of the sea and ended so far overhead that I could not see the tops. I paddled at the base of these cliffs, staring in disbelief and wonder at how rapidly the coast had changed.

The cliffs to the north of Hinahina Cove looked like something out of an extreme climbers' magazine: Sheer walls of rock with hardly a crack or fissure shot out of the sea and climbed straight up for hundreds of feet. There were great slabs of the same rock that formed narrow chimneys next to the parent cliff, slabs that must have separated when the island was formed by the upheaval of tectonic plates. Dark shadows and glaring light combined to form angular lines that fooled the eye into seeing ledges and rifts where there were none. The shadows shifted as I paddled closer. I saw what I thought was a chimney of rock was really nothing more than the shadow of a higher peak. I tried to see it again as a rock chimney, and suddenly it was there again. I switched back and forth between shadow and rock formation until my angle had changed and I could no longer play the game.

I wanted to paddle right beneath the cliffs, to reach out and touch the rock that reminded me so well of Ireland, but the 3- to 4-foot swell made the waters too choppy to venture close. If the seas were as big as they had been in the last week, I would not have dared to be even as close as I was. I paddled with my thighs firmly gripping the cockpit thigh braces. Resting the paddle across the foredeck, I could slip the camera out from its bungee-cord harness and try to capture the interplay of light and shadow. By now I knew the boat well enough that I could sit and shoot photos in relative comfort despite the waves. If the boat started to go over too much one way, I raised the corresponding knee a little higher and brought the boat back to a level position. The scene in the camera's viewfinder tilted one way, then suddenly back the other. If I stayed focused on one spot too long, my vision would begin to blur and my stomach would tell me to either get the picture or put the camera away.

I slid beneath the cliffs, taking pictures and soaking in the visual feast that was so different and welcomed from that of the last 600 miles. My eyes were accustomed to horizontal lines of sea meeting sky and of ever-diminishing lines of bluffs disappearing in the sea haze. Now in the span of a half-day's paddle, the lines had shifted to near vertical, and my normal perspective was standing on its edge. My progress seemed to have slipped to nothing, all apparent speed lost beneath the massive scale of cliff against sky. I paddled into their cool shadow, hoping to rest my eyes from the sun's glare, then quickly changed course to regain the warmth of the sun. The air temperature was somewhere around fifty degrees, not cold, but after so many days of wind, clouds, and of course just being wet from the sea, I relished the warm sun like a reptile.

I paddled into Cannibal Bay, where, in the past, the sea had uncovered skeletal remains of the native Maori people. The Maoris were known to have practiced cannibalism, but there was never any proof that these bones were evidence of that. For some reason the name had stuck, though the tranquil oasis of crescent sand beach and dunes was far from anything I associated with cannibalism.

I chose the west end of the beach to land because of the southwest direction that the swell was coming from. On the east end of the half-mile-long beach, the swells broke a long way out. They didn't look very big on the outside, but in the confines of the bay they were steeper and were running

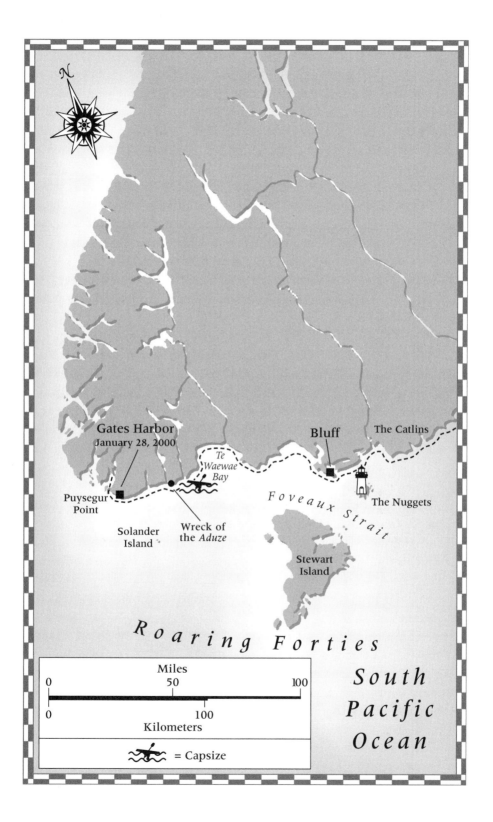

N

Gates Harbor
January 28, 2000

Bluff

The Catlins

Te Waewae Bay

Puysegur
Point

Solander
Island

Wreck of
the *Aduze*

Foveaux Strait

The Nuggets

Stewart
Island

Roaring Forties

Miles
0   50   100

0   100
Kilometers

= Capsize

South Pacific Ocean

faster, or so it seemed. They looked close to 5 feet, and I would have had to run four lines of their breakers. In close to the rocks on the west end, the swell wasn't as big. The beach was fairly protected from the cliffs, and if I sneaked in close to the rocks, I thought I could get ashore without getting wet at all. There was also just a single line of surf where the waves broke over a sandbar instead of the four breakers on the far end of the beach.

Two hundred yards behind me the sun glinted on the face of a low roller that looked smaller than the previous sets. I waited for just the right moment before starting in, trying to estimate the distance to the sandbar and both the speed of the boat and the approaching roller. I looked quickly in front of the boat for the line of suspended sands that mark the sandbar, then just as quickly spun around to watch the oncoming wave. Ideally I wanted to be just outside of the sandbar as the wave rolled under me and broke. If it all went right, I'd have the maximum amount of time to paddle over the bar before the next roller came in.

With every third or fourth stroke of the paddle, I looked over my shoulder and checked on the progression of the wave, which was quickly growing larger than I thought it would. It didn't take long to figure out that I had misjudged everything—the size of the wave, its speed, and the fact that it was going to break farther out than the sandbar due to its greater height. Though it wasn't a huge wave, it was big enough to get my heart pounding, and I knew that I was in for more of a ride than I had planned.

When the wave overtook me, it lifted the boat and shot me toward the sands like a catapult. I was able to ride it for a brief 50 yards before the boat started to carve a hard right turn. As the stern was pushed around to the left, the bow was under a blur of sea washing onto the foredeck and holding the boat on its course like a car tire stuck in a frozen rut of ice. It was impossible to get the boat back on course. Rather than try and fight the forced turn, I let the boat run diagonally across the face of the wave and waited for the next maneuver.

As the wave hit the shallows, it curled over and buried the boat in a glare of broken water. As it heaped itself onto the deck, I leaned sharply into the breaker with the extended paddle jammed into the wave on the right side. By keeping my right elbow tucked against my ribs to protect my shoulder joint and lifting the shore edge of the boat with my left knee and hip, I could ride the wave sideways in a semicontrolled, upright position. If I let my knee drop even a few inches, the edge of the boat would grab the water it was sliding over and in half a heartbeat I would get "window shaded," a term someone aptly coined for the speed at which the sideways roll occurs. The ride was a wild, crashing and thumping sideways slide in front of the wave that eventually grew gentler as the wave lost it power over the gently sloping sands. The boat eventually bumped the hard-packed bottom, skipped over another ridge, and came to rest floating peacefully in water that barely covered my ankles when I stepped out. Quite suddenly, I was where I wanted to be— high, dry, and safe.

I set up camp on the edge of the beach close to the rocks, where there was a little patch of grass. I pulled the boat alongside the tent, tied one side of the rain fly to the deck lines and the other side to pegs driven into the soft sand and weighted with rocks collected from the base of the cliff. It was a precaution that may not have been necessary, but it was a habit I had gotten into of making each camp as windproof as possible regardless of the forecast. When I was done, I stepped back and looked at the dark-green dome of my tent. Its shape and color matched the grass-covered dunes, and I liked how it fit in, tucked close under the rocks. I felt secure and protected, a solid feeling after so much exposure on the waves.

After the tent was set up, I took a stroll down the beach, leaving the tent in the shadow of the hills. I was still wet from the ride through the surf, and the far end of the beach looked inviting in the long, soft light of evening. I shouldered the camera and walked the hard-packed sand of the previous high tide, feeling its firmness on my heels, then rolling onto the ball of my foot and twisting my foot enough to dig my toes in with each step. After all day on the water, there was a simple joy in just feeling the land.

Halfway along the beach I saw what looked like a log half buried in the softer sands up near the dunes. As I got closer, the pale, almost white, color of the sun-bleached log changed shape and became a sleeping sea lion hauled out above the reach of the tide. I left the ease of the wet packed sand and approached the sea lion from directly downwind until I was moving in a crouch less than 10 feet away from its whiskered face. Flies hovered and landed on the sea lion's fur where it hadn't been able to cover itself in sand. Other flies buzzed around its nose and closed eyes. I watched its belly expand in a deep breath, then deflate for such a long time I wondered if the breath was the last one it was going to take as if maybe it had hauled itself onto the sands to die. After a long wait while I barely breathed myself, the belly inflated again, and a few cakes of sand fell off the dried fur. I knew from the long snout and 7 or 8 feet of length that it was a Hooker sea lion, a fairly uncommon breed that visits the tip of the South Island but lives much of its life farther south. I took a picture, then carefully crept away and left him, or her, sleeping in the warm sand.

The sun was slipping farther behind the hills, casting longer shadows over the last stretch of the beach. I watched the rollers come in from around the cliffs glistening in the last of the sun, then fan into the crescent of the cove. Most of the rollers missed the west end of the beach but lined themselves up in clean ranks, four breakers deep, on the east beach. It was a textbook-perfect case of wave dynamics affected by the cliffs on one side, the gradually sloping sandy beach, and the hydraulics of the waves. I stood and watched the rollers become waves, the waves become breakers, and the breakers form the long lines of surf that started at one end and ran like a white zipper opening the blue-green face of the sea. The sea's dampness chilled my face while a colder, drier air mass drifted down from the higher elevations, found its way over the dunes and beach, then touched the back of my neck with its night whisper. I was hungry and thinking how the inside of the tent awaited with its curved walls of soft welcome. Part of me wanted to settle in for the night, but another part didn't want to miss the last of the sun's rays bathing the surf in rich, low-angled light. I wandered farther east, drawn along by the spell of the surf.

Ten minutes later, just before I turned back for the tent and dinner, a black dot appeared through the last of the small surf that ran over the sand flats. Out of the white line of bubbles, the dot popped up and was suddenly standing and hesitantly walking toward the dunes where I was half hidden by the fading light and the backdrop of hills. A few feet from the water, it picked up speed and beelined for the safety of the dunes behind me. There was no mistaking the classic walk of a penguin, its very erect posture and the way it waddled from side to side in an attempt to lift its webbed feet clear of the sand. I had seen penguins out on the sea, but they had always been wary and would dive long before I could get very close. I lowered myself into a crouch beside a tangle of beach legumes and hoped the penguin would enter the labyrinth of sandy hills by choosing the dune valley where I was crouching.

The penguin didn't waste any time in crossing the open expanse of beach. It left a line of tracks as straight as an arrow until it hit the first rise of the dunes, then wandered to one side until it could climb the steep, soft sands. By luck it waddled and climbed to within a dozen feet of me. I could see its yellow and red-rimmed eyes and the feathers on its chest, which moved with each breath. The penguin stopped, looked around as if to get its bearings, then silently ducked under some dune grass and all but disappeared for a few seconds. I stood straighter and caught a glimpse of its brownish-black sides and back as it weaved a path through the grasses and low bush. It was moving steadily but not in a hurry toward the back of the dunes. I looked around and noticed for the first time other tracks that matched the close-stepped, outward flare of webbed feet that the penguin had left in its passing. I was in the middle of a penguin highway of sorts and immediately felt like a trespasser. I looked back to the surf and saw, farther down the beach, two more penguins emerging from the sea. I crouched down again and slowly sneaked back toward camp, staying high on the edge of the sands just below the dunes and hoping I hadn't disturbed the penguin's daily search for their night burrows.

The south coast had such a vastly different feel to it than the east coast. The cliffs, the hidden coves, and the thicker swells coming in from the southern ocean all added a dimension of rugged exposure that had not been part of the east coast. The penguins and the sea lion were also reminders of how far south I had come.

Later, after I had scrubbed the cooking and eating pot with a slurry of sand and seawater, I sat and studied a small-scale map of the South Island. The map showed the entire South Island from the distance of a satellite, a fly-over view of the island sitting in the South Pacific Ocean on its north–south axis. Looking at the map I could not even find the tiny cove where my tent was set up. The map showed only the curve of the land as it left the relative shelter of the east coast and bared itself to the sudden emptiness of the southern ocean. The map didn't show the cove, the tent, the sea lion, or the penguins. On an even smaller scale, it showed none of the tracks of the penguins or the drag marks left by the sea lion as it lumbered out of the surf and finally slept in the soft sands below the dunes. The map placed me on a point of the earth, but it could not tell the full story of discovery and wonder that one experiences when traveling at the pace of other creatures.

I estimated my position on the map, then looked farther west by the width of one fingertip, two-days' paddle. The area inland from the sea was known as The Catlins, a region with few roads, and those that do exist are so infrequently traveled that it is easy to imagine what New Zealand was like fifty years ago. On my bike tour of the South Island, I remembered riding along unpaved roads through this region of native bush and hardwoods, of scant signs of settlements, and of finding the few roads that penetrated the native bush and wound their way down to the sea. The roads were dusty and bumpy, and the pace was even slower than the already relaxed pace I had found farther north. I had camped wherever night found me, my only concern being the weka, a brown flightless bird the size of a small chicken with the kleptomaniac tendencies of a master thief and the arrogance that anything left around the tent was fair game.

Six years later I was now seeing The Catlins from a different perspective: from the sea looking inward at the forested hills and the cliffs that protect the soft underbelly of the land. The sea relentlessly hammers at this coast, sending geysers of mist out of blowholes, smashing waves onto rock faces, and forming scalloped coves where the land seems to offer itself to the onrush of the sea.

Beyond the walls of the tent, darkness had settled in, and the roar of the surf drowned out any of the small sounds of night. Within a few hundred yards of the stretched nylon of the tent were the sea lions and penguins that had sought the same refuge of the cove that I had for the night. I liked knowing this, of being part of the whole.

For the next couple of days, I explored the rocky shorelines and headlands and was content to wait for the strong westerly winds to abate. The winds were not gale force but just strong enough to make any real progress a debt of expending too much energy for the miles gained. It was better to spend the time hugging the shoreline, tucking into coves and peering into sea caves than pushing into a head wind. Offshore paddling was exhilarating and the way I could make the most miles, but I couldn't paddle on that level every day. It was exciting but it was also taxing, physically and psychologically.

The inshore days were when I could get a close look at the cliffs and the side coves that I would normally miss from 2 miles out. If the swell wasn't large, I could paddle within 100 yards of the rocks, sometimes a good bit closer, and hide from the winds that were farther out on the water. Despite the reflecting waves and the lack of the certainty of safe landings, I was more comfortable paddling along this cliff-guarded coast than along the long expanses of beach on the east coast. I liked paddling in close, feeling the backwash of the swells and seeing the rock formations: the veins of white quartz, the folding of sedimentary rock, the uplift of giant plates of gray-black monoliths beside sheer walls. In close I could see the occasional fur seal hauled out above the surge and white water breaking over rocks that looked like the teeth of hunger waiting for the seal to get washed into its maw. How the seals got onto those rocks was a mystery to me. How they slept just above the reach of the surf—so relaxed, with their heads rolled to one side and eyes shut with dreamy sleep—was also a mystery. When I was this close to the rocks, I was constantly looking seaward, ever watchful for the rogue wave that could throw me onto the rocks, below these sleeping rolls of brown fur and blubber. The snoozing seals didn't seem to share my concern.

The cliffs also offered a sense of protection from my greatest fear, that of getting blown out to sea. Along a low, featureless coast, there is no place to hide from the exposure of either the sea or the wind. This double exposure— this dual threat of something so visible as the ocean's waves and something so invisible but equally as dangerous, the wind—is what is so wearing. There is nothing to seek refuge behind, either on the sea or on the land, when the day's work of paddling is over and the next job is to find shelter for the camp. It is human nature to want the security of a safe haven, to know there is a place of certain rest and quiet to repair to. Here on the south coast, where the island seemed to erupt out of the sea rather than melting into it, there was that security of knowing there was shelter in the coves, in the outcropping of a headland where there was a reprieve from the winds, and in the safety of tilted rocks hundreds of feet high that blocked out the noise of surf and redefined the understanding of horizon. In this drama of two worlds colliding— the vertical world of cliff refusing to give in to the relentless pounding of the waves rolling in from the south—there was a feeling of paradoxical belonging, of knowing I was more alive because of the beauty and the severity of the raw power that was in evidence no matter where my eye wandered, and also in knowing that I was here only because the sea was relatively calm.

I in fact did not belong here, not as the muttonbirds did, or the fur seals, the sea lions, the dolphins, or the penguins. They played and fed in conditions that would terrify me. On days when I was challenged to my limits and feeling the strain of muscles and the fatigue of hours of work, they rolled in the surf, basked on the rocks, and slipped through the waves without concern. The remains of a shipwreck in Cannibal Bay—a hunk of riveted iron covered in thick scales of rust and streaked with red and brown—was a stark reminder of how limited we humans are in existing in this world where the sea meets the land. There was nothing subtle about this coast, neither its beauty nor its potentially destructive power. Its very nature seemed to demand that one be alert, watchful, and wary.

There was no use in complaining when the winds didn't do as they were "supposed" to do, even when the marine forecast predicted winds out of the southwest at 10 knots and I would plan a 5-mile crossing accordingly. The winds might shift due west and then build to 15 or 20 knots, but by the middle of the crossing it was too late to do anything but dig deeper. The memory of wind-free days and warm sun faded quickly when the boat pounded into the waves and the wind grabbed at the high paddle blade and threatened to roll me over.

I had left the cliffs of The Catlins behind and was now paddling point to point across multiple small bays and coves. The cliffs had given way to thickly forested hills that rolled out of the interior and ended with steep bluffs spilling the native bush onto gravel beaches. My goal for the day was a place on the map called Papatowai, a river mouth that hopefully would allow a safe landing and access to sheltered camping farther up the river.

I paddled around Long Point, a prominent headland that marked the eastern boundary of Tahakopa Bay. By hugging the low cliffs, I was able to stay out of most of the southwest wind that was tripping the waves into whitecaps a quarter mile out from shore. As soon as I rounded the point, I would lose the shelter of the land and the full force of the wind would be on the left forward quarter of the boat. This was one of those days when the forecast didn't quite match with the actual winds. What happened to the predicted 10 knots of wind was a moot point when it was obviously blowing close to 20 knots. The 5-mile crossing was going to be a slog.

The waves were not big, 3- to 4-footers, with the occasional 5-footer in between. Because these waves were not the product of a storm way out at sea, they did not have any of the associated volume; instead they were local wind-generated waves that were short and steep, whose pattern was difficult to find. The boat plowed along, throwing water into the wind, which was whipped back and would cover me in its salty sheets. As each wave hit the bow and was sent flying back, I would tuck my chin and attempt to shield my face with the bill of my hat. The bill blocked most of the spray, but still my eyes felt as if they had sand in them, and the cracks in my lips burnt like fire. In smooth seas, even if they are large swells, there is time between each stroke for a minute rest as one stroke finishes and the next begins. When the sea is short and choppy, though, there is no rest; the sea is too broken up for the boat to have any glide.

After a couple miles of paddling hard, the burn in my shoulders was something that I couldn't ignore. All I wanted to do was to put the paddle down and shake out my arms. To do that, however, was to rapidly drift off course and then have to turn straight into the winds to regain the line I was trying to maintain in the crossing. The burning never went away; neither did the stinging in my eyes or the pain of my cracked lips. It all somehow became part of the crossing—the miles, the pounding, the sea spray, and the slow definition of the opposite side of the bay, where I could distinguish a line where the river cut through the forest and out onto the beach.

I watched the approaching waves, which were now breaking more frequently. My neck was beginning to ache from constantly looking to my left, watching, measuring, and anticipating each wave. The urge was to press on quickly, to pick up the pace and try to reach the far side a little faster. But two thirds of the way across the bay there was no getting out of anything quickly. There was only the job of continuing, of reaching forward with each stroke and of thinking that with each stroke I was 3 or 4 feet closer to the calm of the river.

This situation prompted me to play a mental game of work and reward: I looked back at the headland, at Long Point, and saw how far I had come. I was far enough out that I could no longer see clearly the actual rocks and cliffs rising out of the sea. From where I sat in the waves, the land appeared to pour off the higher ground in distant folds of green barren rock. The land fell gradually, and then more abruptly as if the weight behind Long Point was pushing the headland reluctantly out to sea. The view from the glance over my shoulder was the reward that kept me focused on moving forward, as slowly the distance traveled grew greater than the distance yet to paddle. The bush-clad coast ahead was now close enough for me to pick out individual trees, and I could actually see the dunes above the surf line.

If I could only escape the noise of the wind, which sounded like a continuous and amplified slow tear of paper an inch from my ear, a noise that stood between me and the work that I had to do to keep the boat on course and upright. If I could have somehow turned off the noise of the wind, the stress levels would have been halved.

On top of the wind noise, there was the rasp and hiss of the waves that broke with a sharper tone. The boat dropped off one wave and hit the next with a crash that I could hear, and also feel in my left leg, the one that was pressed against the side of the boat. My other leg was jammed under the cockpit on the right side and holding the right edge of the boat high so that the boat didn't "trip" over its edge as we were inevitably blown in that direction. All of this was like dancing with too many partners at once and trying to mind the music at the same time.

I could see the beach clearly now, but I couldn't pick out where the lines of surf ran up the river mouth. The wind continued to tear past my ears with the same deafening noise. All I wanted was for it to quit for just a minute so that I could think clearly and make the right decision on entering the surf zone. I decided the best bet was to paddle beyond the bluff, then turn and run back toward it with the waves and wind at my back.

When I was upwind of the bluff by a quarter mile, I stopped paddling, pulled the life jacket on, then popped the spray deck and grabbed the helmet. By the time I had everything buttoned up again, the boat had drifted in line with where I thought the river was. I turned the boat and caught the first wave that sped me into the surf zone. The closer to the beach, the easier it was to see the river pouring silt-laden waters into the blue-green waves.

The ride through the lines of breakers was almost anticlimactic after the two hours of struggling out on the open waters. The farther up the river channel I paddled, the more protection there was from the winds, and the quieter my world became. I let the boat glide to a soft landing against the mud of the riverbank and just sat there. The sudden quiet and the firmness of the mud holding the bow allowed me to let go of the strain of the day's paddling. I suddenly felt the weight of exhaustion, of wanting to just sit there and do nothing but let my chin drop and listen to the quiet. The minutes of calm were part of the reward and the satisfaction of completing the crossing. I sat and listened for a minute, then popped the spray deck and began the work of getting the boat to high ground and setting up camp.

An hour after landing I was finally in the tent, smearing and slapping at the dozens of sand flies that peppered the tent fabric. They were no bigger than a pinhead, but when they landed on my neck or wrists, they burrowed in with a fiery bite that left an itchy, burning welt. I remembered the clouds of sand flies along the west-coast section of my bike trip. As long as I was moving, they wouldn't bother me but as soon as I stopped or was in the process of trying to set up the tent, they descended by the hundreds to feast on any exposed skin. The west coast is infamous for the "little buggers," as they are politely called. I was close enough to the west coast that from here on out the sand flies were going to be my constant land companions whether I liked it or not.

A short walk up the beach from my riverside camp was a "motor camp," the Kiwi solution to providing tourists and travelers with inexpensive accommodations. The dozens of motor camps around the country compete with one another for the cleanest, quietest, most serene settings, complete with tent and camper sites, communal kitchens with pots, pans, dishes, showers, and even washing machines. I decided to take the next day off mainly to rest my body but also to get cleaned up and just get away from the noise of the surf.

When I walked into the campground office, the lady at the counter must have seen the obvious. She said, "I'll bet you either need change for the shower or laundry soap, right? There's soap on the end of the second aisle, and I'll give you change for the showers and the machines."

The host's quick assessment suddenly made me feel overly conspicuous in my salt-stained paddling shirt and my daypack stuffed to overflowing with the rest of my dirty clothes. I walked the dozen or so steps to the end of aisle two and thought about her comment. Before I left my camp I had given myself a quick inspection and had felt pretty good at what I could see from the chest down. Sure my pants were a little wrinkled despite the palm pressing I had given them, but all things considered, I thought they looked pretty good. A young couple with bike helmets dangling from their fingers was shopping for camp food along the three aisles in front of the counter. I had noticed them when I walked in and now was very conscious of how tidy they looked as I slipped past them. It was wet, cold, and windy outside, but they still looked like bicyclers do everywhere—fit, tanned, and streamlined in multipaneled spandex shorts and cycle shoes that clicked on the wood floor from the cleats that held them in their bike pedals. I could feel the grit of sand between my toes, and there was a squishy sound every time I took a step. I knew I was leaving wet tracks everywhere I walked.

I returned to the counter with the laundry soap, two bags of pasta, a loaf of bread, too many chocolate bars to carry very effectively, and three satchels of powdered-juice mix. On the way back to the counter, my backpack caught on the revolving postcard stand and almost pulled it over. The groceries sort of spilled out of my arms and onto the counter. I felt the lady's eyes on me, then noticed she leaned a little to one side and looked at my tracks leading around the aisles. She had started to ring up the items when I thought maybe I hadn't gotten enough chocolate bars. I squished back to the middle aisle, grabbed three more, and hurried back to the counter.

I suddenly felt like a bumbling idiot. Rather than just leave it at that, I made matters worse by trying to explain. "I'm traveling on the water. In a kayak. Actually on the ocean. I paddled into the river and saw the trail, and someone told me you had showers and a washing machine. I was just hoping to get cleaned up a bit, then camp on the riverbank, just for the night."

The lady hadn't even asked for an explanation, but there I was, spilling my scrambled story out to her as the groceries lay all over the counter. Those were the most words I had spoken to anyone in over a week, and it all sounded as though it had come out way too fast. Now all I wanted to do was to cut my losses, get out of the office/store, find the showers, and get back to my camp.

The middle-aged lady was methodical, polite, and much to her credit, tactful and tolerant. "I didn't think you looked like a bicycler or a car camper, but we get lots of travelers coming through." Then as if to double-check on what she thought I had said, she asked, "You're in a kayak?"

"Yes. It's a sea kayak. It's designed for the ocean." As if that would wrap everything up in a nice clean explanation.

"We have people visit who paddle in the river, but I've never heard of anyone out on the ocean. You'd better be careful out there. There's not much between here and Bluff, and we're about the last place I can think of for any food. Where did you start from?"

I really didn't want to go through the entire explanation and then answer the questions that were sure to follow. I just wanted a hot shower. My toes were freezing, and I kept thinking how nice it would be to pull on freshly washed and dried fleece clothing.

"Well I started in Picton a little over a month ago and . . ."

"You're not the fella that was in the paper, are you?" The lady was suddenly very interested and looking me over, head to toe, with a very different look than just a minute earlier.

"Well yes, the Christchurch paper did an article, and the Dunedin paper did one as well," I replied.

Thankfully the bicycling couple walked up just as the conversation was heading for one of those well-intentioned but embarrassing on-the-spot interviews. I paid for the groceries, thanked the lady, and made a beeline for the showers.

Later that evening I was inside the tent writing letters to friends and family when a tall, thin, middle-aged fellow walked up to the tent. He asked if I was going to be staying long and told me that camping on the riverbank wasn't really allowed. Too many people in the past had camped on the floodplain and left fire rings and trash behind them.

For the second time that day, I explained where I had come from and that I was going to stay only one more night. As soon as he heard my story, the fellow rescinded his earlier stiff suggestion about my having to leave. He explained that he was a local naturalist who had been influential in protecting the land on the opposite side of the river, a stand of thick forest that I had been looking at through the mesh opening of my tent. He told me the forest was one of the last old-growth stands outside of Fiordland National Park and suggested I paddle over and walk the trails around the peninsula. He then told me a little about the early history of New Zealand.

Before the Maoris came from the Polynesian islands, there were no mammals other than bats and seals on New Zealand's islands. Without predators many of the birds like the kakapo, the kiwi, the weka, and the moa never developed the need to fly. They had no defenses against the dogs and rats that arrived onboard the sailing canoes of the Maoris, and their numbers soon began a steady decline. The fellow also told me that prior to man's arrival, there had been eleven species of moas on the South Island, some the size of an overgrown turkey and the largest growing to a massive-boned ostrichlike bird almost 10 feet tall. The moas were easy fare for the Maoris, and within a couple of hundred years, the last of the flightless birds had been hunted to extinction. Bones of the moas had been exposed over the recent years as the river flooded and eroded the soft sands at the forest edge.

After the fellow left I slid the empty boat into the river's ebbing current and with a dozen swift strokes was on the far side. I left the boat nosed into a crumbling bank and found a sandpacked trail leading into the forest. Once under the cover of the canopy, the sound of the surf faded to hardly a murmur and was replaced by the songs of birds and the smells of decay and moisture underfoot—a shaded world so different from that of the open coast I was familiar with. I had never learned the naturalist's name—it was one of those meetings where an introduction never came up—but I remembered him telling me some of the trees that I walked under and around were 1,500 years old, already 500 years old when the Maoris first arrived and old enough to have sheltered many of the flightless birds, including the now-extinct moas. I tried to imagine how the moas would have moved through this dense entanglement of greenery. Surely they would have stayed on the high ground, where the present-day trail avoided the swampy earth to either side. With the melodic songs of birds and the limited vision of the trail twisting around thick trunks, and tangles of green leafed bush, the word *extinction* was suddenly something far more tangible than anything I had felt before. Amid the smells, the dampness, the ferns, the small-leafed bushes, and the large ancient branches of the climax forest, only one thing was missing—the giant moa.

With the absence of the noise of the surf, the forest breathed its silence. I paused often to listen to the subtle and intricately layered voices of the woods: the gentle rustle of something scurrying away a few feet off the trail, the multiple songs of hidden birds, the snap of a twig, the buzz of a cicada, and the soft rush of the breeze in the canopy high overhead. Life in the forest was so different from that of the open ocean, yet it left me with the same feeling of being small and of being a visitor that knew so little.

When the forest light faded, I retraced my way back to the edge of the woods, stepping out of its shadows and into the evening light and the noise of the surf funneling up the river. The tide had dropped to its lowest level, leaving a mudflat thick with the smells of calf-high, black shiny ooze through which I dragged the boat. Occasional squirts of water shot into the air, marking the place of mollusks. The first drops of rain left tiny circles on the river's surface. At the water's edge I sat in the boat with my legs out of the cockpit, washing the smooth, slippery mud off and looking at the dark forest above. From a distance of 50 yards, close enough to see individual leaves on the shore trees, I couldn't hear any sounds of the life that moments before I had stood beneath. Along the riverbank a few gulls were digging with mud-covered bills. The gulls left web-toed tracks of their hunting, and despite walking upon and probing the mud with yellow bills, they somehow kept their breast feathers spotlessly white. I finished scrubbing the last of the mud from my feet, refloated the boat, and with two strokes of the paddles glided across the drained river.

Later, as I lay in the sleeping bag recalling the day and listening to the distant surf, a morepork—a forest owl—called out from the far side of the river, "More pork . . . more pork . . . more pork." It must have been right on the edge of the forest. I sat up and looked out the mesh netting as if there might be something to see of this night caller. A few seconds later there was another call farther away, "more pork . . . more pork." And then silence, as if the owl or its mate had announced it was standing watch over the night.

Chapter 7

G O O D - A S - G O L D   M E R I

Ships that pass in the night, and speak each other in passing,
Only a signal shown, and a distant voice in the darkness;
So on the ocean of life we pass and speak one another,
Only a look and a voice; then darkness again and a silence.
                    —Henry Wadsworth Longfellow

IT WAS A THREE-DAY PADDLE FROM PAPATOWAI to the fishing village of Bluff, where I would wait for the final push to Puysegur Point. Bluff had been my focus for the past week, the last place to stock up on food, pick up my mail, and to decide when to fully commit to the next leg of the trip, the west coast.

I was approaching Chaslands Mistake, an oddly named headland with towering vertical cliffs less than 20 miles from Bluff. The seas were running 5 feet straight out of the south and hitting the cliffs with enough force to reflect back out and turn the sea into a confused mass of sharp-peaked pitching waves. The waves weren't a great threat but enough for me to tighten up in the seat, pushing my back firmly into the back band and making firm contact with my toes and thighs. As I approached the headland, the almost sweet smell of an outboard engine brought back memories of fishing with my father and older brother on New York's Long Island Sound—one of those memories that instantly transports you thousands of miles and half a lifetime from the present. After a while the smell, faint though it was, began irritating my nose and I realize how sensitized I had become after living on the sea every day for the last month and a half. Long before I spotted the two sport-fishing boats rolling violently in the confused sea, I knew they were somewhere ahead of me. Eventually the spray of their bows hammering into the waves, and the sound of their engines pinpointed them against the cliffs. The boats were small: a bright red, seaworthy-looking rigid-hull inflatable, and the other, a deep-blue aluminum sport-fishing boat. Both boats had multiple fishing rods, the invisible monofilament bending their tips into tight arcs as the boats trolled, bucking and rolling in the seas. The blue exhaust that I had smelled earlier curled out of the twin engines on both boats as the four men in each held onto whatever they could. The two boats rolling in the seas and splitting the waves with their bows gave me an unusual perspective of seeing how rough the water really was. It didn't look like much fun to me, the men looking as if they were spending more time fighting for balance than enjoying the fishing. Of course they were a lot drier than I was, but because I was so much lower in the water, the seas didn't have the same effect on my boat. The waves that were knocking them side to side and smashing into their bows simply rolled under me, then set me back in place.

When one of the fishermen finally spotted me farther offshore, and no doubt looking as though I was the one that was crazy for being out there, he pointed in my direction. I could see a lot of gesturing as the first guy tried to point out where I was in the waves. Every third or fourth wave would take them from my sight, so I knew they would have a hard time seeing me. As soon as the helmsman of the inflatable located me, the lines were rapidly brought in as he turned the boat in a sharp banking turn and started over in my direction. When the boat was within shouting distance, the skipper turned it back into the waves, and one of the fishermen at the side of the boat called out, "Are you OK?"

I felt I should be asking them the same thing; they were all hanging on with knuckles stretched white around the cockpit railings and bumping against one another as the boat pounded into the waves. I yelled back, "I'm fine, thanks. How's the fishing?"

The fellow must have thought I was nuts because he didn't answer but called out again, "You sure you're OK?"

"Yeah, no worries. I'm heading for Bluff, should be there by tomorrow." Then as much to get the attention off me and onto something else I asked, "Do you know what channel the local marine weather is on?" I had drifted out of the range of the last forecaster and hadn't gotten a weather report for two days.

The fisherman repeated my question to the fellow at the wheel, then shouted the skipper's answer back, "Channel 61, Bluff Fishermen's Radio." The skipper had maneuvered closer, so we didn't have to yell quite so loud above the noise of the waves. He then leaned away from the wheel and called out, "Meri gives the weather twice a day, 7:05 in the morning and again at 7:30 at night. She knows every boat that's out here."

The boats were too close now. I wanted to find out more about whoever Meri was, but I was more concerned about getting caught under the bow of the fishing boat. I backed away as the aluminum hull sent a shower of water onto my bow. All four of the men on board were crowded onto the starboard side, looking down at me one minute, then directly across the next.

"Where are ye going?"

I didn't know who had asked the question because I was more concerned with keeping an eye on the surging distance between the two boats. After back-paddling again and holding my position 10 yards off, I answered, "I'm trying to paddle around the South Island."

My reply got the usual looks of stunned disbelief and of course the next obvious question: "Where did ye start?"

"Picton, a month and a half ago," I yelled back.

It was a direct answer to a direct question. Any other time I might have been more inclined to elaborate, but this wasn't exactly the place to be carrying on a conversation. The look on the crew's faces was the same look I had seen on everyone's face that had asked the same question—slack-jawed shock and raised eyebrows. I knew there would be another barrage of questions coming, but I was having trouble holding the boat in one spot and trying to keep upright at the same time. It was one thing to be paddling through rough water but quite another to be just sitting in it. The skipper kept working the throttles forward and back, spinning the console wheel and adjusting his position with the twin 100-horsepower outboard engines. It should have been obvious that I didn't have the same advantage. I could tell if I didn't break off the conversation, I was going to be in for a grueling round of questions and maybe get knocked over by all the confused seas, plus the boat's reflected waves.

"Well, I better get going before the winds pick up. What was that lady's name in Bluff again?"

One of the other fishermen shouted out, "Meri Leask. She lives right on the front street. A brick house with lots of antennas on the roof. You better stop in and see her."

"I'll do that. Thanks."

I lifted the paddle in a short wave of farewell, then let a wave carry me away from the noseburning fumes of their engines. The skipper paralleled my course at low speed. I could see him talking on his radio while the others stood braced and watching my slow progress through the waves. In another minute the other fishing boat growled up from astern and took up a course alongside the first boat. It was a little like being a bug under a microscope. After a while the fishermen must have been convinced that I was going to be OK. They turned slowly back toward the cliffs, waved, and then sped back to their fishing. I was glad to eventually have my own space back and to settle into the rhythm of paddling again. The encounter had been fun—interesting to be that close to another boat and to see how much more effect the seas had on them and to have had even a few minutes of conversation. I had also found out about the radio connection that I would need for this stretch of coast. I didn't know who Meri was, but I figured I would find out when I got into Bluff.

The approach to Bluff seemed to take forever. The low swells that had been a challenge against the cliffs of the Chaslands were now almost hypnotic as they rolled in from the south and washed onto the steep gravel beach that ran for miles east of Bluff. The sea had that smooth, glassy look and feel to it, the kind of sea that rocks you to sleep, if only there wasn't the need to stay upright and paddling a mile away from land. To my left were several small islands 6 to 8 miles offshore, and farther to the west was the dark outline of Stewart Island, a much larger and higher island, which was serviced by a high-speed ferry out of Bluff. Between South Island and Stewart Island lay Foveaux Strait, a 25-mile slot that funneled the tides into powerful currents ebbing to the west and flooding to the east. Fortunately I had the ebb tide pulling me steadily past the long expanse of gravel and gradually drawing me closer to the houses I could see on the hill above Bluff.

The closer I paddled to Bluff, the more defined the harbor became. A line of small, neat homes lined the coast and looked out on the approach to the outer harbor. Any boats coming or going would have to sail within a stone's throw of the houses and the coast road, which led deeper into the village. As I paddled into the outer harbor, I looked over the edge of the boat and could see 20 feet down through crystal-clear water. Long ribbons of kelp waved in the last of the ebbing current, and schools of small fish shot away as the shadow of the boat passed over them. The farther into the harbor I paddled, the narrower the channel became. Piers with multiple creosoted pilings, cross-braced with thick square timbers, ran parallel to the shore. Steel-hulled fishing boats were moored with lines as thick as my arms holding the boats into the ebbing tide. Some of the boats looked as if they hadn't been to sea in months. They were mostly smaller boats, one-man operations that must have fallen on hard times. Their hulls were streaked with rust, their rigging slack, and their portholes boarded up with plywood painted black. There was a look of despair and resignation about them, as if the best thing that could happen would be for a strong ebb tide to part the frayed mooring lines and take them out to sea.

Other boats were obviously well cared for—40- and 50-footers that had the sheer and the high bows of boats that work in big water. Thick-wired lobster pots and orange buoys with coils of line were arranged in neat order on the foredecks and open sterns, as if the captain was just waiting for the next tide. The boats still showed the wear and rust of working boats, but there was a professionalism and pride about them that spoke of the respect that the skippers, whoever they were, must have had for the sea.

Behind the piers were the ice-making plants, the fish-packing houses, and the boatyards, where several masts jabbed higher into the air and marked the marine railways that hauled the boats out of the water for repairs. I eased out of the main channel, where the current was pushing the green channel marker over at a sharp angle. The current was too strong to paddle against, especially at the end of a long day, and it would be much easier to paddle under the piers. I lined the bow up with a 4-foot opening between two pilings and slid into the underpinnings of not only the pier but also the very thing that supported the village: the fishing industry. Old fishing line, electrical cables, and water lines looped in the shadows and hung between the uprights. There was the strong smell of creosote and the amplified sounds of the tide dripping off exposed seaweed and mussels growing on the pilings. Cormorants—sleek black diving birds that fed on the small fish living in the shadows—surfaced and dove again in a panic as the boat sliced into their world.

To my right, through two or three lines of black-sheathed pilings, were the hulls of the fishing boats with their bows cutting into the current with an inverted V. Old tires hung on the outside of the pilings, where the boats nudged against them and occasionally bumped one hard enough to make the pilings creak loudly in protest. Cooling water shot out of the side of one of the boats that was rumbling in a low diesel throb, and farther out in the channel a boat was riding the ebb tide to the sea, its engine barely audible.

In the span of less than a half mile, I had left the freedom and the gentle swells of the open water and slid into the confines and the challenges of civilization. Now I had to find a place to camp, find a store and the post office, make a phone to call my parents and friends, and find out who Meri was and what information she might have on the west-coast weather. My focus had shifted from that of the sea to that which I had to accomplish ashore. The trick to these solo trips was in making this transition and in making hundreds of more minute transitions, of being able to immediately shift from one task to the next.

◆ ◆ ◆

It didn't take long to see that there wasn't much more to Bluff than what I could see from the water. I landed at a concrete boat ramp that angled sharply into the swirling waters and walked down the main street back to the piers. It was late evening, and the only signs of life were the occasional cars that wound along the shore road and disappeared up a side street. The air was damp and cold, not ideal weather to be out walking, but I wanted to get a feel for the village and to find the post office and store for the next morning.

The main street ran past a fish-and-chip shop, a hotel turned youth hostel, a couple of pubs, and eventually a line of shops with the post office in the middle. There wasn't much to the village, but I didn't need much. I returned to the boat, drifted back down the harbor, and found a small beach to camp on that was barely above the high-tide mark. After camp was set up, I found a phone and placed two calls to the United States, the first to my folks in New York. The phone rang twice before my Mom picked it up.

"Hi Mom, it's Chris."

"Oh Chris, it's good to hear from you. Where are you?"

My mom is pretty good at disguising worry in her voice, but after years of calling home from places all over the world, I could hear the real concern in her voice. I knew that two of my sisters who had computers were sending copies of the Web site that covered the trip to my parents, copies that told of the gales and the difficulties of the paddling. A friend in Port Angeles, Al Zob, had designed the Web site and was faithfully updating it as I sent him e-mails. In the e-mails I hadn't elaborated on the storms, but my Mom knew me as well as I knew her; she suspected the weather had been more of a problem than what I had alluded to on the site.

"I'm in Bluff, at the bottom of the island. I'll be staying for a couple of days. Everything's going pretty well, and it looks as if the weather might be getting a little better."

My mom then cut to the chase. "How is it going, Chris? It's harder than you thought it would be, isn't it?"

I could hear the back door of the house open and thump gently shut. My mom whispered, "It's Chris; pick up the other phone."

In another minute my Dad's voice broke into the conversation. "Hi son, I'm on the other line." It was my Dad's way to just listen for a few minutes.

Both my parents had been on the receiving end of a lot of these phone calls. There was no use in denying what they probably already had read via the Web entries.

"Well, it hasn't been a normal summer down here, more wind than normal, but I'm optimistic. Right now the forecast is calling for moderate southwest winds in the Straits. Things might start to lighten up."

"You're right in the Roaring Forties, son," my Dad broke in. "I remember coming through there on the way to Australia in 1945. Crystal-clear blue skies but the biggest seas I've ever seen."

I wished he hadn't said that. He knew from his days as an officer in the navy just how big the seas in this part of the world were. I thought it was better if we didn't dwell on the weather or the seas. I changed the topic and asked about my brothers and sisters.

"Everyone is fine here," my mom answered. "All the kids ask about you, and we fill them in when they call. Did you get your mail?"

"No, not yet. It's almost ten at night here, but I'll check the post office first thing tomorrow."

"We won't keep you, Chris. Get some sleep and eat well while you're in town."

"OK. I'll call before I set off again. It's good to hear your voices. I love you both."

When I hung up the phone, I could picture my Dad coming out of their bedroom and walking into the kitchen, where my mom would have been. It all seemed so tangible, though so far away. They would probably look at the South Island map I had sent them. They had it pinned to a corkboard in the breezeway and had marked the mail drops that we had agreed upon months before. Bluff would be circled at the lower extreme edge of the map. I didn't like thinking how they must worry. Even though they had always told me that I should do what I wanted in life, I knew my lifestyle wasn't easy for them. Out of the six kids, I was the only one without a regular job, a partner, and children. We are a family that has always kept track of one another, though everyone is scattered throughout the country. My folks have always been the ones who keep the circle of information flowing, letting each of us know what the others are up to. Now my Mom would call around and tell them that I had called and where I was.

The second phone call was to Sam and Martha Baker in Port Angeles. Sam, Martha, and another friend, Gay Hunter, were coming to New Zealand to hike for four weeks and also to fly in a much-needed food cache for the Fiordland stretch of the west-coast paddle. Without the food cache, it wouldn't be possible to cover the distance to the next place of resupply—Milford Sound, almost 250 miles away.

A month before I had left home we had all met for dinner, then had cleared the table and unfolded a map of the island. In the lower left corner was Puysegur Point, the start of the west coast. To the north the land was indented with fifteen fingers of blue water reaching into the green of Fiordland National Park. The third fiord to the north of Puysegur was Dusky Sound, a long reach of narrowing blue that penetrated 25 miles into the park and ended at a place called Supper Cove. A tiny black dot on the edge of Supper Cove marked the spot where we had agreed to meet, a Department of Conservation hut that was the terminus of the Dusky track. We had studied the maps and charts for the trip, figured how many miles it was from Picton, then tried to figure the number of days I might have to sit out because of bad weather. It had been a real long shot, nothing short of a good guess, but we decided that February 7 was the day we would meet where the black dot was circled on the map. Now months afterward it was time to check in and make sure everything was still on schedule.

When Sam answered the phone, he was typically wild with questions of how the trip had been so far. Sam is a kayaker, competitive Nordic ski racer, and marathon hiker. He is also the type of person who throws himself completely into whatever he does. We have a lot of the same energy, though I wouldn't even try to keep up with him on skis or in the mountains hiking. He was just getting ready to retire from 30 years of orthopedic surgery, and their trip to New Zealand was his and Martha's first retirement trip overseas. Martha is the opposite of Sam: I don't think there is a competitive bone in her body, but her passions for life run as strong as do Sam's. She loves hiking, dancing, gardening, and the theater.

I knew what one of Sam's first questions was going to be as soon as there was a pause in the conversation.

"So, Chris, how's the boat?" There it was. It was so much like Sam, direct and to the point. We both had the same design of boat, and one of the big questions we had before the trip was how it was going to handle the surf and the big following seas.

"It's better than I thought it would be, Sam. I've gotten rolled a few times, but it comes back around easily, and the big cockpit isn't a problem. Even in the surf I can lock myself into it and not feel as though I'm going to get pulled out. So far, so good."

I was almost out of time on the phone card, so the rest of the conversation was on scheduling our meeting.

"I have three weeks from tomorrow to make it to Supper Cove. The weather looks a bit dicey, but I think I have a pretty good shot of making it on time. I've left a cache of food with Kevin Beaumont in Te Anau for you to pick up. Once I leave Bluff, there won't be any chance of my contacting you, so let's just hope for the best. If I'm not there when you fly in, just leave it at the cabin, and I'll eventually get it."

"OK, that sounds good. Hopefully we'll see you in Supper Cove. Hey, Chris . . . be careful."

"You bet, Sam. Have a good flight. And I'll see you in three weeks."

The phone clicked down, and suddenly I was back in Bluff, standing on the edge of an unlit street, in a dark phone booth. I always looked forward to phone calls to family and friends; they were major goals and rewards for reaching designated places along the way. But the transition from camping and paddling to suddenly talking with loved ones on the other side of the world was almost too much. I always hung up feeling as if I had said too much, yet not enough; I had touched on too many things but hadn't begun to tell them what it was like to live the fullness of the trip. The phone was too limited, too one-dimensional for me to even begin to explain all that had taken place since leaving Picton.

I walked along the empty main street and across to where the crown of the tent was just visible in the night. I kept thinking about the phone calls, how they made me feel both lonely as well as very connected.

The next morning I was at the post office as soon as the interior lights went on and the door was unlocked.

"Good morning," I greeted the lady behind the counter.

"G'day. Fine morning, isn't it?"

"Yes, it sure is. Maybe we're finally in for some good weather."

"It's not been much of a summer, has it? Well, what can I do for you?"

"My name is Chris Duff, and I'm wondering if you might have any mail in general delivery for me?"

"Duff it was? Oh yes, I thought you might be coming in. We've been getting mail for you for the past couple of weeks," she replied.

I watched as she went to a cubbyhole and pulled out a stack of letters bound with a thin yellow rubber band. My day was starting off on the right track.

"Thanks very much! Can I leave a forwarding address to Greymouth for any more mail that might arrive here?" I asked.

"Sure, we can do that," she answered. "There's a form to fill out, but then anything we get, we'll send it off."

I filled out the form, thanked her and walked out into the sun with my bundle of mail tucked into the top pocket of my backpack. I checked off "post office" on my list of things to do while in town and circled the next item, "check on weather," which meant finding out who Meri was that the fishermen had told me about. I walked back into the post office and back to the same lady who had just helped me.

"Hi again. I forgot to ask if you might know Meri Leask? Some fishermen told me she broadcasts the weather here in Bluff."

"Oh sure, Meri does the Bluff Fishermen's Radio report. Good-as-Gold Meri, we call her. She and Ian live just down the road across from the war memorial. It's a brick house, one story, with antennas on the roof. She should be home now. Just go up and knock on the door."

"OK. Thanks."

I stopped by the tent and boat to check the height of the tide, then recrossed the street and quickly found the Leask house, just as the postmistress had described it. I pressed the doorbell and waited, wondering if it wasn't too early to be calling. A minute later I was greeted by a very pretty middle-aged woman with large gold earrings and a necklace that looked startling against her dark skin. In the background a radio squelched some static, a man's voice split the air, and then all was silent again.

"G'day, can I help you?" the lady asked.

"Good morning. My name is Chris Duff. I hope this isn't too early to be calling."

"Not at all. I'm just finishing the morning radio sched. What can I do for you?"

The morning radio sched? I didn't know what that meant, but I didn't want to get sidetracked by asking, at least not yet.

"I was out off the Chaslands two days ago and a fisherman told me to ask for Meri Leask here in town. I hope I have the right house."

"Yes, I'm Meri. You wouldn't be the kayaker, would you?"

"Well, yes I am."

"Oh yes, one of the boys radioed me and told me they had seen you out there. Are you really paddling around the South Island?"

"Well, I'm trying to. I'm just in town to restock the boat and trying to figure the best way to stay in touch and to get weather broadcasts once I'm around Puysegur. I understand the mountains block a lot of the frequencies and reception is sketchy."

"Yes, that's right, unless you have side ban, but you probably have VHF so that could be a problem. Come on in while I finish the sched; then we can talk."

Meri swung the door wide into a sunlit, immaculately clean living room with overstuffed chairs and a caged cockatoo that shuffled sideways on its perch as I walked past.

"I'll just get my husband. How about a cuppa tea?"

"That sounds great, thank you."

Meri's husband came in and sat down with me as she went around to the kitchen and finished talking on several different radios. He didn't say much as we listened to Meri in the other room. At the end of each transmission, she would sign off with "Good as gold then, I'll talk with you on the evening sched."

Now I knew why she was called "Good-as-Gold Meri." I also knew what a "sched" was. It was short for schedule, as in radio schedule.

Meri wrapped up her radio work and came back into the living room with three cups of tea, sugar, and milk on a tea platter.

"So tell me again where you started and where it is you're headed," she said.

I explained everything up to arriving the day before in Bluff and how I had met the fishermen who had suggested I call in on her.

"Well, you haven't had the best summer for your trip. Have you done this kind of thing before?"

I explained about my other trips—the 8,000-mile American trip, the circumnavigation of Great Britain, and then Ireland.

"Well you certainly sound like you know what you're doing. So let's see what we can do to keep you in touch so you can get the weather."

She sat back and sipped her tea, thought for a moment and then methodically came up with a plan.

"Most of the boys have taken their quota already, so you won't find many boats beyond Puysegur Point. A month ago there would have been plenty of boats that you could get the weather from, but they're all offshore for the tuna. Right now there's only Jim on the *Reliance*, but he'll be heading off as well before too long. What I'll do is let Jeff know at The Lodge that you're coming. There are several boats in the sounds—the *Breaksea Girl* for one—I'll call her as well. The *Oraki* might be working up the sounds later this summer; I can find out and at least let everyone know you're out there."

Meri was clearly a woman who knew her business. But how she got into this business of knowing which fishing boats were where didn't make any sense to me. Back in the United States, it was the job of the U.S. Coast Guard to monitor boat traffic, not a lady with a house full of radios. And what was The Lodge? It was a bit confusing but it looked as though Meri was going to be the key to my getting up the west coast.

"How did you get into the radio business, Meri?" I asked half jokingly.

"When Ian was fishing, I would keep the boys posted on the weather," she explained. "If there were any emergencies, I'd be the one back here that did the organizing. I guess it sort of grew from there. Now I look after the boys while they're out, and even yachts call up for the weather, or maybe they need help or a land-line. There's a fella sailing around the world right now. He left Tasmania a couple of weeks ago. I tracked him across the Tasman. He's halfway to the Horn, and I talk with him every few days. I get Christmas cards from all over the world, from people that I never met, but I remember their boat names."

While Meri explained her role as guardian angel of the fishing and sailing fleet of the south and west coasts, Ian sat quietly beside me drinking his tea and looking across the immaculately kept living room with his eyes focused on something I couldn't see. As I listened to Meri's stories of a plane crash in Foveaux Strait, and the ensuing search and rescue effort she coordinated, I quietly watched Ian. His hands may not have had the saltwater cracks and calluses of a fisherman, but his body still had the tone and stature of someone who had spent years aboard a vessel at sea. He sat seemingly content, sipping his tea while framed pictures of a large fishing boat and a happy crew looked down from the living-room walls.

Meri didn't miss much and must have seen me watching Ian.

"The day Ian got hurt, the boat had been hauled out for repairs. They were pulling the mast . . ." Meri began to explain. "She's a motor sailor that Ian designed so that when we retired from fishing we could cruise with her. They were lifting the mast when it caught on something on deck. When it let go, it hit Ian and knocked him right off the deck. She's a big boat, and it was a good 20 feet to the ground." Meri paused and looked gently over toward Ian. "It's been five years now, hasn't it, Ian?"

Ian nodded and quietly replied, "Five or six by now, I guess."

"The doctors say it could be ten years before Ian's fully recovered from the head injury."

"Do you still have the boat, Ian?" I asked.

"She's tied up down at the docks. You would have paddled past her. She's for sale. A fella from Auckland is supposed to come and look at her later this week."

I changed the subject back to a topic that I thought might have been easier for them both. "What are the waters on the west coast like this time of year?" I asked.

"In the sounds it can be flat as the harbor," Ian softly answered, "but it can be rough on the outside."

I imagined what "rough" translated to in the eyes of a fisherman who had spent a good portion of his life pulling cray-fishing pots from the waters of the Tasman Sea.

"If it's blowing a gale, the outside is nowhere to be in a kayak," Meri added. "Between here and Preservation Inlet there are, what, Ian, maybe three places he could get ashore?"

Ian sat thinking a few seconds; then in that same quiet manner he said, "There's Colac Bay. And in anything but an easterly there's Port Craig, might be a boat or two in there if there's a westerly blowing. Next place this side of Puysegur is Gates Harbor. No matter what the wind does, you're safe in there."

"You mentioned The Lodge, Meri. Where is that?"

"That's not until you get into Preservation Inlet. Jeff's the caretaker there. It's the only privately held land in Fiordland. Years ago a fella had a plan to build some kind of resort there. He started building, but after all the court battles with the Department of Conservation, he eventually went bankrupt. Now there's a group of businessmen from Auckland who own it. They finished the main building but only come down a few times each year. It's a pretty amazing place—in the middle of nowhere there's suddenly this huge complex. If you can get around Puysegur, it would be a good place to sit and wait for the weather."

In an hour of sitting with Meri and Ian, I had learned more about the next leg of the trip than I could have learned any other way. Meri was fully supportive of letting the fishermen know I was heading in their direction. She would be in touch with any of the yachts, fishing boats, or even the Department of Conservation research vessel that sometimes came down to the lower sounds. Whoever checked in with her would be advised to be on the lookout for a solo paddler in a yellow sea kayak.

"You'll be able to hear me on channel 61 almost all the way to Puysegur, but from there north to Haast, the mountains are going to block any reception except if you're way offshore. If you see any fishing boats, don't be afraid to call them up. The boys will do anything they can for you."

Meri then showed me a video that the national television had filmed on her home-based rescue-and-weather operation. I hadn't realized until the tape was playing that Meri was somewhat of a legend. She had been the primary coordinator for several rescues in Foveaux Strait as well as farther around in Fiordland Park. When the weather got rough, or when there was a fire aboard or someone was injured, Meri was the one that the fishermen depended on. When I finally left Ian and Meri, I knew I was in good hands as long as I was in radio contact. After that it was a matter of luck with the weather and hopefully contacting a fishing boat when I needed it.

I stayed three days in Bluff, stocking the boat with food, making minor repairs to the equipment, and impatiently waiting until the weather would allow me to paddle to the next sheltered landing, the village of Riverton. A series of minor low-pressure systems kept moving in from the South Tasman Sea, bringing near-gale-force winds that made the straits impassable. Riverton was 20 miles west of Bluff and would be a perfect place to sit and wait for just the right winds before setting off for Puysegur Point. I could use the strong ebb tides in Foveaux Strait to pull me toward the point, but any wind against those tides would make the straits dangerous. Meri and Ian had told me there were three safe landings between Riverton and Puysegur, a distance of almost 90 miles. Paul Caffyn had also warned me that this stretch of coast was the crux of getting around to Puysegur. If a large south swell were running, regardless of what direction the winds were coming from, any landing except Gates Harbor would be difficult. What I needed were calm winds and a low swell to cover the 90 miles safely. Once around the point I could tuck quickly into the safety of Preservation Inlet and again wait for favorable winds and seas to continue up the west coast. Getting through the straits and into the inlet was going to take patience and a bit of luck with the weather.

Finally, after three days, Meri's forecast called for near-calm southeast winds and a low 2-meter swell. It was the break that I needed. I shoved the heavily loaded boat off the beach and let the strong ebb tide pull me past the channel marker surging and sweeping side to side in the current. It was going to be a fast ride to Riverton.

It took three hours to cover the 20 miles to Riverton, three hours of the calmest winds and seas that I had seen on the entire trip. It was hard to believe that here in Foveaux Strait—second only to Puysegur in terms of wind—I would find such a calm.

As I was approaching Howell's Point, just on the outside of the village, the gentle southeast winds that had been at my back shifted to the predicted southwest winds and quickly turned the calm waters into choppy, breaking seas. The boat slowed to a crawl as the oncoming waves buried the bow, washed over the deck, and swept up to hit me in the chest with the last of their strength. In front of me a line of heavy clouds marked the approaching frontal system. The sun shone over the top of the growing bulk of massed energy, mixing its light with the gray anger that seemed ready to boil over any second. Between the boat and this frontal system, the seas were brilliantly illuminated, highlighted by the dread and darkness that was sweeping over the sea to the west. With land less than a mile in front of the bow, there was little threat in the increasing wind. I was close enough to safety to dare the winds to blow hard and let me work off some of the pent-up energy of sitting for the last three days. Ten minutes after the winds shifted, I caught a small wave and surfed in between two massive boulders guarding a lovely crushed-shell beach. A stand of flax plants with their long, sword-shaped leaves provided a perfect barrier from the winds.

It hardly seemed worth the work of breaking down the camp in Bluff just to set up another camp three hours later. But at least I was 20 miles closer to Puysegur. That was 20 miles less to paddle when the weather would allow me to make the big push to get around the point and into Preservation Inlet.

The front that had looked so threatening as I approached Riverton never developed into anything very severe; it was just enough to make progress any farther a bit too risky. That was the hardest part of the trip, knowing when to sit tight and to wait for optimum conditions—conditions that may or may not ever develop—and when to go, even when the conditions were borderline. What it came down to was something I remember my father calling "prudent seamanship," which I interpreted as judgment and risk assessment. It wasn't always the easy choice to stay ashore on days when the seas were marginal, but it was what had gotten me this far into the trip. Foveaux Strait had all the components that make for a potentially dangerous piece of water: fast-moving tides, high winds, and the potential for an offshore storm to send in big swells. Until I was certain of a fair chance of making it around Puysegur, I wasn't going to risk setting off.

For four days I sat on the outskirts of Riverton and waited. I filled the days with reading, getting caught up on sleep, and walking along the coast road into the village. After the initial excitement of a new place to explore, I soon became restless with being shore bound once again. If the weather had been rainy, dull, and cold, I would have been happy to find shelter in one of the village cafes, but the weather wasn't the problem—it was the wind. From a grass-covered hill on Howell's Point, I could look across Foveaux Strait and watch the waves glistening white against the deep, clear blue of the strait. The waves were straight out of the southwest, spinning off the gale-force winds at Puysegur that Meri forecasted each morning. Despite the clear skies I was stuck until the winds died down. I grew tired of sitting beside the tent and looking at the sea that I didn't dare venture out on, yet walking into the village was hardly any better. With my hands stuffed in my pockets and my backpack filled with the weight of camera, film, radio, and journal, I wandered along the coast road, kicking stones into the grass. I was restless and it was obvious even to myself that I was out of my element. The land felt hard beneath my feet, and after a day of walking, the skin between my toes was clogged with the dust of the road. After spending three days in Bluff and now another four in Riverton, I felt as though I was losing the momentum of the journey. I missed the full body connection that the paddling offered and the near-constant motion of the sea beneath the boat. With each passing day I felt my impatience with the wind growing and the pent-up energy building with my concerns of looking out on the "crux of the trip"—this stretch of water noted for its winds and lack of safe landings. While there were plenty of folks out for evening walks, and music flowing from the cafes and pubs, I didn't want the company of people and the distraction of noise. I needed to stay focused, quiet, and withdrawn, conserving the mental and physical energy I would need for the south-coast crossing.

When the southwest winds finally blew themselves out, I didn't waste any time in setting off. Meri's forecast called for southeast winds, the perfect winds to push me westward on the ebbing tide. As soon as I cleared the Riverton Rocks, a series of ledges that marked the deep water of the straits, I called Meri to let her know I was heading out.

"Bluff Fishermen's Radio, Bluff Fishermen's Radio, this is Sea Kayaker One, Sea Kayaker One. Over."

"Sea Kayaker One, this is Bluff Fishermen's Radio. How are you, Chris?"

Meri's voice came across the 20 miles of coast as though she were standing on the beach watching me. Her voice was sweet and clear, reassuring me and chasing away the worry that had been chewing at my insides ever since I made the decision to break camp.

"Hello, Meri. Good to hear your voice. I'm about a mile off Howell's Point and heading west. I've got a slight east wind and almost flat seas. This is the day I've been waiting for. Over."

"Ah, roger, Chris. We've got southeast winds predicted, so you should have a good day. Where are you heading for tonight? Over."

"If the winds stay as they are, Meri, I'll shoot for Port Craig. Over."

"Good as gold then, Chris, I'll tell the boys to keep their eyes open for you. Bluff Fishermen's Radio out."

"Thanks, Meri. Sea Kayaker One out."

I slid the radio into the hatch behind the seat, checked the boat for the tenth time to see that everything was in place, and then set the bow on a westward heading.

Across the blinding glare of Foveaux Strait, Stewart Island rose out of the sea, spread itself across the near horizon, and disappeared into the clouds that hid half of its bulk. To the west the straits were wide open, a corridor of calm blue stretching clear to the curve of the earth and beyond to the emptiness of the greatest expanse of ocean in the world. The southeast wind barely stirred the surface of the water, and as long as I stayed offshore, the low swell was hardly noticeable. The moon had been full two nights earlier, creating the highest tide in a month, a powerful ebbing tide that swept me through the strait and toward the very goal that I had wondered, worried, and lived for over the past year—the South Island's west coast. I had dreamt of this day—of crossing the bottom of the island, of feeling the expanse of an ocean that encircled the globe, and to purposefully pull the boat deeper into that exposure and into the untouched beauty of Fiordland. I was rested, well fed, fit from two months of paddling, and fueled with a mix of excitement as well as anxiety.

Pushing off the beach from Riverton was an absolute commitment to myself, of believing that I had the paddling and the judgment skills to meet the unknown demands ahead. I had heard a lot of stories of the west-coast surf and how remote most of the coast was. There was no denying the fear that I felt every time I thought about how big the surf might be, but I also knew what I could do in this boat, which had become an extension of my body. If the time came when I had to run really large surf, I would do it, and I would come through the other side. That confidence came from knowing not only the boat but also from knowing myself and how I react when faced with a physical threat. The key would be in staying calm and believing in myself and in my abilities.

Chapter 8

Expect nothing.
Be prepared for anything.
—Samurai saying

IT DIDN'T TAKE LONG TO SEE WHY THE SOUTH COAST could be such an inhospitable place if the southerly swells were big. West of Te Waewae Bay the densely wooded foothills of Fiordland National Park rolled off the heights in steep plunges of shaded ravines and bare-rock buttresses that ended 50 feet above the boulders and gravel of low tide. Beneath the first totally clear sky in almost three weeks, the offshore waters ran aqua blue over a sandy bottom. Dark-green patches warned of the rocks and ridges that tripped the swells into long lines of reef breaks. With just a hint of a southeasterly breeze at my back and an ebb tide for six hours of the day, I felt as if Puysegur Point was drawing me like a magnet along this formidable coastline and toward the safety of the fiords.

With no wind and the swell running an average of 4 to 6 feet, I decided to paddle within a half mile of the shore, threading my way through the shallows by watching the breakers up ahead and skirting the darker waters that indicated the reefs. The swells were coming from the southwest, off the port bow, which gave me ample warning of the occasional larger set breaking on the reefs up ahead. When a big set came through, I would angle the boat well away from any dark water but still keep the boat steadily moving west. I could have gone a mile or more offshore to avoid the reefs altogether, but that would have taken time, both to paddle out as well as to eventually paddle back in. With each stroke of the paddle, I was closer to Puysegur, and any detour would only leave me more exposed. I also wanted to be in close so that I could register how fast I was moving. When the tides changed, I didn't want to be a mile out and not able to read the currents against the rocks or the occasional red-and-white or black-and-white crayfish buoy anchored to the reefs with yellow floating line. Being inside the reefs, as long as the swells remained fairly low, allowed an intimacy that offshore paddling did not.

Meri had told me that any winds out of the east quadrant weren't going to last long and that I would have a maximum of three days to get into the protection of Preservation Inlet. At the end of the second day, I landed through a slot of moderate surf at the mouth of the Waitutu River. Ever since leaving Colac Bay, I felt I was in a race against time and the wind, a race that I was winning but just barely. The swell was definitely building the farther west I paddled, and all night long the darkness was filled with the crash of the swells against the boulder beach that awakened me from a fitful sleep. When sleep came again, a vague image of Puysegur Point filled my dreams—a blur of a headland—or maybe it was just the fog of stress that I couldn't escape. The headland had become a twenty-four-hour focal point, something I couldn't erase even in sleep. All I needed was one more day, maybe two, and I could put it behind me.

I kept thinking of Kazutomi Yoshida. He had left Riverton with the same weather that I had and then had gotten nailed by high winds that forced him to retreat back to Riverton to resupply. So far our trips had been very similar, with much of the same weather problems. I was fed up with the weather and felt I had paid my dues and deserved a fair crack at the west coast. No doubt Kazutomi had felt the same. On an exposed coast, however, there is no bargaining with the winds or the swells, and no claim to any right or privilege of passage. There is just persistence, endurance, and an around-the-clock awareness that keeps one on edge but also begins to wear one out. The goal of sheltered water becomes the mirage in the desert, an oasis that is just around the corner, one that occupies all the moments of the day. Along an inhospitable coast one either slips by unscathed, gets caught by an unseen wave, or spends a week hiding from a sudden change in sea and weather conditions, all at the whim of the weather gods and of pure luck or lack thereof. The next day as I came around Long Point, that message of safety and luck was driven home in a way that left me feeling as though I was way out of my league.

Paul had warned me about Long Point, about giving it a wide berth because of how far out its ledges reached beneath the sea. The swell was running 8 to 10 feet, still out of the southwest, but with twice the volume of just two days earlier. From more than a mile away, the point was easy to pick out against the continuum of green hills spilling their ridges of native bush onto the short beaches. Even from that distance the size of the waves breaking over the extended reef made my stomach churn. With a limited horizon in the big swells, the reef looked as if it extended miles out to sea. I paddled a little closer, then swung the bow straight offshore to get a better angle of approach. It still looked terrifying, but in the deeper water I could see there was an easy way around it.

I was a half mile from land as I drew even with the point—a half mile, but only a few hundred yards from the first breakers that turned the smooth rollers into racing cascades of fury. From the top of the swells, I could see where the forest suddenly ended above a band of broken cliff and tumbled rocks. A tower of rock as big as a three-story house shielded a small cove from the brunt of the waves. The swell dropped me into the next trough before several seconds later lifting me so that I could again see the point. In the confusion of distance, and the mist from the reef break hanging in the air, I was sure I had seen a boat in among the explosions of white water. Meri had said there may be the odd cray-fishing boat working the reefs this side of Puysegur, but it didn't seem possible that there was enough room to maneuver a boat in that close.

As I passed the reef, I looked back and now could see clearly that there was a boat in there, except that it wasn't fishing; it was washed high on the rocks and laying well over on its port side. I sat abeam of the swells, bracing into the seaward side and trying to see if there was anyone around the wreck. The boat had to be a good 45 feet long, a commercial fishing boat that looked as though it had been tossed helplessly aside like a toy. The bow was angled up the steep face of the gravel-and-rock cove pitching the blue-and-white radar sphere on top of its pilothouse at a weird angle. It looked as though a wave had hit it just moments before, driving it onto the rocks, then receding and leaving it high and dry. For five minutes I sat and watched each time the swell lifted me atop its crest. There was no sign of anyone near the boat. I could still raise Meri on the VHF if there was a need to, but it was clear that the wreck had been abandoned. Whoever had been onboard had either been rescued or was long gone in the waves. I watched for another ten minutes, one eye on the wrecked boat and the other on the seas breaking over the reefs around me. It was easy to see how a wave could catch a boat off guard and swallow it in the walls of roaring white that didn't end until they swept onto the blackened rocks. All it would take was one wave a little bigger than the rest. If the wave broke offshore, there would be a mere few seconds to try and turn the bow out to sea and to pour on the power and hang on. I wondered if the fishermen had any warning of what had hit them, or if their only warning was the sudden lifting of the deck beneath their feet and the awful realization of their misjudgment of the sea. I watched the wreck for another few minutes then crept away, hyperaware of every boomer that unleashed its power and raced white toward the rocks. I tried to put the wreck out of my mind, but the image of its hull thrown high onto the rocks kept coming back like a dream. Was it bad luck or just carelessness that had put the boat on the rocks? Either way the image haunted me. I eventually left Long Point behind and got back to the task of getting to a safe landing.

Paddling the south coast was a mental game of trying not to get psyched out by the sheer power of everything. To my right the mountains soared out of the sea in walls of dense greenery, shadows of ravine and sunlight highlighted by long scars of bare rock where the roots of the native bush had been ripped away in avalanches of rain-sodden, thin soil. Shearwaters tore past on their flight westward while massively thick swells rolled in from the same direction and buried the rocks guarding the mountain bases. On the face of those mountains, the wings of those seabirds, and the backs of those massive southern ocean swells, there was that terrible yet wonderful beauty of raw vulnerability, a conflict of terms and emotions and the very stuff of the psyche and the natural world that had drawn me here. Between the two worlds of the land and sea meeting in violent collisions of glory, there was no place for error or the carelessness of inattention. There was only the focus of being finely alive and present, stitching an awed awareness with the steady sewing-machine rhythm of the paddle blades pulling me toward Puysegur. It was a tightrope act, holding the boat and the mind in carefully balanced tension.

In the early morning of January 28, I left the shadows and the shelter of Gates Harbor, a perfectly spooned-out oasis of calm just 7 miles east of Puysegur Point, and paddled into the warmth of the sun edging over the mountains. The previous evening I had sat tense and hard-muscled on the outer edge of the same natural harbor, watching huge sets of waves nearly close out the narrow entrance in cataclysmic reverberations. Paul had told me that I would have to paddle just beyond Gates Harbor before I would see the narrow slot angling back between the rocks. If I hadn't been in close and watching carefully for the third landing on this coast, I would have easily missed it. Once inside the gauntlet of refracted and booming waves, the sea had flattened, locked out of this hidden oasis by the rocks that stood like sentinels at the gates, allowing only a gentle rise of swell to penetrate. Suddenly the stress of eight hours of paddling had melted away.

Now as I paddled out the same narrow channel, a slight breeze touched my right cheek and warned of the weather change that the previous night's clouds had forecast. The wispy "mare's tails" that had looked so innocent meant that the southeasterly winds that had escorted me across the south coast were going to change within twelve hours. A low-pressure system was building over the south Tasman, and gale-force northwesterlies were predicted. My window of opportunity for the south coast was closing.

A mile beyond Gates Harbor the compass swung in its liquid sphere and settled on 330 degrees. For the first time on the trip, the bow was heading almost due north, slowly following the curve of the coast and swinging toward the final approach to Puysegur. Under a sky that was streaked with high cirrus clouds and diffused with filtered sunlight, I came around Windsor Point and suddenly saw it, a blunt finger of land reaching out from a rocky wave-pounded bay and pointing straight into the Tasman Sea. After 800 miles of paddling, dreaming, and worrying about this mythical headland, I was finally looking at it—Puysegur Point!

"Wow!" The single word slipped out on an exhaled breath that left me sitting with the paddle unconsciously resting in a low left brace. Thoughts, words, song, and poetry slipped in and out of my mind, silent words that attempted to capture and preserve the moment, to freeze its image amid all the other emotions of the past few days so that I could register where I was, sitting in a boat and looking at something suddenly too real, too big. I tried to gather in the last two months—people, camps, beaches, capsizes, waves, and winds—and the last year of planning—a log book that was 7,000 miles away with columns of dates, wind speeds, swell heights, and the names of nine places around the South Island, with one name standing above all the others—Puysegur Point.

"So this is what you look like," I whispered.

Long and low, the point was windswept and treeless on the top, with boulders piled at the base of its cliffs where the seas relentlessly clawed. It looked battered and ravaged, worn down by whatever the South Pacific Ocean, the Tasman Sea, and the lows out of Antarctica had thrown at it since its first uplifting.

"Yes. Yes. Now just give me another hour, just one more, and I will be around you." I talked to it as if we knew each other.

Across the final 3 miles, the point gradually grew larger and more detailed, the sun playing across its length and the bush-clad ravines on its south side and shadowing its tip where the heavy swells lifted, curled, and spewed their smoking tops. The 3 miles gave me time to study the point and to let my arrival sink in. I wanted to cherish the time, let it wash through me as my reward. Two months of living purposefully, persistently, and deliberately had brought me there. One person in a world of six billion, slicing a thin, black paddle blade into the mixed currents of two oceans and feeling so very tiny and, in truth, so insecure.

The closer I got to Puysegur, the larger it became until I could see the individual windowpanes in the old lighthouse and the slowly revolving light inside. I turned around in the cockpit and looked back at the Marshall Rocks, thimbles and islets that blocked my view of points south and east. Beyond the rocks the coast led back to Riverton, Bluff, and Meri and Ian. By the grace of the winds, I had crossed the 90 miles without so much as a wave breaking over the bow. Shearwaters filled the air as they raced past and circled in broad flight patterns that brought them repeatedly back to where I sat beneath the point looking east, then turning and looking north to the headland that had been so pivotal on this journey. Part of me wanted to linger with the birds as if I had the comfort of flight to take me in minutes away from the threat of increasing winds and vulnerability against the cliff. Another part was feeling the north wind and seeing the first whitecaps to the northwest. Once again the choice wasn't mine to make. Survival on the sea meant a vigilance that didn't languish in a calm. I waited for a large set to roll in and break white against the cliff, and then I started around the point.

I had just rounded the point, paddling forward but looking over my shoulder at the lighthouse, when twenty or thirty shearwaters raced up from behind and spilled helter-skelter out of the air and headfirst into the sea. Gulls appeared out of nowhere, squawking and making crash landings onto the sea, then sitting there and screaming their complaints as shearwaters popped to the surface, pivoted their heads frantically around, and dove again as more shearwaters dropped from their flight and joined the feeding frenzy. Amid the confusion two white albatrosses glided in on 10-foot wings, hovered for a second, then gracefully settled on the water with wings still spread, and stabbed at something beneath the surface. Ten, maybe fifteen seconds passed, and suddenly the shearwaters flapped into the sky again, taking with them the slapping of wings, the high-pitched screams of the gulls, and the splash of water. The albatrosses turned into the freshening wind, spread their wings, and lifted magically off the sea as dignified and as silent as they had arrived. Whatever the birds had spotted had either dove deep or veered suddenly away. I watched the shearwaters form up again in their circle and immediately fall again from the sky in another mass attack a hundred yards away. The gulls were right behind them, followed by the albatrosses, landing just as the first shearwaters once again took to the air. The thousands of shearwaters I had been watching for the last three days had obviously been heading for this point, where the ocean currents tossed up schools of small fish and left them easy prey for the birds.

Beneath the black bungee cords on the foredeck was a laminated chart of Fiordland National Park. For two months it had lain flat against the curve of the hull in the forward compartment, nearly stuck to the fiberglass by the daily compression of the sleeping bag, sleeping pad, and rammed fleece clothing. Now droplets of seawater beaded up on its shiny surface, which showed the details of Puysegur Point, Preservation Inlet, Coal Island, and Long Sound. Up until this point the only navigation I had to worry about had been keeping the land on my right side, but suddenly that wasn't enough. In front of me were multiple islets, islands, and peninsulas that overlapped one another in a labyrinth of fingers amid the glistening light of watery passages. By picking out points and islands and comparing them with what was on the chart, I gradually made sense of what lay before me. Against the backdrop of Gulches Head, I could see what must have been Coal Island, and farther to the north still was Chalky Island, or at least the tip of it. Balleny Reef was where the swells piled in mounds of broken white water a quarter mile off Gulches Head, and way to the north was what must have been Cape Providence. The coastline was confusing, but after the exposure of the south coast, its inlets and sounds were a welcome sight. Now no matter the winds and the cantankerous seas, there would always a safe place to hide.

A half mile into Preservation Inlet a low, white building appeared nestled against the forest and sitting above a cobbled beach. Even from a distance it was obvious that it was well past its prime. Ian Leask had told me the building was the old gear shed for the lighthouse before it was automated in the early 1980s. Cray-fishermen now used it to occasionally store fishing pots and extra fuel—a kind of depot on the edge of the Fiordland wilderness.

I landed and pulled the boat up the cobbles then onto the heavy planked ramp that led from the mid-tide mark into an open bay at the end of the shed. A slack cable snaked its way across the planks and was married to a winch that had long ago rusted itself together. Yellow-and-black bumblebees the size of my thumb buzzed around purple flowers and inspected the boat like miniature humming birds. I left the boat resting on the ramp and felt the stretch of calf muscles as I walked up and explored the old shed.

Inside the creaky hinged door was a barrackslike room with rusted-iron-spring beds and moldy mattresses stacked neatly but taking on the smells that all old buildings have regardless of where they are in the world. On a crude wooden table were several unopened cans of beans, two tiny boxes of camp matches, and the snubbed-out inch of three candles with puddles of wax cementing them to the soot-covered wood. The windowless room had the feel of a squatter's shack, a place to hole up and hide from whatever was beyond the exposed 2-by-4 studs.

The saving grace of the building was the history written in a variety of penned scrawlings between the studs. Some of the graffiti had dates and names—dates going back fifteen years, when the shed had been abandoned with the automation of the lighthouse. There were tallies of fishing parties: "Three days in Preservation, lots of blue cod, sea bass, and plenty of crays. Dolphins in the inlet." There were diving reports: "Storms and high winds, poor visibility. Some crays and black coral." And there were accounts of hunting parties apparently dropped off for a week at a time and left until a boat could come out from Riverton and pick them up again: "Three deer in a week, boat overdue."

I walked around the room, stepping over a broken chair and between the cold iron beds, where spiders had woven their mists of web. Between two wall studs, a little higher than eye level was a penned scribbling that jumped out at me like a snake hidden in the rafters: "Louis Hart and Bevin Walker storm bound for ten days—paddling from Milford to Bluff."

Paddlers!

Between the lines I read the untold musings of frustration, boredom, and waning patience with the weather. Ten days of sitting and waiting, eating the limited food that a kayak can carry and listening to the winds that must have whistled through the shed walls. I imagined the daily walks up to the light-house to break the boredom, and the closeness that can grate like sand even between close friends. Between the spacing of another two wall studs was a nearly identical record of paddlers waiting ten days for a storm in March 1995.

I made a circuit of the large open room, then returned to the table and noticed a moldy covered notebook lying next to the cans of beans. Inside were pages filled with names, dates, and comments from ten years of visitors, plus a history of the lighthouse. There was mention of a graveyard in back of the shed where four crosses could be found. The graves marked the burial place of three separate drownings when boats loaded with supplies—oil, fuel, and food for the lighthouse keepers—were capsized as they tried to run the

Above, some of the hundred pounds of gear that would sustain me during the expedition. Below, paddling into the "Roaring Forties."

Above, east coast pinnacle. Below, Marlborough Sound sheep station.

Above, Cape Campbell—a starkly beautiful and arid coastline. Below, the rich warmth of evening light north of Kaikoura.

Above, driven by following seas and making miles. Left, a joyous escort near Kaikoura.

Above, brilliant sun and fresh snow following a southern gale. Below, good-as-gold Meri Leask in her kitchen station.

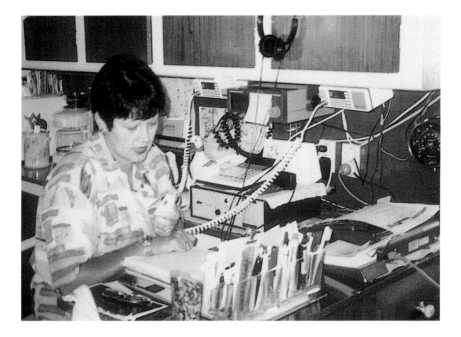

A Hooker sea lion waking from a nap in Cannibal Bay.

Above, Foveaux Straits—pushing into the waves. Below, Puysegur Point—the beginning of the west coast.

Above, waiting for the seas to calm, writing in the journal. Below, surrounded by playful dolphins near Dusky Sound.

Above, Ray and David Haywood aboard the Oraki. *Below, Hare's Ears, the rocks that guard the entrance to Doubtful Sound. Opposite page, the rains and fog lift, revealing the beauty of Acheron Passage in Fiordland National Park.*

Above, morning magic in Thompson Sound, Fiordland National Park. Below, bands of promise that the storm is breaking. Opposite page, Commander Peak— 5,000 feet straight up out of Doubtful Sound.

Above, some of the damage after the forced landing. Below, entering Milford Sound.

Above, a full moon rises, marking the fourth month of the journey. Below, a peaceful camp at the end of a long day.

Red sky at night, an ocean paddler's delight.

reef break in front of the shed. Much later, the reef was dynamited and a channel provided safer and more regular resupplying. The note went on to explain that the fourth cross marked the burial place of one of the keeper's children. What the child died of it didn't say.

The inside of the shed would have been a welcome refuge in a storm, but the messages written on its walls and the notes in the visitors' log book were like looking into a family's troubled past. There was a closeness about the place that left me with an uneasy feeling, as if the door would suddenly be thrown open against its weighted pulley and an oilskin-clothed ghost from the past would stand silhouetted against the light of the outside. The shed held the memories of not only those who had penned their stories in ink between the wall studs but also the years of toil, storms, and tragedy that the lighthouse keepers had lived with. I felt like a trespasser reading into the lives of those who died or had left a child buried at this place they had called a home. I closed the book, left it exactly as I had found it, and let myself out, pulling the door firmly into its latch.

It wasn't difficult to find the small cemetery. It appeared out of the tall grasses and was backed into a steep hillside, which gave it a sense of intimacy and protection on two sides. A low picket fence, painted white but over-grown with knee-high grasses and a few ground-hugging flowers, surrounded the simple wooden crosses with the dates carved and painted into the cross-pieces: 1895, 1914, and 1925. One did not have a date but stood on its own in a tiny enclosure. Bees hovered over flowers. The winds softly swept through the tall grasses, and the sun warmed the small plot of level ground looking out across Preservation Inlet.

Around the back of the shed, an old tractor path cut through the hillside and angled up through flax plants and lovely arched branches of beech trees that rustled in the north winds. Between the parallel ruts that must have first been cut for hand-pulled carts, soft grasses covered the once-packed earth track and cushioned my sandaled feet. Native bush crowded the path, and heavy rains had eroded gullies into the route from the supply shed to the lighthouse. Overhead, clouds raced with alarming speed across the face of the sun, shading the path in cool shadows one moment and unleashing pinpoints of burning ozone depletion the next. Through breaks in the beech canopy, stands of thick manuka, tea trees, and flax, I could look across Preservation Inlet and out toward Cape Providence. Since I had landed, the calm winds, which had escorted me safely into the fiords, had shifted to the north and now blanketed the sea in whitecaps that reached out to the horizon. By some stroke of luck, I had slipped past Puysegur with little more than an hour left in the calm before the gales.

By the time I hiked to the lighthouse, the northerlies were strong enough to halt my pace across the remains of the foundation of the keeper's house. Thick clumps of clover and stunted grasses shuddered in the wind, and gulls hung motionless over the slowly revolving light. To the north the mountains melted and overshadowed one another in purple undulations that faded in the sea haze. To one side of the light tower was another tower with a locked metal box at ground level and solar panels up higher. Out of the box ran several wires leading to an anemometer, which was spinning in a blur at the very top of the tower. I thought of how many times I had logged onto my computer at home and had read the wind speed that the little prop-driven instrument had recorded. I had studied this place on the map, plotted its weather for over a year, and listened to the VHF marine reports every morning for the last two months. Now that I was safely standing atop the point, I could look into the winds and see the next leg of the trip. The dream of paddling the west coast of New Zealand was right there in front of me— laid out in a patchwork of greens, ribboned with silver channels and an imag- ined line meandering north, hugging as remote a coastline as any on the face of the earth—a place where the ocean's energy met the stubborn resistance of temperate rain-forest mountains pushing straight up from the depths and standing green against the sky. To the south there were no more than a dozen rocky, uninhabited islands between Antarctica and me. This was a coastline of extremes, the Tasman Sea meeting the mountains of the Southern Alps: two forces uninfluenced by man and pure in their own rights of power over this bottom edge of the globe. This element of purity and raw wildness was what I had come to experience.

I left the windy summit of Puysegur with an image of the islands and the sounds running cinemalike through my mind. From Puysegur to Milford was 150 miles, with fifteen fiords along the way to explore. Sam, Martha, and Gay would be bringing food into Dusky Sound, and I would have another food drop arranged once I got into Milford. Beyond Milford Sound I would be back to dealing with the exposure of a straight coastline without any safe harbors, but that was too far away to worry about for now. I was here in Fiordland, and I was going to see as much of it as I possibly could as long as the winds and the weather allowed.

I walked lightly back down to the supply shed and around to the ramp where my boat rested on its edge. Even out of the water she looked as if she was built for serious work: the low rear deck that made rolling it back around so easy, the slight rocker in the hull that was only apparent when she was high and dry, and the soft chines just below the cockpit area, which combined with the rocker to make it maneuverable in following seas. The black keel strip, which Nigel Dennis had glassed in for abrasion when he built the boat, was getting thin near the bow but was holding up pretty well. After so many miles the boat still looked sleek and well cared for except for a few scratches on the bottom where I had dragged it over the sand and rocks, but other than that it looked as it did when I pulled it out from the shipping container with Kevin and Dawn.

Looking at the map, I was as near to being halfway around the South Island as I could be. The only piece of gear that needed replacing was my paddling jacket, which had delaminated from the constant rotation of my torso and the continuous exposure to the sea and the sun. Sam was bringing in a new top from the manufacturer, and I would send the worn one back out with him. Before I left Bluff I had mailed my dry suit to Kevin and Dawn in Te Anau because I needed every last square inch of available space for food. There was nothing in or on the boat that was superfluous, and as I looked at it resting so easily on the ramp, I felt ready for what lay to the north. I was still strong and uninjured and, more important, I still had the psychological edge that I would need once north of Milford. The key would be in maintaining that edge for the next 800 miles, plus being lucky with the weather and sea conditions.

Chapter 9

*Only those who will risk going too far
can possibly find out how far one can go.*
—*T. S. Eliot*

THE WINDS THAT BLEW IN FROM THE NORTH brought with them a dramatic change in the weather. Instead of blinding white sun and blue seas, I was now paddling beneath a low sky that hid the mountains behind the weight of clouds piled up like mounds of gray cotton. Vague shadows of islands appeared, then faded like apparitions in the drifting mist. Five miles inside of Puysegur Point a large bay opened up to the south. Somewhere in that void of light and definition was "The Lodge," which Meri had told me about. She had assured me I would get a warm welcome from Jeff Sweney, the caretaker. Now it was just a matter of finding him.

I was sitting in the middle of this wet world of mist and cloud when across the calm of the bay came the high-pitched buzz of an outboard engine. The mosquitolike whine grew louder with the seconds until it seemed as though whoever was at the throttle must have had an inner radar aimed right at where I sat. Out of the curtain of gauzy gray appeared a small aluminum pontoon skiff with a fellow kneeling with one knee at the center console and the other leg extended out as he leaned into a tight turn. The fellow must have seen me as soon as I saw him. He immediately throttled back, and the boat came off its plane and settled back onto its stern. The last hundred yards closed rapidly. He cut the engine altogether and let the boat glide up to within a few yards of me.

"You must be Chris," he called out. "I've been expecting you. Meri said you'd probably stop by for a visit. How about a cuppa and a hot shower?"

A "cuppa" I knew was a cup of tea, and a hot shower didn't need any translation.

"Tea and a shower sounds great. I was looking for the lodge when I heard you coming. I was hoping you weren't going to run me over."

"Ah, no worries, it's a little thick today but not too bad."

I looked behind him and tried to imagine how the fog could be any denser.

"A bit wet, but I thought I'd check the pots. Got a few nice cod for dinner."

"How far are we from The Lodge?" I asked.

"Ah, not far at all. Cromarty Bay is right in front of us. Just follow me. You can almost see the float."

I looked in the direction his bow was pointing and couldn't see anything but the shadow of a flying gull appear, then fade just as mysteriously into the gray. We were sitting in a vacuum.

Jeff gave the outboard a pull on the starting rope and slipped the engine into gear with a clunk. With a push of the throttle, the skiff leapt out of the water and was instantly back on plane and disappearing into the mist. A minute after I lost sight of him, the whine of the engine was cut again. I followed the last of Jeff's wake and found him straddling a four-wheeler and backing a boat trailer down a gravel-and-sand beach. The boat sat floating in the silk-smooth water a few yards offshore. By the time I landed, he had hauled the boat clear of the water and was coming back down the beach to help me lift my boat above the tide.

Jeff chuckled and shook his head as he walked up in his hip boots. "That's a little boat to be going all the way around the South Island. What was Puysegur like?"

"Well, actually it wasn't bad," I answered. "A bit of a westerly swell but no wind, so it was pretty easy."

"Supposed to be gales tonight out on the point—40 knots and maybe higher. We'll have a listen for Meri's sched at 8:30."

The sand flies had descended on us in swarms as we lifted the kayak from the water's edge and carried it, grunting up the steep beach. They flew into our ears, our noses, and eyes and settled onto the tender skin between our fingers.

"Damned little buggers are bad today. They like the wet weather. We'll have a cuppa. Then I can show you around the inlet if you want."

Jeff seemed to be running on high octane. He talked fast and didn't stop for a full introduction. The fact that Meri had told him to be on the lookout for me and that he had nearly bumped into me in the fog and mist was the only introduction I apparently needed. He set off at a quick pace into a break in the forest, then down a worn, wide path that curled through and around the trees. I followed this short, stocky figure in a ragged dark-blue sweater,

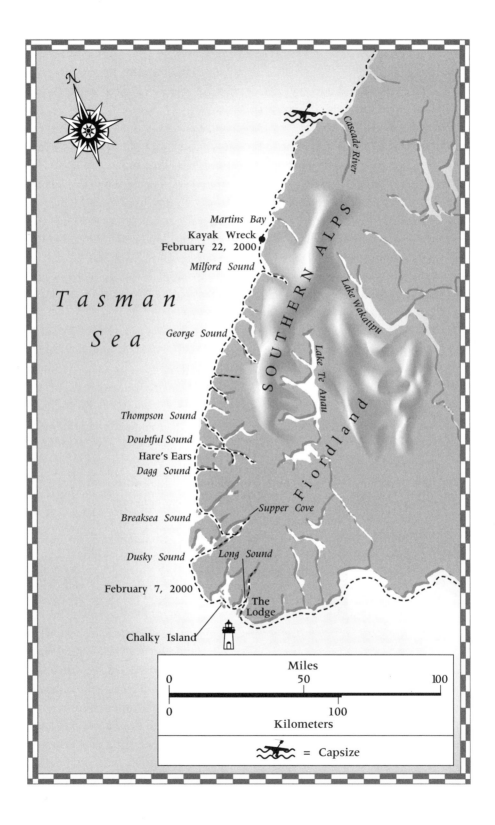

N

Tasman
Sea

Cascade River

Martins Bay
Kayak Wreck
February 22, 2000

Milford Sound

George Sound

SOUTHERN ALPS

Lake Wakatipu

Lake Te Anau

Fiordland

Thompson Sound

Doubtful Sound

Hare's Ears

Dagg Sound

Supper Cove

Breaksea Sound

Dusky Sound   Long Sound

February 7, 2000

The
Lodge

Chalky Island

Miles		
0	50	100

Kilometers	
0	100

= Capsize

his hip boots slapping against his thighs. Less than 200 yards into the forest a clearing opened up and revealed a massive, two story wooden building with a wraparound veranda and circular driveway of gravel.

"Welcome to The Lodge," Jeff exclaimed, as he led the way through the front door and into a high-ceilinged room with several head mounts of elk, deer, and mountain goat hanging from the rough-sawn siding of the great room. A big dining-room table, three overstuffed easy chairs, and a pool table at one end of the room stopped me in my tracks. Ninety miles from the nearest village and surrounded by a national park was a building that looked as if it belonged in a travel brochure for the rich and famous. I followed Jeff through a doorway that led past a bar and into a well-lit, commercial-sized kitchen that looked out on the central court in front of the lodge. He showed me the walk-in pantry, the chest freezer filled with venison, fish, crayfish, and frozen vegetables.

"How would you like venison steaks and spuds for dinner?" he laughed. "I've even got a little fresh lettuce from the garden. There's cucumber, and I think there's probably a tomato or two left as well."

Everything was a bit of a shock to me, and I hadn't been saying too much other than the occasional "Wow, this is really something else." Jeff must have noticed. We were back in the front room. He stopped midway from pulling his wet sweater over his head and explained, "If it seems like I talk a lot it's just because I haven't seen too many people lately. The fishermen 'ave all gone north, and I've been out here pretty much on my own now for almost three months. I like the solitude, but it's nice to have visitors too."

Over a dinner of thick, juicy, red venison and roasted potatoes with plenty of melted butter, I learned a lot more of Jeff's life. He had grown up near Hokitika on the west coast, an area that even at present is hard pressed with high unemployment. He trapped possums for 50 cents a skin and started hunting deer for the venison market when he was fifteen years old. He'd get a dollar a pound for the deer and had a 50cc Honda motorbike to which he strapped the deer and rode the whole affair back into town to collect his money. Like most of the mammals in New Zealand, the deer were imported and released for sport hunting. But like so many other introduced species, their numbers soon multiplied faster than anyone could have imagined, and the native bush started disappearing at an alarming rate. Hunters were hired to cull the deer herd, and Jeff switched from trapping to hunting to make a living. He was in his twenties, living in the bush for a week at a time, hunting and collecting the tails as proof of the kills he made.

"I'd have five or six tails on my belt before lunch. A good day was fifteen animals," he explained.

Once Jeff started reminiscing, the stories came as fast as his mind could recall them. He was a wonderful storyteller as we sat and drank strong, sweet tea beneath the glass-eyed stares of the mounted heads looking down at us. Jeff had worked as a logger, a bulldozer operator, a surveyor for the Department of Conservation mapping the high peaks of Fiordland National Park, a hog farmer, a businessman selling sphagnum moss, and a financial advisor. He was a hard worker and one who didn't take to sitting around. And then suddenly, at age thirty-five, he suffered a massive stroke that left him completely paralyzed and immobile on his bedroom floor. His doctor told him it was caused by too much adrenaline and stress.

"So here I am in the most beautiful part of the world, working at a job that I can't believe I get paid to do. Every day I'm out in the boat exploring and just being thankful I'm alive."

Jeff was a philosopher, a gentle man who loved the native life around the lodge but who also saw how fragile that life was. He explained how the government had imported rabbits decades ago and how they had completely overrun the country. The government then brought in the stoat, a weasellike animal that was supposed to keep the rabbit population in check. Instead of killing rabbits, however, the stoat, which will kill just for the sake of killing, went after the easier prey of the flightless birds. It wasn't long before some of the rarest birds in the world, the kakapo and the takahe, among others, were nearly wiped out. Jeff was trying to trap the last of the stoats, which had somehow made their way across the mountains of Fiordland and into the otherwise pristine wilderness of Preservation Inlet. He showed me the leghold traps he set along the beach and the root hollows of the trees next to the house. He then told me how he loved watching the oystercatchers out along the shore rocks, and the tomtits and fantails that made their home in the rafters of the porch in front of the large picture windows. He was a man who knew the woods and the waters that surrounded him very intimately and seemed to be looking after the native birds and plants as if they were his family. He could name most of the plants around the lodge and identify all the birds by their song. He could also overhaul the diesel generator that supplied power to the lodge and do all the mechanical maintenance on the outboards and the "bike"—the four-wheeler that hauled gravel from the beach to the circular drive in the front and also hauled the boat in and out of the water. Jeff was a free-spirited blend of part naturalist, historian, philosopher, and general mechanic who was just as interested in the sea and the forest as the inner workings of a four-cylinder diesel engine. He seemed to have an endless energy for learning.

At 7:30 Jeff got up and turned the side ban radio on. In a few minutes Meri's voice came over loud and clear. "Bluff Fishermen's Radio, Bluff Fishermen's radio calling The Lodge, are you there, Jeff?"

"Yeah, Meri, I hear you loud and clear. Over."

"Right, Jeff. How's the weather looking out there? Over."

"Not too much happening right at the moment, Meri. A bit of rain and no visibility but no wind here at The Lodge. I've got a visitor though. Chris made it in this afternoon. Over."

"Ah, good as gold then. Ian and I have been wondering how he was getting along. He'll be glad for your cooking and a place to wait out the winds. A low pressure is moving in with gale-force winds tonight, going up to storm force tomorrow. Over."

"Right then, Meri. We'll sit tight and wait it out. I'll let you get on with your sched. Thanks for the weather. We'll talk in the morning. Lodge out."

"Good as gold, Jeff. Bluff Fishermen's Radio out."

Jeff hung the mike up beside the radio and turned the volume down so that he could barely hear the other stations and boats checking in. "Meri's a saint, I tell ye. A wonderful lady she is."

For the next two days, the weather was just as Meri had predicted. The rains lashed the windows and blasted the lodge with gusts and bits of flying debris from the bushes and trees that surrounded the clearing. Jeff kept the woodstove stoked up and the meals miraculously appearing from his cupboards and freezer. In a lull between gales, he towed the skiff back to the beach and took me on a high-speed historical tour of Preservation Inlet. He showed me where the first whaling station in New Zealand had been built in the late 1800s and where, not far from the present lodge, an old gold-mining town had briefly prospered with a population of more than a thousand people. He then turned the boat toward the more protected waters behind Coal Island and, over the noise of the outboard, told me about the "Lost Tribe" of the Maoris. This legendary tribe had broken from the main east-coast tribe and had taken refuge after fierce fighting and cannibalism had splintered the tribe. Jeff later showed me a book that recounted how a Maori guide in the late 1800s had brought some anthropologists from a British museum to an island cave where the body of a Maori chief had been laid to rest. The body had become encrusted in the mineral-rich drippings from the cave ceiling.

When the guide learned that the archaeologists were going to take the mummy back to England for display, he returned to the cave and removed the body. The anthropologists returned to find the elevated platform where the body had rested empty of its mummified remains.

As Jeff motored just beyond the threat of the heavy surf at the cave's entrance, it was easy to see why the tribe had chosen such a well-defended lookout across the inlet.

"I landed here on a calm day and walked up over the back of the island. There's a natural tunnel out the back of the cave that disappears into the forest." Apparently there was more to the legend of the "Lost Tribe" than mere myth.

The second evening with Jeff we sat next to the radio and again listened to Meri's report: "4-meter seas off Puysegur with 50-knot winds." The low-pressure system was slamming the outer coast. Meri was checking in with the *Reliance,* which was bound for the shelter of Doubtful Sound and for some reason was not answering her call. We could hear the worry in her voice as she talked with other boats and asked if anyone had been talking to Jim, the skipper. There was some talk of his hiding up one of the fiords and probably just out of radio range. Meri then called up a yacht that was rounding Farewell Spit after transiting the west coast. It was north of the front and in another few hours would be safely into Golden Bay, and she could take it off her list of contacts to check. She was also tracking another yacht out of Hobart, Tasmania, which was somewhere in the middle of the South Pacific and heading nonstop for England. She would monitor and worry about it until it was beyond her radio's range. Listening to the concern in Meri's voice while the weather beat against the windows almost brought tears to my eyes. No wonder the fishermen loved her as they did. All they had to do was to pick up the radio, and she'd be there for them.

I asked Jeff what he knew about the wreck I had seen near Long Reef Point.

"That's the *Aduze.* The skipper was in close checking his pots, and a wave caught her off guard on December 8. The captain and crew were thrown into the water and had their clothes ripped off them by the time they got to the rocks. They started a fire with some flares and were rescued by a helicopter." Then as if to explain why they lived through the wreck, he said, "They were lucky."

Later he told me how he was pulling a crab pot close to the rocks and a wave knocked him out of the skiff. "I broke one of the cardinal rules of the sea: Never turn your back to the waves. I was just lucky that I got back into the skiff before the next one hit." Again it seemed that luck played a certain role in living and working so close to the sea.

With Meri's nightly radio schedule and the weather reports that she collected and passed on, it was clear that the trip up the west coast was going to be a matter of sitting tight in the safety of the sounds and only going on the outside when the weather allowed. The problem was that the VHF radio was almost useless in the mountainous regions of the park. Once I left The Lodge, I would be on my own with no way of predicting the weather unless I came upon one of the few fishing boats still working the maze of fiords and sounds.

The anemometer at Puysegur was reporting northwest winds holding at 40 knots and gusting to 50 out of the north. The swells would be running 4 meters plus, and it would be several more days before the winds and the sea calmed enough to continue. Until the low pressure passed, there was no point in even thinking of what lay to the north. I decided to explore Long Sound, which reached 20 miles into Fiordland Park. A side trip up the sound would be the perfect escape from the storm.

I left Jeff at 10:00 A.M. under overcast skies and a soft drizzle. Drifting mist and cloud half hid the vertical world of mountains meeting the sea. Where the water had been gin-clear just a few days earlier, it was now stained the color of strong tea from the dozens of waterfalls tumbling and cascading with the same tannic-stained waters out of the mountains. Giant tree ferns called pungas stood 30 feet tall, surrounded by lancewood and manuka trees draping and entwining themselves with smaller ferns and mosses. In the profusion of the rain forest, the pungas stood out like round-faced oracles greeting any visitor that was willing and blessed to press into the primal depth of the sound. I passed Useless Bay, an aptly named dead end, then paddled through The Narrows, where the flooding current swept me through the break in the mountains. For hours I paddled in close to the shore and watched the currents swirling around the rocks, the very last hint of a swell melting over granite boulders and chasing oystercatchers off their slopes of mussel-covered rocks. In the quiet of the sound, tucked out of the wind, there was a silence that was so rare on the outer coast. The winds kicked up whitecaps in the middle of the sound, but they were confused winds that never blew from one direction for very long. It was the mountains that blocked the rage of the winds and protected the inner waters.

Around one point of rocks, I surprised a yellow-eyed penguin standing beneath the dripping branches of the bush that hung over the tide-bared rocks. The penguin stood huddled out of the wind and looking out across the narrowing finger of sea, its flippers, or featherless wings, hanging at its side. As I came around the point, the penguin stood up straighter, and with a dignified shuffle and with flippers held out to either side for balance, it hopped onto a rock and waddled out of sight behind a large boulder.

Five hours after leaving the outer waters of Preservation Inlet, I paddled around the last rocky outcropping of the narrowing sound and sat looking up at a massive waterfall throwing a torrent of brown water over a 50-foot ledge. The cliff, with its thundering falls, marked the terminus of Long Sound and the farthest point that I could penetrate the mountains. High overhead the fog and clouds were lifting, revealing for the first time the dramatic rise and the faces of bare rock thousands of feet straight up. In front of me was a mountain wilderness as thick and impenetrable as any jungle on earth could be. I let the brown river of fresh water catch the bow and swing me slowly around so that the mountain peaks spun in a circle against the clearing sky. The bow came to rest, pointing back to where I had started the day—in the direction of the open sea. Ridges and cliffs that forced the sound to twist and curve out of sight seemed to block the passage back. Two hundred yards in front of the bow the fresh tannic waters mixed with the salt water in clouds of salient layers.

I had ridden most of the way into the back of Long Sound on the last of a flooding tide. Now, against the shore were rocks that showed the first lines of green seaweed, which dripped with the receding tide. I found a level, semidry piece of land and set the tent up looking across the last reach of the sound and upward to the mountains in the background. The roar of the falls was the last thing I remembered hearing as I fell asleep.

I was back at The Lodge by late afternoon the following day. The brief respite from the rains had ended, and the low visibility and drizzle had returned. The closer I had gotten to the open coast, the more evident the winds had become and the more the swells reached into the protected waters and broke on the shallows and rocks near shore. It was clear that the seas on the outside were still running wild. I had called Jeff on the VHF and asked him if he minded another visit while I sorted out the weather and made a plan to try and get around Gulches Head, the headland north of Preservation Inlet. He had the tea brewed by the time I landed and told me he had been worried that I would set off for the headland without checking in for the weather report. Another low-pressure system was building over the south Tasman, and gales were again expected off Puysegur with more of the same 3- to 4-meter seas. I was starting to worry about the days slipping past, with me no closer to Dusky Sound and my rendezvous with Sam, Martha, and Gay. It was only 50 miles from Preservation Inlet to the hut, but with the winds straight out of the north, it might as well have been 500. Once again I was shore bound with the winds, waiting and listening to Meri's evening radio reports, which called for steady north winds peaking at 45 knots.

On February 2 I decided I couldn't wait any longer. The forecast called for a sudden shift to 20-knot southerlies, shifting back to 30 knots out of the north within twelve hours. The seas would still be big from five days of northerly gales, but by the time I got out to open water, the southerly shift in winds might knock the swell down a little. Once I made it to Chalky Island, I could land and sit out the northerlies again. If nothing else, I would be 7 miles closer to Dusky Sound.

Jeff helped me carry the boat back to the beach and then stood in the same mist that had introduced us five days earlier. He was dressed in the same worn and tattered blue sweater and stood as solid as a forest stump at the edge of the beach as I slid into the cockpit of my boat. Over the last five days, he had shared his stories, his food, and his thoughts on life with me as we listened to the woodstove crackle and burn and drive the dampness and cold from the air. We had already exchanged addresses and had shaken hands at the top of the gravel beach. I had told him the previous night that I would be leaving in the morning. As I pulled the spray deck on and prepared to settle into the boat, he said, "I couldn't sleep last night worrying about you taking off. If it all turns to custard, you gotta just sit tight somewhere, ye hear? Your friends'll know that if you're not in Supper Cove, you've just run into bad weather. I don't want to be the one that finds you battered on the rocks, you hear me?"

Jeff had told me grim stories of searches he had been on in the mountains that had ended in tragedy, all because people were trying to "get out on time" and not waiting for the right weather. The image of him awkwardly watching me ready the boat for the launching and the worry on his face would stay with me for weeks.

"I'll be careful, Jeff. Don't worry," I replied.

I back-paddled into deeper water, turned the boat with a sweep stroke on the right side and a backstroke on the left, and then raised the paddle in a farewell.

Jeff called out, "I'm with you on this journey, mate. You take care of yourself."

"I will, Jeff. You do the same. Thanks so much for all your help."

There wasn't anything left to be said. We waved once more, and I finished turning the boat toward Weka Island. Beyond Weka was the faint outline of Coal Island and the shallow passage between Coal and Step Two Island. From there I would get a good look at Gulches Head and decide if it was worth attempting to get around it. I turned to look back twice before the mist swallowed Cromarty Bay in its muffled emptiness. The first time Jeff was standing there watching me; the second time I looked, the beach was empty, with just the dark green of the forest closing in on all sides of the bay and hiding the trail that led into the clearing and The Lodge.

After hiding from the swells and wind in the safety of Preservation Inlet, the exposure of coming around the north side of Coal Island was unnerving. Eight- to ten-foot swells, thick with the volume of the open ocean, crashed and rebounded against the rocks, throwing the heavily loaded boat around like an empty bottle on the waves. I moved steadily away from the islands and reflected waves and farther out into the wind and the bigger swells, which were wrapping around Gulches Head 2.5 miles off my starboard bow. I was now out of the wind shadow of Coal Island and feeling the 15 knots of southerly wind grab at the high blade and trip the smooth crests of the swells into small breakers. Shearwaters knifed through the winds and cut tight circles around the boat. Off to the northwest the sun broke through a bank of dark clouds and arched a brilliant rainbow of colors over Chalky Island. Everywhere else the sea looked as black and tempestuous as the water in the eye of a hurricane.

The closer to Gulches Head I paddled, the larger the swells grew. They were 20 or 30 yards apart and broad, backed with the steamrolling power and memory of the high winds that had formed them. With the dramatic lighting and the size of the seas, the exposure was both intimidating and frighteningly beautiful.

A half hour into the crossing a massive rogue wave lifted and rolled out of the sheen of the black seas. The long climb up its smooth face lifted me high into the air and then opened a trough behind it that was so enormous I stopped paddling and just stared at what didn't seem possible: a lightless valley of moving water so deep and broad that it overwhelmed any sense of scale. The true size of the wave had been disguised by the drama of thick rolling clouds above and the 8- to 10-foot swells that I was watching explode on Balleny Reef a half mile up ahead. Until the trough opened up in front of me, I didn't realize how mammoth the wave was. Down into this maw of colorless, bottomless, empty space, the boat slid. All reference points suddenly disappeared: The reef break, Gulches Head, and Coal Island were gone; in smooth, terrible slow motion, everything but the gray boil of sky directly overhead vanished.

The trough seemed to be dragging me right into the bowels of the ocean, opening deeper and deeper until I could almost feel the sea floor beneath the hull. When the boat finally settled out of its downward slide, I looked across at 30 or 40 yards of flat lightless water. Beyond was a hydraulic expanse so frighteningly large that if it, for some godforsaken reason, should break, death would have come in an unimaginable horror of hundreds of tons of crushing water. For the briefest second the boat seemed to stall at the bottom, in the belly of this monster. There was no sense of motion or measurable distance, only the feeling of being at the very bottom of something so huge and out of all proportion that it completely overwhelmed any sense of scale. What made it so frightening and foreign, so sensuously vacant, was the total absence of any sound. There was no wind, no noise of breaking seas, no call of gulls, and no slap of waves on the boat—nothing but walls of water, moving walls that slowly swept under the boat. Gradually at first, then more rapidly as the sky seemed to grow larger and larger, they began to lift smoothly and then very swiftly thrust me out of the bottomless valley and into the endless horizon of the surface sea.

"My God!" The words escaped from my breath that I must have been unconsciously holding. I followed the rogue wave with my eyes as it rolled away behind me, toward the land that it would explode against and shake the air with its power. I swung my head back around and tried to recapture reference points, tried to reach out for the scale of things that must certainly still be there. The wind immediately rushed past my ears, and I saw the explosions of white seas breaking over Balleny Reef and racing on toward Gulches Head. I was still on course, aiming for the quarter-mile slot between the reef break and the sea stacks off the headland.

As soon as the rogue wave passed, I concentrated on settling myself back down. The wave was gone; it was only one, and it was unlikely there would be another one. These thoughts ran through my mind as I slowed my pace and locked my attention on the boomers just out from the headland: "Pay attention; stay focused; settle down." I was coaching myself off the adrenaline-fired high that had stressed every muscle and mind cell through the rogue wave's passing.

I was back to my measured pace, gauging the buffer between me and the rocks of the Gulches, noting the angle and speed of the waves and pulling one stroke at a time, head-on into the seas. Gradually the headland slid abreast of me, and I changed course to a more northerly heading. The steep seas were erratic and confused by the rebounding waves coming off the headland. They came in from both sides, tossing the boat high on a peaked crest one second, then dropping out from under the boat the next. Twice a wave collapsed from the seaward side, burying the boat in broken white water, knocking the stern off course and sending the bow pointing straight out to sea. Both times I instinctively reached out with a low brace to port, holding the boat upright on its edge until the broken water subsided and released the boat.

Straight ahead Chalky Island had all but disappeared behind a heavy rainsquall that was closing in from the north. Behind me Gulches Head was a jagged fortress of sea stacks, crashing waves, and confused seas, all set against a coal-black sky. The only thing lacking in the picture would have been a three-masted ship wrecked on the teeth of the rocks below the cliffs.

I had the rain hood on my paddle jacket pulled up and snugged around my head when the squall hit. I was now out of the rough waters around the headland and almost into the protected waters behind Chalky Island. The rain pounded the front deck and drilled against the fabric of my hood in a deafening roar. Fat, cold pellets bounced and ricocheted off the boat, off my head and hands, and off the sea around me. What looked like a low blanket of fog on the water was actually a haze formed from the rebounding rains, driven out of the sky by some force of temperature difference and a pressure that was firing billions of drops onto the sea's surface.

Ten minutes after the deluge began, the squall moved southward. The curtains of water slowly thinned and then were gone, leaving Chalky Island bathed and glistening in crystal sunlight. I paddled around the back side of the small island, then around to the north side, where aeons of storms and waves had scalloped a crescent of sand beach out of the eroded sedimentary rocks. Ledges of red-brown rock reached out from the thickets of flax and wind-combed bush that covered the tiny island. In less than an hour, I had gone from the complete exposure of rounding Gulches Head to this oasis of sun and sand, an island sanctuary that was completely sheltered from any wind or wave threat. What was more shocking than finding the sheltered landing was seeing a small, green-metal-roofed building breaking the soft contours of the island's junglelike canopy.

A small wave surfed the boat over the rippled sands until it bumped gently onto the island. I pulled the boat into the drift logs and then found a thin, winding track that led from the top of the beach through a tunnel of green and eventually to the roofed porch of a newly constructed cabin. The door to the cabin was locked, but through the windows looking out to Cape Providence, I could see leghold traps, a map of the island, and charts of the Fiordland waters. On a shelf was a radio, connected to a set of batteries below a workbench. I had heard of several islands in the fiords that were being cleared by the Department of Conservation of the same stoats, rats, and predators that Jeff was attempting to wipe out at The Lodge. The DOC was carrying out this eradication program in the hopes of creating refuges, and perhaps breeding grounds, for the last of several species of nearly extinct flightless birds.

Two Quonset huts cabled to the earth with rebar and concrete sat to one side of the hut. I tried the door of one and found the tiny, arch-roofed room to have been converted into a four-bed bunkhouse. Someone had left a lighter and a couple of half-burned candles on a crosspiece between the wall studs. Three copies of *Reader's Digest* lay in a neat stack beside one of the bunks, and there was a box filled with emergency food under another. I closed the door and returned to the porch, which overlooked the tops of the bush and out toward Cape Providence. The cabin and huts were obviously new and looked as though they had been set up as a base for studying the island. Tucked under the crown of the island and into the protection of the natural cove, it was a perfect place for me to wait out the weather. I could watch the seas off the cape and decide when to attempt the 15 miles of cliff-and-rock coastline that would lead into Dusky Sound. I was happy to have the porch roof over my head for the afternoon and maybe even throw my sleeping bag on one of the bunks for the night.

At 1:30 I turned the radio on and listened to channel 67 for the weather. The forecast called for southwest gales at Puysegur, swinging to the northwest and rising to 40 knots by the next day. After coming around Gulches Head in only 15-knot winds and seeing what the seas had been like, there was no way I was going anywhere until the seas and the winds calmed. The weather broadcast was weak and broken with heavy static. I tried to raise first Jeff, and then Meri, to let them know where I was, but there was no response.

During the next day and a half, each weather report continuously contradicted the previous one. The forecasted 40 knots out of the northwest went down to 30 on one report then back up to 45 on the next. One twelve-hour outlook called for 10-knot southwesterlies that never developed but instead stayed at 40 knots out of the northwest, then shifted suddenly to 30 knots out of the south. The fronts were moving through faster than the forecasters could track them, and the winds were all over the place.

These were exactly the conditions that Jeff had warned me about: unpredictable weather, a scheduled meeting that was becoming less likely to make with each passing hour, and a growing impatience and restlessness as Cape Providence would appear out of the mist and fog one minute and then vanish the next. I remembered Jeff's warning, "I don't want to be the one to find you battered on the rocks just because you had to meet up with your friends." It was hard to be patient when the rendezvous day was just around the corner and there was no indication the winds were going to settle down. The thought of my friends flying in and just leaving the needed food when I didn't show up was almost too much to imagine. I had worked too hard to get this close and not see them. It seemed that Puysegur Point had innocently let me slip past and then had sprung this wind trap on me. Where were all the southerly winds that had harassed me on the east coast? Now that I was on the west coast, those southerly winds should have been pushing me steadily north; instead, the winds were mainly out of the north, with brief and violent shifts to the south. I thought of a letter from my Dad that I had picked up in Bluff. The first line of his neat handwriting spelled out his understanding of the sea: "By now you are well into the voyage—let's hope you have gentle following seas, but that seldom happens." My Dad couldn't have called the shots any better than that. The winds that blew so erratically and churned the sea into a mass of confused large breakers were anything but gentle, and they certainly hadn't been at my back for most of the trip. All I needed were five hours of calm winds and seas to get into Dusky Sound. Once I was in the sound, it wouldn't matter what the winds on the outside were doing. I could always find a lee shore to paddle and to work my way 25 miles into Supper Cove.

On February 4 the 1:30 P.M. forecast called for southwest winds at 20 knots, dropping to 10 knots by evening. Maybe the winds were finally dying out? A few seconds later the twelve-hour outlook shattered any hope of that. The outlook called for a shocking 50 knots out of the north! If I was going to get off the island, it had to be that evening or I could just as well write off the rendezvous. In front of the hut, visibility was down to a quarter mile, with a steady drizzle and a 10-knot northwest breeze. The forecast was calling for southwest winds, not northwest. I could see the weather, and it was nothing like what was coming over the speaker of the VHF.

I debated. A north wind at 10 knots was the best that it had gotten in the last three days, but I didn't like the low visibility. Would I be able to see anything on the outer coast if I chanced an attempt? On the chart the outer coast was marked "Unsurveyed." The fact that it was unsurveyed just added to the anxiety that the unstable winds and the inaccurate reports had been fueling. I was tired of basically sitting for the last week and was impatient. Despite the low visibility I decided to go for Dusky Sound and take my chances on the 20 miles between Chalky Island and the safety of the sound.

In a rush I packed everything off the porch, where I had set up a temporary camp, and carried it all down to the boat which was sitting behind a drift log above high tide. I made two sandwiches with the last of the bagels and peanut butter and jam, then measured the mileage for the tenth time from Chalky Island, across to Cape Providence, then along the outer coast and into Pickersgill Harbor 6 miles into Dusky Sound. The harbor had sheltered Captain Cook's ship, the HMS *Resolution*, when he sought a lee shore to resupply the ship in 1773. The harbor had been named after his first lieutenant onboard.

If the north winds did blow up to 50 knots, I needed the same protection from the seas that the *Resolution* had sought. It wasn't good enough to just get around South Point—the entrance of Dusky Sound—because it was wide open to the north. If I left the protection of Chalky Island, I had to get all the way into Pickersgill Harbor. That meant I needed more than six hours of stable weather: an hour to get to Cape Providence, four hours along the outer coast, and maybe another hour to reach the safety of the harbor. That was six hours if everything went just right. Once beyond the cape, there were no bail-out points on the chart, just a straight, rocky coastline. If the north winds picked up, I would have to turn around and retreat to the cape and find a landing on its south side or come back to Chalky. Because of the fog and mist, I couldn't see how large the waves were running. No doubt they were still out of the north and running fairly high after the last two days of wind. Even if they were smooth-faced swells, it wouldn't take much of a wind to drive them into steep breakers.

The options and doubts rolled around in my mind and turned my stomach into knots. The boat was packed, and I was standing with the spray deck on, looking across at where the cape should have been visible. Leaving

Chalky Island with no visibility, a questionable weather report, and a pattern of shifting high winds was a gamble that I didn't like.

I remembered my friend Candace's words at my going-away party. She had stood across the packed room and read a note that she had prepared. With tears on her face, she had finished her blessing and wishes for my safe journey. The last words she had spoken were, "I give you my trust that you will not take any unnecessary risks."

I had told her then that I wouldn't take any risks if I were given a choice. Now I was faced with just such a choice. Her words, and my promise, made the decision for me: The risks were too great. I stripped off the spray deck, dropped it in the cockpit and pulled the boat back behind the log. With that decision I gave up on making the rendezvous.

Later that afternoon I hiked to the south side of the wooded island, following a newly cut trail through the brush and around thick-stumped trees bent and twisted by the winds. I found a place where the land dropped precipitously to the waves below and I could look back on Gulches Head. I tried the radio again, "Any vessel, any vessel, any vessel. This is Sea Kayaker One, Sea Kayaker One, over." There was no response. I adjusted the squelch and tried again. Still nothing, just the rumble of the surf on the base of the cliff on which I was standing.

By the time I got back to the beach in front of the hut, the skies had cleared, and for the first time I could clearly see the cliffs on Cape Providence 2 miles away. A small patch of blue to the north of the cape had opened up, and it looked as though the seas had calmed. Was it possible? Maybe this was the lull before the predicted 50-knot northerlies? Two hours earlier I had resigned myself to sitting out the coming storm-force winds on the island. Now it looked as if maybe I had a chance of getting into Dusky Sound after all.

I had unpacked the boat in anticipation of setting up camp again. There was gear up at the hut, food bags, and loose gear in the cockpit and an untidiness about the boat that was not typical. With the patch of blue sky now extending over the cape and growing larger by the minute, I suddenly had the opportunity I needed. I ran through the bush and up to the hut, grabbed all my gear, and dashed back to the boat. In five minutes everything was stuffed into the hatches—not exactly where it normally belonged, but at least it was in the boat. I sprinted up the trail one more time to double-check that I hadn't left anything, then ran back and jumped in the boat as I shoved it off the sand and into calf-high water. It was exactly 3:00 P.M. as I took the first strokes that pulled me away from the beach. If all went well, I would be in Dusky Sound just as nightfall settled in.

The crossing over to Cape Providence took fifty minutes. I was watching the time, gauging my paddling speed and mentally clicking off the miles. A 6- to 8-foot northerly swell was running with a 3-foot tidal chop directly in front of the cape. It was a wet ride, with the smaller waves pouring over the front deck, washing up and soaking me as I shot through the tidal rip. Farther offshore the seas were smoother—big thick rollers that lifted the boat high enough for me to see 3 or 4 miles down the coast—a view of heavy surf piling in lines of white upon the rocks and the base of the cliffs.

A mile north of Cape Providence I looked back at Chalky Island disappearing around the curve of the coast. The last of a north breeze lightly touched my face and seemed to be dying out. A few scattered cat's-paws rippled the surface of the swells but then just as quickly faded. I was paddling into the only calm window of weather there had been in over a week. Three quarters of a mile to my right, the din of the surf was like a warning: "Don't even think about finding a place to bail out."

For the moment I had everything going for me. The miles were slowly dropping away, and the sun was actually warm enough for me to strip off the paddle jacket and dig in harder, driving the boat a little faster and eating away at the miles that lay between me and sheltered water. This was not a coastline to sit and photograph or to ponder its remote wildness; it was simply one that I wanted to put behind me. The forecasts of the last few days had me spooked. If the winds shifted, as they had so often in the last forty-eight hours, I would be in more trouble than I wanted to imagine. Each time my mind started going down the path of "what-if," I would shake my head clear of the thoughts, dig in harder until I couldn't hold the pace any longer, and then settle back into a high cruising pace. I needed to stay focused and just kept pushing the boat over the smooth faces of the north swells, then down their sloping backs and onto the next one.

Slowly the time began to slip past—the first hour, and 4-plus miles leading into the next hour and becoming 8 miles. I would try not to look at my watch but then would give in and see that only a half hour had elapsed, which meant a little more than 2 more miles covered. A puff of wind would stir the surface waters and blow a faint warning onto the skin of my hands and face. At every puff, my brain would snap into alert and trigger the release of a little drop of adrenaline that ran like firewater through my veins and into my stomach. And still the surf pounded the distant rocks. I moved a few hundred yards farther offshore to get away from the noise, but it was more of a mental game than anything that really made an audible difference.

Somewhere near the halfway point I began to settle down mentally, perhaps knowing that I was over the hump and on the downward run of the distance yet to paddle. I was still on the defensive, however, pushing the high blade and pulling the low blade with more energy than normal, but I was starting to loosen up mentally. Now I was beginning to let my mind play with the images of meeting my friends. I tried to imagine them meeting up in Te Anau, Gay having been in New Zealand for two weeks already, and Sam and Martha just arriving. They would pick up the thirty pounds of food I had prepackaged and left with Kevin, who would make arrangements for the floatplane that would fly them out of Te Anau, over the Southern Alps and into Dusky Sound. I tried to imagine what they would see flying over the Alps—the glaciers and river drainages, the rock faces of cliff, and the endless miles of forests that would look so much like the interior of Olympic National Park, where we all lived. I also tried to imagine our meeting in the cabin— their faces, their smiles, the stories they would bring of home. With each passing mile I was getting closer to Supper Cove and to that tiny dot on the chart that we had all studied so many months earlier.

While my mind was 40 miles away, filled with the excitement and expectation of meeting my friends, the physical part of me was still at work pulling the boat past the line of cliffs, ears listening to the surf and eyes unconsciously searching the near waters for threats, watching the bow wake and scanning the horizon for anything that indicated a change. Every five or six minutes I would twist in the seat, scan the horizon behind me, then return to the automated fluid pull of the blades.

On one of these horizon scans, a white dot floated out of the swells a half mile to the left of the bow. I forgot all about Supper Cove, and mountains, and home, and even friends, as the white dot slowly drew closer and larger, veering in its slow, graceful turns over the swells and swinging in closer toward my course. The nerve-rattling exposure and the total lack of any safety net along the 20 miles of rock and cliff was instantly transformed into something else—into the grace and beauty of an albatross soaring over this ocean wilderness. I watched the albatross slowly draw closer, watched it disappear for long seconds at a time, then glide back into view on outstretched, graceful white wings, gaining height for its next sweeping turn. At the height of each climb, it seemed to stall, then, with a dip of its wing, glide swiftly down to wave height again and settle in front of a rolling mound of sea, diagonally surfing the air currents. As our courses intersected, the albatross floated out of the trough in front of the boat and hung suspended overhead and slightly to the right. Everything about the white giant of a bird was detailed against the blue of the sky: its massive hooked beak and regal serene face, the long tapering wings, and its feet tucked cleanly beneath a belly of pure-white feathers. God, what a beautiful creature! For no more than a few seconds, it hung on the air currents, silently holding its position and height above me. It hesitated for just a few seconds longer, then was instantly gone, sweeping behind me and dropping smoothly to wave height again and continuing its silent patrol. During the rest of the passage, three more albatrosses would repeat the first one's visit, altering their flights to come over and investigate the yellow boat and paddler slowly moving north.

By the time I reached South Point, the warmth and mellow light of the evening sun had dropped behind a thickening bank of clouds that lay low on the western horizon. Five Fingers Peninsula jutted out from Resolution Island 4 miles across the mouth of the sound. In closer, Anchor Island formed the south channel of Dusky Sound, which led farther inland and would gradually give more protection from the swells coming in from the north. An hour after rounding South Point, I was gliding effortlessly along on flat water past rock outcroppings and tree limbs that almost touched the sea. After the company of thick ocean swells, and booming surf filling the air with noise and ocean mist, the quiet of the sound was almost deafening.

In the very last light of day, I almost ran the boat aground on a submerged ledge, which marked the mouth of Pickersgill Harbor. It had taken five and a half hours to paddle from Chalky Island. I found a gravel beach to land on, scratched out a level spot for the tent, and turned in without bothering with dinner. The paddle hadn't been a long one, but it had drained me emotionally. I lay in the bag listening to the soft tingle of wavelets on the stones and a light drizzle on the tent fly. It was February 5, two days to go and I would see my friends. I had made it!

By the time the predicted storm-force winds hit the outer coast the next day, I was paddling down the middle of Cook Channel, with Long Island on one side and Mount Evans rising 3,000 feet straight up to my right. Behind me gray-black contorted clouds raced in from the north, boiled over the peaks of the outer islands, and began filling the mouth of the sound with dense, wet clouds. Up ahead the mountains were bathed in eastern sunlight, the higher elevations holding a ridge of cold air mass that temporarily blocked the inflow of warm, moist marine air. The mountains would hold the winds at bay for a few hours, but eventually the winds would erode the last of the high-pressure dam formed by the mountains. When the dam broke, the winds would funnel up the island channels and roar into the mountains with an unleashed vengeance. For several hours I paddled and raced, with a west wind at my back beneath the developing storm. Blasts of wind hit Cook Channel, lifting wavelets and throwing beads of water off the tiny waves. The short-lived winds were the precursors to what would come later. These winds had been deflected off the peaks and were scouting out the lees and slowly filling the quiet waters and bays of Dusky Sound. Each time I turned to look back toward my previous night's camp, the view had changed dramatically, the storm rapidly pressing in behind me.

The problem with camping in fiords is that the glaciers that form the classic narrow and steep-sided rifts often leave nothing in the way of flat ground to camp upon. The fiords are a world of rock rising straight up from the depths and ending in a neck-craning ridge of peaks that overlap and scrape the bottom of the clouds. The moisture-laden clouds are cooled by the elevations they are pushed up against and wring out more than 20 feet of rain each year. One has to find not only a level place but also one that is protected from the winds and the sudden downpours that can change an innocent trickle of a side stream into a raging brown torrent.

Before the storm hit the inner waters of Dusky Sound, I stumbled upon an island with a hidden entrance of offset cliffs and granite boulders that protected a sanctuary of calm water. At the back of the quarter-mile oasis, a stream bubbled and murmured out of the forest, flowing over smooth-faced rocks stained brown with tannic acid. To one side of the stream, the forest floor opened up with a nearly flat piece of ground no bigger than the footprint of my tent. I was within 10 miles of Supper Cove and a day early. If the weather didn't ground the floatplane out of Te Anau, I would see my friends the following afternoon.

I didn't know if it was the wind or the torrential rains drumming against the tent fly that woke me first. All I knew was that in the middle of a pitch-black night, when trees were snapping in the forest and the winds were shrieking and slamming into the canopy overhead, sleep was not something that came easily. Hours later the rains still hammered the fly and had filled the gully where I had set the tent up. The tent floor floated on a pool of water as I curled into a tighter ball on my sleeping pad and pulled the bag in closer around me. Sometime toward dawn the noise of the winds and rains abated, and I finally slipped off into the exhaustion of sleep. When I awakened again, it was to the roar of the stream 50 yards away that had swollen to four times its previous size, pouring thousands of gallons a minute into the protected harbor. A new day was dawning as I unzipped the tent and looked out on a forest dripping in sunshine.

Beneath the canopy of beech trees, and a sky partly filled with scudding, puffy clouds, I mixed the last of the granola and powdered milk and then hastily broke down the camp. As I rolled the sodden fly of the tent into a bundle and stuffed it into the middle compartment of the boat, I tried to imagine where my friends were at that same moment. Were they waking up in the hut at Supper Cove after listening to the rain and wind all night? Or maybe they were still in Te Anau, waiting for the weather to lift for their flight over the mountains? After so many months of planning and paddling, it didn't seem possible that in a few hours I might actually see them, these friends who had sat with me at a kitchen table half a world away studying a chart of the waters that now surrounded me. I slid the boat into the tea-colored tannic runoff and retraced my route out of the little oasis I had found the night before.

A two-hour paddle would be necessary to reach the back of Dusky Sound where it split into two arms, the left arm reaching into Supper Cove. The morning paddle had been a marvel of one cascading waterfall after the next streaming off cliffs thousands of feet overhead. Some streams could be traced from near the tops of the mountains all the way down to the sea. Others would disappear into the lush green of the mountains and reappear hundreds of feet lower, then vanish again until they tumbled and poured into the sea. Through the pristine clarity of the air, the falls at the top of some of the cliffs looked more like hanging columns of glistening white quartz rock than they did waterfalls. The height of the falls was so far overhead that none of the noise of the tons of falling water ever reached the stillness of the sound.

Beneath the heights of the mountains, and the falls that had turned the top layer of the sound almost fresh with the torrential rains, I finally paddled into Supper Cove. My chart that showed the DOC hut as a black dot wasn't detailed enough for me to pinpoint the cabin's exact location. The final half mile of paddling had me searching the shoreline, which ran for several miles in a smooth semicircle around the bay. When I finally spotted the roofline perched 50 feet above the cove, I nearly jumped out of the boat with excitement. After two months of dealing with the winds and weather problems and then almost giving up on getting to Supper Cove on time, I couldn't believe that right in front of the bow was the hut!

I sprinted to within 100 yards of the shore and called out, "Hello-o-o." My voice echoed across the water and was absorbed by the green forest. I paddled another 50 yards and called out again, "Hello-o-o." There was no answering call or sign of anyone. After the push to get around Gulches Head, then Cape Providence and out along the exposed coast leading into Dusky Sound, I had the sinking feeling that the violent weather I had been dodging might have grounded my friends in Te Anau. I paddled up to a small sandy beach to one side of the hut and pulled the boat quickly above the tidal range. Maybe they were in the hut and just hadn't heard me calling? A trail led from the beach, past tree ferns and over exposed roots slick with the rains that had just ended. It climbed steadily from ankle-deep, oozing mud to drier land and then onto the rock ledge where the hut had been built.

I was within a few strides of breaking out of the forest and coming to within full view of the hut when I stopped dead in my tracks. Above the pounding of my heart came the unmistakable whine and throb of a helicopter from somewhere behind me, in the direction of a valley reaching between the peaks of several mountains. I hadn't heard a plane or a helicopter or anything else like that in weeks. For a few seconds I stood frozen, trying to register what a helicopter would be doing in the middle of Fiordland National Park. Then it suddenly hit me, like stepping barefoot on a hot coal. *My friends were on that chopper!* I spun around, leapt off the ledge, and scrambled down off the rocks, over the tree roots, and straight into the mud holes that I had so carefully avoided on the climb up from the beach. By the time I got to the beach, the chopper was closing fast. I jumped into the boat, pulling mud and seawater into the cockpit with me, and then sprinted out from under the trees just in time to see a shiny white helicopter banking and dropping into a tight turn. The rapid-fire throb and turbo whine of the engine was deafening as the pilot pulled out of the turn and hovered for a few seconds, tail down and rotors churning the water into a maelstrom of flying mist and small waves. The chopper inched forward until it was hovering like a possessed whirling dervish, throwing bits of leaves and twigs into the air above a makeshift landing of logs and rocks built out from the shore. The powerful downdraft of the rotors tried to blow the bow off its course as I sat almost under the chopper and snapped a couple of photos. It was the sweetest, most invasive chaos of earsplitting noise and machinery that I had ever heard.

By the time the chopper's metal skids had settled on the ground, I had driven the bow carelessly onto a gravel spit, and I jumped out of the cockpit just as the pilot stepped out of the left side of the helicopter. I could see Martha waving from the Plexiglas bubble, and behind her I caught a glimpse of Sam and Gay taking off the headphones and preparing to climb out. As many times as I had imagined our meeting, I hadn't imagined the flood of emotion that swept over me as Martha suddenly stepped down from the chopper. Dressed in a khaki shirt, hiking shorts, and stout leather boots, she ducked low under the rotors and gave me a great hug that almost squeezed the tears from my eyes. The others piled out of the chopper, with Sam taking pictures and Gay nearly crushing me in a bear hug. She was trembling, and tears filled her eyes. We had both lost a good friend and nearly several other friends as a result of a helicopter crash a few years earlier. Wounds and memories like those don't fade with time, and the flight for Gay had been a rough one. She hates helicopters. The winds over the mountain passes had been violent and the visibility poor. The flight into Dusky hadn't been a smooth one.

Above the high-pitch whine of the turbine, I shouted, "I was afraid the weather had grounded you guys."

"It almost did," Sam yelled back. "We had to change from a floatplane to the chopper. Thick clouds and winds over the mountains."

"When did you leave? When did you get into New Zealand?" My mind was racing to catch up with what was happening, and I started to babble questions. "Who are you?" I asked a strong-looking young hiker with a leather cowboy hat clutched in one hand.

"This is Jon. Jon, this is Chris," shouted Sam. I left it at that as the pilot started pulling backpacks from a red fiberglass storage box suspended beneath the clear bubble of the chopper. When a small mountain of gear was sitting in a pile on the landing, he shook hands with all the passengers, climbed back into the chopper, fastened his shoulder harness, and slipped a pair of headphones on. In another minute the rotors wound up with an increasingly higher-pitched whine, and slowly the machine lifted off the logs and rocks. Helicopters fascinate me. They are noisy and fragile and so brilliant in their ability to maneuver and hover, like a cross between a giant dragonfly and a robotic hummingbird. They couldn't be any further removed from the silence of a paddle knifing into the sea, yet there is something about them that holds my attention. I was watching the machine carefully, trying to see what the pilot was doing with his hands and feet, when Sam grabbed my arm and led me away from the debris-filled air. All of us hung onto our hats and gear as the chopper backed away, once again churning the water into wavelets, then turning and racing for the cut in the mountains leading back to Te Anau.

A half hour later we were all gathered inside the one-room DOC hut, with a picnic table and wood-burning stove in the middle and two long sleeping platforms, one above the other, on the far end. I wanted to know all the news from Port Angeles: How was the skiing? Was it a good snow year? How were all my friends? Where had Gay been in the two weeks since she had arrived in New Zealand? I learned that Jon—a biology major who was traveling throughout New Zealand after doing an internship on the South Island—was from Germany. Gay had hiked most of the major tracks on the South Island one after the other, in her typically full-on love for the outdoors. Sam told me the snow had been piling up in the Olympic Mountains, but he also assured me there would be plenty left for spring skiing when I got back in May. The Port Angeles newspaper had published excerpts about my trip from the Web site that Al Zob had been maintaining. Apparently the entire town was following the progress of the journey.

I asked if they had brought the food I had prepackaged and left with Kevin. Martha replied, "Don't you want to see what treats we brought for you?"

She had a mischievous look in her eye as she started digging into her pack. In a few seconds the tabletop was filled with little boxes and bags and envelopes with bright string tied around them. A bottle of wine appeared out of Gay's pack, along with a huge block of cheese, fresh bread, crackers, chocolate, and tea. Out of Sam's pack came a vacuum bag filled with beef jerky, dried fruit ribbons, and more chocolates.

"The crew at Safeway wanted us to bring down a few goodies," Sam explained. Safeway was the local grocery store where I did my shopping and where I knew most of the checkout folks.

There were cards with the Safeway package that had been signed by customers who were following the trip, and other cards, notes, and letters from personal friends. When everything was piled on the table, it looked like Christmas. I didn't know where to start.

"Here, eat this. You look like you need some fat," Gay said as she pushed the cheese and crackers to my end of the table. "Who wants wine?"

We had a toast to the support crew, to Sam's birthday, which was just a few days away, and then to the continued success of the trip.

I couldn't imagine anything else coming out of the packs and adding to the plethora of colors and foods almost spilling off the rough wooden table-top. I caught a glance between Martha and Sam that hinted there was more to come.

Sam started the presentation with a brief introduction: "The girls at Bonny's Bakery thought you should have a little treat."

On more than a few occasions before the trip, Sam and I had ended our paddling workout at a bakery in Port Angeles. Our favorite selection had always been a cinnamon roll—moist and sweet and full of calories.

Sam reached into his pack and pulled out two of Bonny's cinnamon rolls, two squares of thick, chewy dough, swirled with brown cinnamon and what-ever secret ingredient Bonny drips into them to make them almost melt in your mouth. He dropped them in my hand with that wonderful dense weight that a good cinnamon roll has, pure decadence double-wrapped in cello-phane for the 7,000-mile journey from the pastry display to a cabin tucked into Supper Cove. After eating rice and pasta for most of the last two months and always being aware of how much food was left in the back compartment, I was overwhelmed by all the treats in front of me. I carefully unwrapped one cinnamon roll and sliced a wafer-thin end off one side. It felt too precious to just devour the whole thing, too precious and way too much sugar for my blood. I offered everyone a piece, but they all declined. Sam said, "You need every ounce of fat you can get. It's all yours."

For the next couple of hours, we talked and ate and talked some more. My friends wanted to know about the trip, and I wanted to tell them about it but, like all the gifts and food, I didn't know where to start. The past two months were too much to recall—too complex and too intense and focused. I wanted to give them some perspective on the trip, something the Web site couldn't explain or show, but I didn't know how to do it.

I had hung my soaked paddling clothes on a line over the woodstove and was wearing my fleece pants and shirt. My other fleece jacket was draped over the back of a chair. My sandals were the only footwear I had. Martha looked up at my shorts, fast-drying shirt and paddle jacket.

"Where are the rest of your clothes?" she asked.

"That's all there is," I replied.

"That's it?" she asked incredulously, pointing to the limp garments that dripped puddles onto the cabin floor.

My clothing was a perfect example of how removed and ascetic my life on the sea was. Everything about the trip—the unsettled winds, the higher than normal swells, and the cool weather—had whittled away all the extraneous stuff and had left me with the bare essentials and little else except for an unexplainable drive to continue. I told my friends about the people I had met, the penguins, the albatrosses, and a few memories of the gales I had sat out, but there was so much that I could not find words for: the awe I felt on this trip that was still unfolding, the power of the South Pacific swells, and the raucous nature of the Tasman Sea, which was twenty-five miles away. It was a struggle to make this connection that I so wanted to share. But there was also the shock of too many things in front of me. I couldn't focus on all that was going on—the sheer amount and choice of food, multiple plates and cups, three headlamps sitting on the edge of the table and ready for the evening that would come all too quickly. I was so accustomed to my routine, to moving so efficiently and knowing exactly where everything I owned was. How was I going to fit all this wonderful food in my boat? Where were my gloves and the lighter that I kept tucked in the same Ziploc bag with the toilet paper? I kept trying to keep my gear separate from everybody else's, neatly stacking it in a corner and taking the clothes off the rope above the stove as soon as they were dry and putting them on top of the other gear. My mind kept jumping around and trying to organize what didn't need organizing.

In the middle of all this confusion, I would look at my friends and see again what the moment was all about. They had spent their vacation time and their money to fly all the way from Port Angeles, Washington, to this tiny cabin on the edge of Supper Cove just to support *me*, to bring in the needed food and to be a part of the adventure. It was all so fantastic and, at the same time, overwhelming.

The weather pattern that had almost wiped out our meeting was still a factor with which we all had to deal. The hike out of Supper Cove and along the Dusky Track is the most difficult hike in New Zealand, with four major river drainages to cross. As we sat in the cabin that evening and finished off a communal diner, the rains hammered the tin roof and ran off the overhanging eaves in steady rivulets. The forecast called for clearing weather for two days, then more rain and wind as another front moved in from across the South Tasman. The rains would fill the rivers and make the river crossings difficult. For my part I still had almost 500 miles of the west coast to paddle and all of the questions that had haunted me from the very start of the trip in terms of the surf farther north. As much as I wanted to just relax and enjoy the shelter and the comfort of my friends, I couldn't shut out the thought of the complex route, both physically as well as psychologically, that lay ahead of me. I was already planning the route out of Supper Cove: paddling the north edge of Dusky Sound, slipping into Acheron Passage and then into Breaksea Sound, where I would wait for another break to paddle the outside coast into Dagg Sound. There was no denying that the weather and seas of the last week and a half were beginning to weigh on my mind. I had to keep moving, taking advantage of every single opportunity to move northward. We decided that the next morning I would hike out a couple of miles with everyone to the Seaforth River, the first major river crossing that they would have to make. The hike would give us a few hours together and would also give me a chance to see a little of the interior.

It didn't take long on the trail to see that my friends had four days of tough hiking ahead of them. Unlike most trails in the United States, the Kiwi system of trail design seemed to focus on following deer paths and rabbit runs rather than building bridges or ladders over obstacles. The trail was more often under water than above and frequently went straight up rock faces, with only toeholds and twisted roots to cling to. We hiked in silence for the most part, surrounded by a land that looked like something out of Jurassic Park, with its massive tree ferns, lichens, mosses, and a thread of trail that wound through the thick underbrush of fallen trees and rich, moist forest earth. Sam was somewhere in the lead, 10 yards away and completely swallowed by the dense vegetation that crowded in from all sides as well as from above. Suddenly he would reappear, waiting for the rest of us beside a 20-foot-high tree fern with its fan of drooping greenery beside him.

In the 2 miles from the cabin to the wire cables that stretched over the Seaforth River, everyone's boots were already soaked, and their nylon gaiters were covered in mud. The trail conditions, though, couldn't dampen everyone's spirits. We all wore the same smiles as we stood and looked at the river gushing swiftly past. Three wires, one for the feet to balance upon, and two others at shoulder height for the hands to slide over and hang onto, were strung above the river, running brown and swift over jumbled boulders 30 feet below. This was the first of the four drainages they would have to make, four crossings that would depend upon calm nerves and a steady surefootedness. I crossed first, then took photos of each of my friends as they gingerly threaded their way across, wearing top-heavy packs that made my crossing look like child's play. Martha was the last to cross. Sam had gone back to take her pack, then had retraced his steps and stood very quietly watching. She slowly stepped out on the wire, hesitated, and then, with eyes intently on the wire beneath her feet, worked her way out over the river. There was nothing anyone of us could do to help. Sam's love for Martha is something that is indelibly imprinted in my memory as he watched her take those first steps out on the cable, which swayed and sank with her weight. One step at a time she drew closer to the far side, where we all watched and waited. When she was within arm's reach, Sam reached out and took Martha's hand, which she extended to him.

Months after the trip had ended and I was standing in their living room, Martha had told me how terrifying the river crossings had been for her. The only way that she could bring herself to inch out on the finger-thick cable was to sing a tune her father had taught her as a child as she concentrated on putting one foot in front of the other. With the water flying past below, and the noise of rapids filling her ears, I understood what Martha had felt—a fear that is almost paralyzing but one that you have to confront and move forward with. Sometimes there are no options, no bail-out plans. Whether it is a headland or a river-cable crossing, fear is still fear. There is something of value when that fear is confronted with awareness and a full understanding of the consequences of a mistake. The fear is acknowledged, and the choice is made to cross to the other side.

The hardest part of seeing my friends in Supper Cove was exchanging hugs with all of them on the far side of the Seaforth River and then walking back across the swaying cable that linked our separate journeys. They stood on the rock outcropping above the river with colorful packs, muddy gaiters, smiles, and wet boots. Within five minutes of my paddling into Supper Cove, they had swooped out of the sky in a whirl of rotor blades and churning downdrafts. Now they stood seconds from disappearing into the forest after fueling me with food and love enough to carry me onward. We waved from opposite sides of the river. All the good-byes had been said on the far side and throughout the last hours of our visit. I turned away, took a few steps, and then looked back as their backpacks faded one by one into the forest. In seconds there wasn't any sign of them. The cable bridge still stretched taut across the river, but there wasn't a single hint of sway or sign that four friends had just crossed its thread of steel. The trail that led to Lake Manapori had just taken the last view of my friends from me. In the other direction the trail back to Supper Cove twisted and vanished behind ferns and beech trees.

After the overwhelming love and excitement of seeing my friends, I was suddenly standing alone on a muddy trail in a New Zealand rain forest. It was all too abrupt, the moments passing too quickly and the trails disappearing in opposite directions. Part of me wanted to run up the trail, balance my way across the cable, and sprint to catch up with Sam, Martha, Gay, and Jon. But then what? Another good-bye? We each had a route that we had chosen, one leading deep into the mountains and the other out along the coast. If all went smoothly, by the time my friends were back in Te Anau, I would be well up the outer coast and working my way toward Milford Sound. They would let Meri know that I had made it to Dusky, and she in turn would tell any boats in the area to be on the lookout for me.

I retraced my route back to the cabin, following my friend's lugged-sole boot prints in the mud and on the wet rocks that we had clambered over on the way to the river. It all felt very surreal—the short and intense visit in the cabin and the memory of hiking with them through the rain forest. The boot prints and the food back at the cabin were proof that I hadn't dreamt the last eighteen hours, but like many times on the journey, it didn't seem possible that I was living this life so far from home but so connected to the people that I loved.

Chapter 10

If I knew what it was I was getting into,
I wonder if I would have had the courage to set out.
—Mark Twain

THREE DAYS AFTER WATCHING MY FRIENDS DISAPPEAR into the forest and start their trek back to civilization, I was worried about their safety. Heavy, low clouds and torrential rains obliterated any sign of the mountains, and high, erratic winds turned even the protected waters of the inner sounds into impassable channels covered in whitecaps. If the winds and rain in the mountains were half what they were down on the water, my friends' hike out would be more of a survival epic than a vacation in the park's wilderness. The one consolation I had was that they should have reached a mountain hut at the end of each day of their traverse.

The low-pressure system that Sam had heard about in Te Anau had arrived right on time, bringing the weather that reduced visibility to less than a quarter of a mile. Once again I was holed up and waiting for the calm that would indicate the passing of the front. The difference was that this time instead of sitting in a sodden tent and waiting to see if the tent poles would survive the onslaught of winds, I was warm, dry, and comfortably sitting in the pilothouse of a codfishing boat anchored in Breaksea Sound. While I inhaled a plate of steaming potatoes and the savory aroma of a quarter of roast chicken on my plate, I wondered what my friends might be eating, or if they were even off the trail for the day.

I had left Dusky Sound via Acheron Passage, which cut in behind Resolution Island and connected Dusky to Breaksea Sound. After so much bad weather, I wasn't even tempted to go on the outside of the island and risk getting caught in the predicted winds. As it was, the northwest winds had funneled down the narrow channel of Acheron Passage and forced me ashore at the southern end. After a day of sitting, rereading my mail for the fifth time, and listening to the rain splatter against the tent walls, I had paddled up the passage engulfed in the wet mist that hid everything but the dozens of waterfalls appearing out of the cloud-draped mountains above. For several hours I paddled just yards from the east wall of rock that occasionally sheltered me from the winds and showered me with the free fall of streams pouring off the cliffs. The closer I had gotten to the north end of the passage, the higher the swells had raked the rocks and repeatedly lifted and dropped the bow into each oncoming wave. Progress dropped to near zero, and if there had been a level place to pull off and set up yet another camp, I would have gladly done so. The thought of setting up the wet tent and crawling into a damp sleeping bag, though, wasn't much more enticing than just sticking it out in the boat and pushing into the waves.

By the time I got to the north end of the passage, vague shadows began to form out of the mist between Resolution Island and where I sat on the far side of the narrow channel. Where moments earlier there had been only an opaque world devoid of depth or geometry, now there was some definition and a hint of the heights that my chart assured me were there. In minutes the 2,900-foot peak of Mount Wales slowly took form in the rapidly clearing skies, then stood proudly overlooking the passage. The clearing northwest wind continued to blow the last of the day's cloud, fog and gloom away until I sat stunned by what I had been blindly paddling beneath. Two- and three-thousand-foot peaks crowded the skyline and shouldered into one another half hiding, yet adding depth and stunning power to the panorama. The winds still rolled the waves in and slowed the boat to a crawl, but with the sun shining and the mountains rising in splendor all around, there was a new surge of energy to the day.

Up ahead Entry Island sat in the middle of the point where Acheron Passage joined Breaksea Sound at a right angle. To the left of the island was the route to the outer coast and north to Dagg Sound, a route that would have to await calmer seas. To the right were the inland waters of Breaksea Sound and hopefully a place to sit and wait for the first opportunity to continue north.

I had paddled less than a mile into Breaksea Sound around a point of land that quickly dropped away into a lovely protected cove. At the back of the cove were two commercial fishing boats tied to an old barge. As I entered the cove, the pilothouse door of one of the boats swung open, and a short stocky fellow about sixty came out on deck. He was dressed in the same kind of blue work sweater that Jeff had worn. The fisherman must have been checking on the weather. He looked out across the cove—toward open water and the direction the winds were coming from—and immediately spotted me paddling in. By the time I paddled up to the black hull, another fellow, younger by twenty years, had come out on deck as I came within hailing distance.

"Hello," I called out as the boat drifted with the last few strokes.

"G'day, mate," the older of the two men called out.

"Ye must be the kayaker Meri told us about." He chuckled and said, "She told us to keep an eye out for ye, but I didn't expect to see ye paddle right up to us."

"Well, I was looking for a place to set up camp out of the wind and just wait for the outside to calm down a bit."

The younger fellow hadn't said anything and was just leaning with his crossed arms resting over the railing, looking at my boat, and letting the other man do the talking.

"Where have ye come from today?"

"Oh, I was just on the far end of Acheron—had to sit all day yesterday because of the wind and finally got tired of being in the tent. I can only sit for so long before I get bored."

"Well, ye won't be going any farther today. We were out near Breaksea Island this morning—40 to 45 knots out there and 5-meter swells. Another fella up near Dagg said the swells were 6 to 7 meters. We've got pots out but can't do a thing with 'em till this blows through. Ye want to get outta of that thing and come aboard?"

"Yeah, sure," I replied.

I popped the spray deck and said, "I can probably just tie it off and leave it alongside."

"No, you don't want to do that," the younger fellow said. "We'll just pull it aboard, and you won't have to worry about her."

I unfastened the boat tether from my waist and handed the belt up. As soon as I had stood gingerly in the seat and hauled myself over the steel railings, the two fishermen welcomed me aboard.

"My name's Ray Haywood, and this is my son David," the older fellow said as he held out his hand.

The younger fellow stepped forward and said, "Hi, welcome aboard."

Ray had already turned toward the pilothouse door while David went aft and lifted a hatch on the rear deck that led into the fish hold.

"Come on in and get out of those wet clothes. It's too damn cold and wet to be standing out here," Ray said.

As I stepped over the foot-high pilothouse threshold, a wave of warmth and the heady aroma of roast chicken nearly stopped me in my tracks. Just inside the doorway was an open oven with a golden roasted chicken sitting in the middle of diced and browned potatoes.

"How's chicken and spuds sound for your dinner?" Ray asked as he opened a cupboard and pulled out three plates. "It's not fancy but probably better'n what you can cook up in a tent."

Steam was rising off my neoprene shorts, and I could still taste the salt water on my lips as I tried to adjust to the sudden shift in surroundings. I pulled the paddle jacket over my head and stripped the sleeves inside out off my wrists as I looked around.

"Wow, that sounds great!" I exclaimed as the heat from the stove soaked into my back and melted the goose bumps on my arms.

The pilothouse was low ceilinged and small enough so that you could almost reach across its width with outstretched arms. Thick windows wrapped around the forward part of the cramped space and looked out across the snub bow and the anchor windlass. On the starboard side was the boat's wheel and the skipper's high swivel chair, with its foot braces beneath the split and worn leather seat. Bolted to the overhead were two radios and two radar screens tilted down so that they faced the empty seat. Ray was already raising a wooden drop-swivel table that was hinged to the bulkhead beside the stove on the port side. A single steel leg held the opposite end level. Once the table was in place there was less than 2 feet of room between the sink and where he set the plates and silverware.

"Get in there behind the table and set that cushion up for a back rest." Ray chuckled again as he said, "That's the best seat in the house."

As I squeezed into place, David came in from checking the temperature in the fish hold and joined us. Ray split the chicken and divided it evenly among the three plates, then spooned piles of golden roasted potatoes around the steaming chicken. I didn't even know these guys, and I was about to eat a third of their dinner with them as if I had been expected to drop by. David sat in the skipper's chair with his plate balanced on his knees, and Ray joined me at the small table.

"Every night Meri's been asking all of us if we'd seen you yet," David explained. "She'll give us a call at 8:30 tonight, and you can have a chat with her."

"Man, this is delicious!" I said as I hardly heard what David had said. Paddling all day in the wind and waves had left me starving. The juicy chicken melted in my mouth, and any thought of leaving the crisp skin on the plate was forgotten. I'd worry about my cholesterol another time. In no time at all, amid the clinking of silverware and the pssht of a can of beer opening for each of us, we had cleared our plates. Ray offered the last of the potatoes and a wing that was left on the chicken carcass.

"There's peaches for dessert if you want," Ray explained as he spooned the "spuds" onto my plate. "David's the skipper, and I do the cooking and clean up. We make a pretty good team."

Over the last of the chicken and the peaches that followed, I learned more about Ray, David, and the *Oraki*, the old but solid boat that sat like a rock in the sheltered cove.

Ray and David were home-ported out of Riverton and normally fished for blue cod along the south shore. They had come around Puysegur and into the lower sounds to see if it was worth extending their fishing grounds a bit farther west and north. They ran six cod pots—massive, steel-reinforced pots covered in thick crosshatched wire that weighed several hundred pounds each. Ray would bait the pots, lock the hinged door on one end of the 4-foot-square pot, and check that the lines would run free. At a signal from David, who was watching the sonar screen and noting the exact location of each drop, the pot was tossed over the side. Unlike the crayfish pots, which were checked every twenty-four hours, as soon as the last cod pot cleared the afterdeck, David would head back to the first drop site. The pots would be winched aboard, emptied of any fish, rebaited, and dropped over the side again. It all sounded pretty easy until I tried to imagine what it would be like to work out on the open deck with the boat pitching and rolling in the seas. I had seen firsthand what the waters were like on the outside, where David and Ray fished. They didn't have to elaborate on the dangers.

They had both worked in the "freezer works," the slaughterhouse on the outskirts of Riverton, before it had been closed due to a decrease in the export of lamb. Across the South Island the shakeup in the industry had left thousands unemployed. Ray had been at "The Works" for twenty-five years and David for thirteen. It was a job that sounded pretty brutal: killing thousands of sheep a week, stripping off the skins for tanning, and preparing the meat for export to the United States, Britain, Europe, and the Middle East. When the plant closed, they were left with few options. They had bought the *Oraki*, a thirty-eight-ton ferro-cement boat that was twenty years old, not very fast at 8 knots, but steady and solid in her almost 40 feet of length. For the last nine years they had spent two weeks at a time out fishing, a week back in port to sell the fish (which went to the fish-and-chip shops), then time to restock the boat, and back out for another two weeks. They had settled into a routine of skipper and mate, working as a team and knowing the boat inside and out.

Ray said, "No sense in setting up a tent when we have an extra bunk below. Just bring your sleeping bag in, and you can put anything that's wet in the engine room. It'll be dry by morning."

Later that evening David turned the radio on, and within minutes the radio clicked and squelched, then went silent. "That's Meri," Ray announced. David reached up, adjusted some knobs, then unclipped the mike from the side of the radio and settled back into the swivel chair. A few seconds passed and Meri's voice filled the pilothouse.

"*Oraki, Oraki, Oraki*, this is Bluff Fishermen's Radio, Bluff Fishermen's Radio. Are you there, David?"

"Bluff Fishermen's Radio, Bluff Fishermen's Radio. This is the *Oraki*. Hello Meri."

"Righto, David, just checking in with you boys. How's everything tonight? Over."

"Ah, right Meri, we're in Sunday Cove. High winds on the outside and 5-meter swells. Not much fishing. We've got a kayaker here for the night. He showed up out of the rain this afternoon. Over."

Meri repeated the entire message. I could almost see her scribbling the weather notes into her spiral-bound notepad on the kitchen counter.

"Righto, David, you're in Sunday Cove, you've got high winds and a 5-meter swell on the outside. Good to hear that Chris has made it. I've been wondering where he's been for the last few days. We've got 50 knots out of the north at Puysegur, but it should drop to 10 knots in the morning, going back to 45 by late tomorrow. Is there anything Chris needs? Over."

David looked over at me, sitting warm and snug in the cabin. "He's looking pretty comfortable here Meri. I'll pass you over to him."

David handed me the radio. "Hello, Meri, good to hear your voice again. David and Ray are taking good care of me. I'll be off for Dagg in the morning and will stay put until this front passes. Can you let Jeff know where I am? Over."

"Righto, Chris. I told you the boys would take good care of you. I'll pass on to Jeff that you're in Sunday Cove and heading for Dagg in the morning. Over."

I passed the radio back to David. "Right then, Meri. We'll let you get on with your sched, and we'll talk with you tomorrow. Over."

"Good as gold, David. Bluff Fishermen's Radio out."

We listened as Meri made contact with everyone in the sounds: getting the weather report from Jeff and passing on my message to him, then contacting the *Breaksea Girl*, a schooner anchored deep in Breaksea Sound whose captain was hiding from the same winds and seas that David and Ray were. She then raised the *Reliance,* which was up in Milford Sound doing the same thing. Everyone was holed up just waiting for the next opportunity to move.

If there was a pattern to the weather, it seemed to come in two-day increments: gale- or storm-force winds hitting Puysegur and blowing for two days out of the southwest, then switching to the northwest and blowing slightly less for another two days. A calm would then settle over the west coast for a day before the pattern would repeat itself. After two months of this kind of weather, I had to finally admit that summer just wasn't going to happen, at least not on the lower southwest corner of the island. The sea and wind reports from up north weren't as severe, but there were more than 500 miles of nearly uninhabited coastline between the fiords and the sheltered waters on the north end of the island. Once again it was the folks that I met along my route that made the west coast possible. I don't know what I would have done if it hadn't been for the likes of Meri, Jeff, my shore crew, and now David and Ray.

I got off to an early start the next morning with tentative plans to meet Dave and Ray in Dagg Sound and wait out the next low-pressure system that Meri had warned us about. As I drew even with the north side of Entry Island, I looked over my shoulder to see the *Oraki* steadily gaining on me. David let go on the boat's horn, sending an echoing blast across the morning stillness. At the back of the pilothouse, I could see Ray waving in the sunlight. As they passed 100 yards to my right, I raised the paddle overhead and then settled back into the rhythm of paddling. At 8 knots the *Oraki* plowed into the swells coming into the mouth of the sound, sinking into the troughs, then rising again and pushing her blunt bow into the next smooth roller. It wasn't long before she was way out in front of me, all 40 feet of her sinking into the swells for long seconds before rising again farther out and continuing into open waters.

A half mile behind me, and motoring out of the protection of the inner sound, was the *Breaksea Girl*, her white hull and masts set against the backdrop of the mountains rising straight into the clear sky. It didn't take long for her to close the gap and motor to within 100 yards as she steamed straight up my wake. Eight or ten people crowded the foredeck, leaning into the rise and fall of the swells and pointing video recorders and cameras in my direction as the boat towered above me. As the glistening-white 60-footer eased along my starboard side, everyone waved and called out greetings. The rumble of the diesel engine slackened, then kicked into reverse, sending a swirl of bubbles through the crystal-clear waters. A tall, gray-bearded fellow appeared from the port side of the pilothouse carrying something wrapped in a paper towel.

"G'day, mate," he called down. "We've been watching for you ever since Meri let us know you were in the sounds. My name's Lance. These folks are all scientists conducting studies here in the fiords. We're just heading up to Doubtful to do a little diving before the next front moves in. Thought ye might like some breakfast."

Lance was apparently the captain. He straddled the lifelines and stretched way down to hand me the wrapped breakfast. An aroma of biscuit, egg, and sausage registered as fast as the warmth of the cooked meal in my hands. The weather on this trip may not have been very cooperative, but the hospitality of the Kiwis certainly was. And the way the food just kept appearing out of nowhere was fantastic!

"Wow, now that's service with a smile. Thanks very much!" I exclaimed.

"No worries, mate. Good on ye for getting this far. Maybe we'll see ye in Doubtful."

Lance pulled himself back over the lifelines and hurried aft into the wheelhouse before the swells turned the *Breaksea Girl* sideways in their troughs. The scientists waved as the schooner eased away, then slowly recovered her speed and powered into the swells. Ten minutes later she was off Oliver Point and turning north, her masts raking the sky as she took the 2- and 3-meter swells and troughs broadside. It would be a long 20 miles for the scientists before they were into the calm waters of Doubtful Sound. I wondered how many would be too seasick to make the afternoon dive?

By the time I was off Oliver Point, I had finished off my second breakfast, stuffed the paper towel into the cockpit, and was settling into the work of paddling the 14 miles of outer coast up to Dagg Sound. Without a deep keel like that on the *Breaksea Girl*, my boat simply rose and fell in the same swells that would have turned me green onboard the luxury motor schooner. When I rounded the point and turned north, neither the *Oraki* nor the schooner were anywhere in sight. The sun shone warmly, and the swells rolled smoothly in from the north, 10-footers that had sorted themselves out in massive but nonbreaking sets.

For the first time on this outer coast, there wasn't the feeling of a mad dash for the next protected water. This was how I had imagined the trip would be: paddling on an open expanse of ocean, bordered by high mountains with silvery threads of streams pouring off their flanks. The sun and the lack of any wind made the day so different from other days offshore. I settled into the rhythm of the sea and the sun, working the boat into the swells, pulling hard on the paddle as the bow nosed into the oncoming waves, and backing off just a bit when the boat was high on the crests. The blades came out of the water dripping with glistening droplets, which were flung off the paddle's edges as one stroke finished and the next one reached swiftly forward for the next full grab of water. Except for the shearwaters that tore past me on their search for better feeding grounds, I was alone and supremely happy. It was a rare day to be on the outside with no place to land yet still feeling relaxed.

Three hours after leaving Breaksea Sound I paddled into the mouth of Dagg Sound. I followed the north shore for a mile before the mountains pulled back and formed a small valley, with a river winding through the trees and flowing swiftly out into the sound. The northwest swell wrapped around the outer rocks, rolled in smooth and fast, and then folded over the gravel and cobbles at the river mouth. I waited for a small set to break, then surfed in on the back of a wave that shot me past a cliff face on the right and a 6-foot-high bank of cobbles and flood debris on the left. Swirls of salt and fresh water partially mixed with each swell washing over the cobbles in the river's mouth. A hundred yards upriver was an island where the river had split and left a stand of beech trees, a perfect spot to again sit and wait for the next move.

Later that evening as I was finishing dinner, the *Oraki* steamed past my camp, heading for the protected waters at the back of the sound. I waited until morning, and as the winds began to freshen and kick up whitecaps on the outer waters, I headed into the sound to see if I could find my new friends. Five miles into the wind shelter of the mountains I came around a point and saw the *Oraki* sitting peacefully at anchor.

I had met David and Ray only two days earlier, but they welcomed me once again as if I was a family member. They wouldn't hear of me sitting out the winds and rains in a tent. We pulled my kayak aboard, tied it off so it wouldn't roll around in the swells, and then retreated into the pilothouse.

True to Meri's forecast, the northwest winds went up to 40 knots the first day and then hit 55 knots at Puysegur Point the next. For three solid days the winds and rains obliterated any view beyond the condensation-covered windows of the pilothouse. Ray kept the food coming: eggs or cereal with toast in the mornings, sandwiches or soup for lunch, and two huge meals of ham hocks and beans one night and fresh cod the next. While I ate as though I was putting fuel in the tank for the next leg of the journey, Ray and David shared their stories of fishing in Foveaux Strait and Fiordland.

"So is the fishing life really as dangerous as it sounds?" I asked on the last evening we were together.

David was in and out of the pilothouse checking on the anchor, then back aft to check on what little frozen fish was in the hold. With the rough sea conditions, it had been a far from profitable two weeks of fishing. The pilothouse door swung open, and he stepped in, bringing a blast of cold wind just as Ray was recalling boats that had sunk during the nine years he and David had been fishing.

"There was the *Deborah Jane*. She went down, but everyone got off. Then there's the *Aduze* down off Long Reef Point. Ye must have seen her when you came around Puysegur."

"Yeah, Jeff told me about her. Sounds like the crew were just lucky to get ashore alive," I replied.

"Yeah, damn lucky. Let's see. What are some of the others that have gone down David?" Ray was thinking out loud.

"There's the *Sherwin*," David replied. "But she was recovered. And the *Golden Eagle*—skipper was lost on that one."

"How about the *Dougal*?" Ray asked, and then answered his own question by recalling how she was wrecked on the rocks outside of Gates Harbor.

David was back in his swivel chair in front of the boat's wheel, his feet propped up on the edge of the instrument panel. Ray was sitting beside me with a beer in his hand and two days of beard shadowing his face. The list of near misses, wrecks, and lives lost increased as the two men began recalling one boat after the next that were no longer fishing the waters of the south coast or the sounds; the *Galin Mari*, sunk in Te Waewae Bay, with two lives lost; the *Avenger*, also lost in Te Waewae Bay, with another two lives gone; the *El Ninio*, burned and sunk on Chalky Island; the *Southern Light*, washed up on the beach, with no one aboard.

There was a story, which Ray told with macabre humor, of a boat that had gotten hammered by vicious seas and winds off Puysegur. Ray was laughing so hard tears were welling up in his eyes. "By God, he came into the harbor with damn near nothin' left of the pilothouse—windows were all gone, the forward bulkhead ripped to shreds, and there he was just standing in the wind and hanging onto the wheel. I don't know if he ever went back out or not. I can tell ye I wouldn't 'ave. Ye get away like that only once."

In a little more than ten minutes, the two men came up with the names of more than a dozen boats lost. In the back of my mind, I kept hearing Jeff's advice: "Never turn your back on the sea." What hit me was that I knew most of these places where the boats and crew had come to rest. Names like Gates Harbor immediately brought up the memory and feelings of bridled fear as I had slid through the boomers exploding on the outer rocks that made up the narrow entrance. I also knew the wide-open, unprotected waters of Te Waewae Bay and had crossed it in near calm conditions, nervously aware that there was no place to run to if the winds had suddenly sprung up. If I had read about any of those wrecks and the places where they had gone down, I would have tried to imagine the headlands and islands and the seas that relentlessly exploded against them. But because I had paddled those same waters, I didn't have to imagine them. As I sat listening to David and Ray, I felt I understood what they were telling me, that they knew the risks and the price some fishermen paid for the life they all loved.

Part of me wanted to tell them how I had seen these places about which they spoke and of how I had sat offshore and watched the wreck of the *Aduze* wondering if anyone had gotten off her. I also wanted to tell them I knew what it was like to be in the water next to my boat, flipped amid the rocks off The Lizard—the southernmost point of Great Britain—a different ocean but the same horror of a wreck. I knew what it felt like to get slammed bodily onto the rocks, to feel the impact and the adrenaline, but because of the shock not to have any sense of the pain, to have waves wash over me and to be underneath the boat—hanging on and praying that somehow the waves would miraculously stop, that they would just let up for a minute so that I could spit out the salt water and get a breath. Fifteen years after that wreck I could still remember the noise and my fingers clinging to the paddle, slipping off the overturned boat, and grabbing again for the bowline. I could still feel the hacking coughs, the spitting, and the sting of the salt water in my eyes. Those memories don't go away, even after the bruises and the cuts heal and the scars on the boat have been glassed over.

Part of me wanted to tell them I knew something about getting wrecked on the rocks in the surf, but another part wanted to just listen and learn something from these fishermen who had taken me in. I watched their faces and tried to read their feelings about these stories that could have been their own—or mine. Their faces and posture revealed little; a raised eyebrow or a shrug of the shoulders said more of resignation than anything else. They looked as if they were removed from the storytelling, as if they were talking about something they knew could happen to them and so maintained an emotional distance from it. Each of us was living with the same sea as the one that had claimed the lives of which David and Ray spoke. What I saw in their faces told me something we all knew: The sea was the master, and sometimes, even though you do everything right, it can still punish you severely. I watched David and Ray carefully, listening to their stories and noting small things that seemed to set them apart as skipper and mate, yet unite them as a crew.

David had a wife and three children. He looked tired and unshaven but was still cheerful, in a quiet, unassuming way. He wasn't flashy or loud but moved around the boat with an ease and an acceptance of the life he had chosen on the sea over the life he had left in the slaughterhouse. It didn't seem that he left anything to chance but was constantly checking the holds, the engine room, and monitoring the winds and the radios. I imagined him at the wheel when the sea was nasty. He would have had the same quiet demeanor and competence about him. There are some skippers that take chances, either with the weather or with the tons of fish that can be packed into the hold. Often the risk is based on money: How soon can the boat get into port and back out again for the next load of fish. I didn't think David was the type of skipper who would risk his or Ray's life for the sake of money.

I watched Ray carefully as he told his stories and always gave me the largest piece of chicken or fish or ham. He was always concerned about my "tucker"—my food. He also gave me his seat at the table, the only one with a back support. He was a rough and tumble kind of a man in his younger days, and he had had a rough life; he had suffered through a burst appendix, and 4 feet of his intestines were taken out. He loved American cars, Chevrolets in particular. He was married and had two or three daughters— the stories weren't always easy to follow—plus David, his son and skipper. There's a lot more that could be said about him, but it all came down to looking at both David and Ray and knowing that they were the finest humans I would want to rely upon if I were in trouble on the sea.

We sat in the back of Dagg Sound, holed up and listening to the wind scream through the antennas on the pilothouse roof. In the near dark of the evening, a howling blast off Mount Forbes hit with the rush and noise of a freight train, filling the air with a deafening roar of wind. We each sat there looking at the windows, not through them but at them, as if waiting for them to implode. The *Oraki* took it broadside and was pushed well over on her port side, thirty-eight tons of cement and steel shoved sideways like a leaf on the water. The blast lasted no longer than fifteen seconds. As quickly as the blast hit, it was gone. The *Oraki* righted herself and slowly swung back into the normal winds.

Two hours before dawn on the third day, the whine and catch of the *Oraki*'s diesel engine woke me from wind-filled dreams. I climbed the ladder out of the forward cabin, where the bunks were built into the curve of the bow. David already had the radar warmed up, and the pilothouse was filled with an eerie green glow from the rotating illumination on the screen. A soft red light lit the instrument panel and reflected off the pitch-black windows. Outside, the mountains crowded the edges of Dagg Sound like looming hunched giants silently watching the fishing boat come to life.

The previous night's forecast had called for the winds to drop to 25 knots, the calmest they had been in almost a week. The *Oraki* was low on fuel, and the weather wasn't worth staying longer and trying to fill the fish hold. David and Ray had decided to make a run for Puysegur, then on to Riverton while they had a chance. I would go out with them to pull their pots. Before heading south they would bring me back to my campsite beside the river. Going with them would give me a chance to see the fishing operation, as well as to assess the risks of paddling north to Doubtful Sound.

By the time we had eaten breakfast and Ray had prepped the afterdeck for pulling the pots, the sky had begun to lighten, revealing the first hues of dawn, the soft pink changing to light orange, then yellow, and eventually to powder blue. The storm of the last three days had left the sky clear of all but a few rapidly drifting clouds. As we headed for the mouth of Dagg Sound, I went out on deck to get a feel for the winds. They were coming straight up over the stern; an offshore wind was tripping whitecaps even in the protected waters of the sound. It was early in the day for a wind to be that strong. I didn't like the feel of it but for the moment pushed the nagging worry of it out of my mind. There were the cod pots to pull before I had to decide whether to go for Doubtful Sound or to sit and wait for the next lull in the weather. We had talked the previous night about the short 6-mile run to Doubtful. If all went well, it should only take an hour and a half for me to cover the distance. Ray had been insistent that I make a break for it.

"If ye don't go now, ye could be sitting right here for the next three weeks. You'd run out of tucker before the wind would let you go, and you'd be in heaps of trouble."

Ray had become fascinated with the trip, carefully checking out the boat and asking me all kinds of questions about the gear, the miles I could cover in a day, and what kind of seas the boat could handle. After three days of talking and just hanging out with them, Ray and David probably knew more about the trip than anyone else I had met so far.

"You can make Doubtful in less than two hours. I wouldn't want to leave you here and be wondering for the next month if you ever got out."

I hadn't committed to going, but it was clear that Ray had already decided that I should.

As the *Oraki* approached the mouth of Dagg Sound, the bow rose and fell in thick 6-foot swells that wrapped into the sound from the north. By the time we were offshore and David had located the first orange buoy with way points entered into the *Oraki*'s computer, the sun was up over the edge of the mountains, and the sea had turned a deep sparkling blue. Both men had pulled on chest-high, thick yellow rain pants with black suspenders. Ray was out in the wind and the spray and also wore the traditional heavy rain slicker that most fishermen work in. As the *Oraki* came alongside the buoy, he heaved a grappling hook over the floating yellow line. With quick hand-over-hand hauling, he had the line aboard in seconds. Without a word David stepped from the pilothouse and grabbed the line as Ray took the buoy aft. David fed it smoothly through a system of fairleads and eventually onto a hydraulic pulley. With one hand on a steel control lever and the other on the edge of the pilothouse to maintain balance, he worked the lever in and out of gear as the pulley started taking a strain. Dozens of feet of yellow polypropylene line ran off the pulley and snaked around his feet while the *Oraki* swung broadside and rolled heavily in the swells. When the pot broke the surface, he eased off on the hydraulics, then pushed the lever forward again until the pot was hanging just over the railing, a black monstrosity of rebar frame, painted steel-mesh wire, and intricate one-way funnels that the fish swam into but couldn't swim out of. The 4-foot-square trap was hauled over the railing, and a hinged door was released to empty a half dozen 2-foot-long cod into a bin. The pot was then dropped to the deck where Ray hauled it aft, wrestled it onto its end, and then tied it off to the railing.

While the guys did all the work, I stood out of the way, hanging on to the opposite railing and trying not to slide from one side of the boat to the other. After the first pot was secured, David disappeared into the pilothouse again, and the *Oraki* moved on to the next buoy. Ray in the meantime was gutting the fish, throwing the offal to the shearwaters, gulls, and three albatrosses that had appeared out of nowhere.

One by one the pots were pulled from the bottom of the sea, hauled over the side, and cleaned of their meager catch. Seawater streamed in through the scuppers of the boat, and fish guts and blood streamed out. David kept the *Oraki* as steady as he could in the increasing seas, as Ray kept hauling the pots aft and tying each one off as he fought for balance on the slippery steel deck.

In an hour the pots were onboard, and we were all back in the shelter of the pilothouse and leaning into the swells as David guided us back toward the mouth of the sound. It was time for me to make the decision to either stay put or to head north. On the open water the northeast wind was holding steady at 20 knots, gusting frequently to 25. Waves coming out of the sound were breaking white and tumbling over one another as the winds poured out of the mountain passes. Under the protection of the cliffs, the sea was quieter as the winds were held aloft by the walls of rock rising from the sea. I would be protected from the winds as long as I stayed in close. Still I didn't like the feel of it. Offshore winds scared me; there was no safety net if something went wrong, nothing but empty ocean to port for thousands of miles. Ray argued what I already knew, that I'd be in the lee of the mountains as long as I stayed in close.

"What we'll do is drop you off so you can go in and get your gear, then we'll stay with you till you're into Doubtful," David offered.

"We're not goin' to leave you here, that's for damn sure," Ray added. He sounded almost angry at the thought of just dropping me and heading south for Riverton.

"Well, I don't know," I hesitated. "I don't like the wind. It's still pretty erratic after the last few days. But I hear what you're saying about getting stuck in here if they don't lie down."

I was weighing the risks and trying to justify paddling in winds that I would normally sit out. Six miles. An hour and half, maximum, if I pushed it. What was the big deal? What was I so worried about if it was only an hour and a half paddle? I didn't like the idea of being stranded in Dagg Sound, but the thought of paddling in offshore winds was just as troubling. I could feel the weight of Ray and David's eyes on me as I looked out the pilothouse windows and tried to make a decision. There didn't seem to be many options;

either I sat tight and risked getting trapped like the paddlers had at Puysegur Point, or I gambled on the winds staying high over the cliffs and attempted to get into Doubtful Sound. There was one thing I was not going to do and that was to delay David and Ray from heading south. They had a 14-hour nonstop run to get around Puysegur and into Riverton. We had all listened to Meri's reports of the wind hitting 55 knots at Puysegur just two days ago. If they were going to make it around before the next front, they needed to get going as soon as possible. I had only met them four days earlier, but that was enough time to know they would do anything to help me, including putting themselves at risk. Against my own better judgment, I made the decision to go for Doubtful Sound—alone. It was a decision that in hindsight was wrong.

The boys, as Meri called them, dropped me off in the deep water off the mouth of my river camp and waited while I broke down my camp. In a half hour I had the boat packed and was sitting in the river looking at the swells completely closing out over the gravel bar. Coming into the river had been one thing; breaking out with the heavily loaded boat was another. I timed my exit as best I could and got hammered by a 6-footer that buried me in its break but let me go before surfing me backwards—an inauspicious start to the day.

When I paddled up to the *Oraki*, the size of the swells really became evident. Even at thirty-eight tons she rose and fell in the 10-footers like a cork.

"Thanks for everything, you guys. I really appreciate all your help," I shouted above the winds and the waves slapping against the steel of the *Oraki*. David was in the doorway of the pilothouse, three steps away from the engine controls and the wheel. Ray was back aft, looking down at me with the same kind of concern I had seen in Jeff's eyes. We all knew the risks, and we all felt the friendship that had developed over the last few days.

"Ye be #%* careful, you hear, Chris," Ray shouted down.

"I will, Ray. You take care and have a safe trip home."

We waved, and that was it. I headed out toward the north point of the sound with the gusts of wind whipping the waves into whitecaps and surfing me toward open water. I could hear David slip the *Oraki* into forward and ease in behind me. They would follow me out to the mouth of the sound and then turn south.

The waves running out of the sound were 4-footers, 4-footers that met the 10-foot swell coming in from the Tasman. The wind-generated waves lifted the stern, buried the bow under the wave in front, and raced the boat almost as fast as the *Oraki* could motor. I looked back at David and Ray and froze the image of the *Oraki* firmly in my mind. She was plowing blunt-nosed into the large swells and throwing white water clear over her bow and onto her windows. David was at the helm working the wheel to keep the boat straight into the waves. Ray was braced against the forward bulkhead gesturing in my direction and leaning into each surge of the boat. I waved with the paddle, and David let go with the *Oraki*'s horn. We were underway—friends bound for different ports but united by the same seas.

The first hour of paddling toward Doubtful was fairly smooth. The winds for the most part stayed high, whistling overhead and missing me as I tried to stay as close in to the mountains as I dared with the 10-footers booming onto the rocks. Like so many other times, I would have loved to have seen how small the boat looked against the enormity of the seas and the mountainous coastline. I had been in large seas so often on this trip that it wasn't until something inside of me clicked and I looked around that I became aware of how huge the scale was. On this sunny day with the clouds racing over the mountain peaks and dissipating over the clear sky to the west, there was a glorious tension, a volatile magnificence to the energy that I was keenly aware of. The energy was in the rolling strength of the swells, in the thousands of feet of forested mountains to my right, and in the winds of which I was so fearful.

In this emotionally charged yet isolated raw beauty, there was a tension and a metamorphosis within me that had occurred over the duration of the trip. Looking back it was easy to see that what passed for "normal" had, over a period of ten weeks, gradually raised the performance bar until I was still reaching and pulling with the paddles, but I was so much deeper mentally than I had ever been before. I had developed the necessary ability to immediately shift from the calm waters and the companionship of new friends to the sudden and surreal world of paddling solo in extreme conditions. The transition was a balance act, a tightrope walk of emotions and physical agility that required constant awareness and timing. Once I was away from the security of sheltered waters and friends, I was intensely focused, moving with deliberation and precise balance and so different from the lighthearted person I knew in the company of others. When the conditions demanded it, I was a competitor in the sense that in big seas there was only one option: winning. That meant staying upright and moving forward to whatever sheltered water was ahead.

I was less than a half mile from the Hare's Ears, the sea stacks that I could see so clearly in the afternoon light. Once around the point I would be in Doubtful Sound and could get in behind Bauza Island and out of the wind.

I don't know where the winds came from, what suddenly caused them, or how they so rapidly engulfed me. I just knew that what looked like a low bank of fog a quarter mile in front of the boat was something that wasn't supposed to be there so suddenly. My first thought was that it was simply fog. But fog doesn't develop in seconds, and you don't get fog with a high-pressure system, wind, and a clear sky.

In less than ten seconds after the haze appeared, all my defense alarms went off. The haze wasn't fog: It was wind, high wind that was ripping the tops off the waves and filling the air with vaporized sea spray! I turned the boat sharply toward a rocky cove 300 yards to my right and started sprinting in.

When the first blast hit, it lifted the laminated chart from under three taut bungee cords on the front deck and sent it sailing 100 yards over my left shoulder. The blast grabbed at my body and the high blade and almost knocked me over. "Holy shit!" The words escaped before I knew what was happening.

In seconds the stinging spray blinded me, and the winds seemed to suck the air out of my lungs. I couldn't get a deep breath, and I couldn't see where the land was that I was so desperately trying to reach. The wind stopped the boat dead in the water and started driving me backward. I drove the right paddle blade into the water and felt the huge blade instantly dig in and slow the backward drift of the boat. The left blade was straight up in the air, shoved into the wind that caught it and tried to rip it out of my hand and at the same time throw me over. The blade in the water was the only thing that kept the boat from skidding backward, building momentum and eventually flipping. For long seconds the wind shrieked and rammed its strength against my upper body, the paddle, and the bow of the boat as it rose out of the short, steep seas that had suddenly developed. I was less than 300 yards from the cliffs, which offered some protection from the winds, but already the waves were 3-footers and growing as the winds howled out of the mountains. Each time a wave hit, the bow would dive into it and throw more water into the wind-water that would come straight back and hit me in the chest and face. I was spitting and snorting out seawater, shaking my head to clear my eyes, and trying to tuck low each time the bow dove. When the wind shifted a few degrees off the bow, I would frantically dig in and get a half dozen power strokes to regain a few feet of progress.

All the years of paddling, the thousands of miles of exploring, the whales, the seals, the albatrosses, the sunsets, and the wonder of the sea—all vanished into the awful terror that what I feared most was actually happening. "My God, I'm going to get blown out to sea!" The realization flashed through my mind as the fear soared and started to flare into panic.

"The radio! Get the radio out."

Another blast from the side hit with such force that the boat went over on its edge and hung there for seconds without rolling. The blasts shifted slightly, and the boat recovered with a hip snap.

"Forget the radio."

I didn't stand a chance of opening the hatch behind my seat and getting it out. If I let go of the paddle for an instant, it would be ripped out of the other hand and would be gone, just like the chart.

"Focus. Just stay focused. There's no one to call anyway!"

The bow dove again, and I ducked into the wave that broke over me. I lay low over the foredeck, trying to minimize the sail area of my body and trying to breathe with my chest compressed and the water flying into my face.

I jammed my feet onto the pegs, pushed myself farther back in the seat, and locked my thighs under the cockpit cowling. My legs started shaking from the strain of trying to keep the bow dead into the wind. If the wind caught the bow and swung it off course, I'd never get it back.

The gusts strengthened, flattening the dry-top against my chest and snapping it like a flag at the backs of my upper arms. If only the shrieking of the winds would stop, I could concentrate on what I had to do to regain the focus I needed. The paddle had stopped spinning and was just frozen in the wind and the waves, one blade thrust into the sea and holding on like the claw of a cat not daring to let go for fear of getting knocked over with the wind. Between the gusts I spun the blades like a madman—spitting, coughing, driving for a few precious feet of gain, then digging in while another blast stung my eyes, stole my breath, and shrieked in my ears. In the course of a few minutes, any awareness of the rugged mountainous beauty of the coastline had been ripped away with the scream of the winds and had been replaced with the desperation of fighting for my life. Minutes passed, with the shriek of the winds growing higher and my body reaching its physical limits of fighting. I wanted to fill my lungs with dry, fresh air but couldn't. I took a ragged half breath, spit out some salt water, and exhaled hard from my nose, which was raw and burning with salt water. My fingers, forearms, and shoulders started to quiver. I wanted to drop the paddle for just a second, drop it across the cockpit and just breathe. I didn't know how long I'd been at it, but it didn't matter. I just needed to rest. I had to rest! *"Paddle. Dig in. Drive. Drive. You're going to die if you don't."*

I was at a place I had not been before, nearly powerless against the winds and knowing that if I gave in for just a few seconds, I would be gone. Nothing was happening in slow motion the way the books say it's supposed to. The slashing chaotic winds were turning my fears into panic. Muscles burned like torn fibers, and my chest felt as though someone had me in a bear hug, squeezing the air out of me when I needed it the most. I started to pray in words that came in gasps and in flashes that came in begging pleas.

"Oh, God, I can't do this. Settle me down. Just give me strength."

I tried to find a mantra, a single word I could spit out into the winds through the burn of salt water in my throat. Between gasps of breath I resorted to grunted pleas of help and knew in the deepest part of my existence that I was on the edge of life and losing the last of any hope in reaching the safety of land.

More minutes dragged by, the time eating away my strength. The cadence of the blades had slowed even when the winds allowed me to spin them faster. I wanted to let go, to lay the paddle into a windward brace and just let the winds have me, let them take me offshore. But my mind would not allow it. The fight had shifted into another realm where my body and mind were fighting separate battles; one was ready to surrender while the other was still willing to battle it out. The blades spun a few more turns, then froze, with one blade barely slowing the backward drift of the boat. Nothing mattered but the pain in my shoulders, in my chest, in my lungs, and in every quivering muscle of my body. The breaking point was not far off, and I felt myself letting go.

As soon as that flash of realization was born, something fired inside me, and another battle began to rage. "No, I won't quit!" The fear and weakness were replaced with an anger at almost giving up.

"Something has to give. But it's not me. Not me." I found the mantra and spit the words into the winds and the waves that washed over the top of the boat and cut into my face.

The blades slashed when they could and dug in with short, deep strokes that held firm when the winds returned and tried to drive me back. With each shift of the winds, I would spin the blades as hard as I could and drive the boat inch by inch toward the safety of the cliffs. I couldn't see clearly. I shook my head and caught a glimpse of the cliff, but the next wave threw another sheet of water into the air, and the wind drove it into my eyes again. The cliff didn't look any closer, but it had to be. I *had* to be gaining.

Time was transformed into something that wasn't measured in minutes: It was measured in desperation and in the pounding of my heart in my ears and in my upper jaw, where I could feel my heart slamming blood through my head. *"I'm gaining. I'm winning."*

The inches turned to feet and the feet to yards as the wind shifted more often and gave me the breaks I needed. The wind was higher on my body, buffeting my head but not stripping the tops off the waves as much as before. I was getting under the protection of the cliff! The blades slipped through the winds more easily. I spun them as fast as I could, grabbing big chunks of water and throwing them behind me! My heart still pounded in my chest, but for the first time I could get a full breath and drew air into the bottom of my lungs.

In another few minutes the air was suddenly very quiet. Short, powerful gusts touched down briefly but then were gone. I paddled to within 60 yards of the cliff and the carsized boulders that appeared and then vanished in the surf. With the back of the paddle resting on the seaward side of the boat, I tried to calm my breathing.

"OK, settle down, Chris. Think surf. Think surf."

I talked to myself as though I were a separate identity, someone needing reassurance and coaching for the next obstacle right in front of me. My voice sounded uncertain and thin after the shrieking winds and now the roar of the surf that crashed on the boulders. Minutes slid by as I slowed my breathing and rested in the swells while studying the surf zone and trying to catch glimpses of the beach. The north side of the cove was out of the question— too many exposed rocks poking up through the surf and nothing but huge boulders on the beach.

I kept looking over my shoulder, wary of the 10-footers that were relentlessly rolling in. A set of five or six huge ones washed under me, and then a mega wave, which made the others look small, began forming out beyond the others. I spun the boat away from the beach and paddled like a possessed demon straight into the wall of green that was steepening with every yard it raced over. The boat climbed up the face of the wave, cut through the crest, and was instantly airborne as the wave folded and crashed behind me. The boat slammed down and lost most of its momentum as it dove into the next wave. I dug the blades in deep and got the boat moving again. I was losing the protection of the cliffs but was more worried about another rogue wave catching me off guard and throwing me onto the rocks. Twenty yards of hard paddling had me on the outer edge of the cove, safe from the surf for a moment and still out of the wind. After a couple of minutes of watching the waves, I moved cautiously back toward the surf and again sat watching the sets of waves.

I remembered the panic, the jittery, weak leg and arm muscles, and the nausea of past surf encounters. There was none of that this time. It was all very analytical: studying the surf, gauging the risks, racing for deep water when the rogue wave struck, and then moving back in toward the surf zone again. I had the helmet and life jacket on for collision protection, and I was in survival mode. Nothing mattered but the crash landing that I had to make on the beach.

I sat, waited, and watched the sets for a lull. Another set of five or six big ones rolled in. A roaring din filled the air as each green hump of water folded in a dumping implosion on the boulders. On the southern edge of the cove was a giant slab of rock that a landslide had left jutting into the surf. The big sets hit the slab at an angle and smashed up against its vertical side. When the waters receded, a channel opened to the left of the slab where two boulders on the beach formed a fairly flat slot that was filled with rocks the size of soccer balls.

A smaller set of waves followed the big set, and I watched the slab landing carefully. Two more sets of large waves and two more of the smaller ones hit the beach with the same impact. If I timed it just right and caught a smaller wave, I could land in the channel and drive the boat between the two boulders. I shoved the water bag, which was under my thighs, forward of the foot pegs and out of the way of my feet. If the landing worked, I needed to jump out as soon as the bow hit the rocks, run forward, and pull the boat higher before the following sets hit.

When the next small set rolled in, I was already as close as I dared to the point where they were breaking. The second wave broke 5 yards in front of the bow. I paddled as hard as I could to get right on the back of the wave and sprinted to stay as close to it as I could. The boat surfed in behind the slab of rock and hit the channel as if was on a laser-guided path. While the boat was flying over the shallows and rocketing through the narrow slot, I popped the spray deck and was already half out of the seat as the keel slammed onto the rocks. I jumped out, stumbled over the wet rocks, and grabbed the bow just as the next wave hit. As the wave washed under the stern, I ran and fell over the boulders higher on the beach, dragging the boat with me as I went. By some miracle I outran most of the wave and managed not to break my ankles on the rocks.

As soon as I landed, the sand flies seemed to rise in a cloud out of the very rocks that I stood on. I dragged the boat higher and, at the same time, tried to wipe the hundreds of black spots off my arms and legs. I had never seen them so thick and so painfully persistent. After everything else I had been through that day, the sand flies were almost enough to drive me into a state of manic overload. I frantically pulled off the front hatch, slapping and smearing at the burning white welts that appeared on my wrists and bare legs and, at the same time, trying to pull on long underwear, socks, gloves, and the head net. By the time I had the boat hauled high above the threat of high tide and had set the tent up, I was exhausted to the point of collapse. I crawled into the tent, zipped the mesh opening shut, and fell into a comalike sleep beneath the cliffs.

That night I wrestled with the demons of my dreams, dreams where my gear disintegrated in front of my eyes. In other dreams it was scattered all over the place where I couldn't find it, and when I eventually did find it, I kept losing it again. I also dreamed of paddling with Paul Caffyn and other experienced paddlers. In the dream I didn't know what I was doing and was afraid these Kiwis would see how inept I was. I normally don't recall dreams, and when I do, I can never remember details. This night was different: My dreams were filled with vivid details of boat designs, some with rudders and some without. I saw my stove—the fine details of valves and O-rings; I saw the faces of people I didn't recognize but felt certain that I must know them; and I could feel the paddle shaft in my hands and the pull of the blades through the water. I half awoke several times to the crunch and roar of the surf, then curled into a tighter ball and slipped back into the fragments of mental and physical exhaustion.

The next morning I woke long after the sun had risen. The tent stood in the cool shadow of the mountain, but already the sea and the sky mirrored the deep blue of a cloudless day. Rather than waking quickly and feeling refreshed as I normally did, I felt as though I had been drugged. My shoulders, upper arms, and finger joints felt inflamed with aches, and when I crawled out of the tent, I could feel the strain on my thighs that had locked me into the boat during the fight to get to shore the previous day. For the first time I had to admit that the slow accumulation of the last three months of stress was wearing me down. I needed to get into sheltered water, get away from the endless crashing noise of the surf and hide in the safety of the mountains, where the offshore winds and the incoming swells couldn't reach me.

Two days after my near miss with the winds and the surf, I was deep in the protection of Doubtful Sound. The horror and the memory of nearly getting blown out to sea were still fresh in my mind. The shrieking winds, the desperation, the panic, and the taste of how close I had come to being another casualty of the sea were only a thought away from the calm waters I now paddled. The winds had shifted to the west and were blowing a steady 15 knots at my back, kicking up small whitecaps and gently surfing me beneath the 3,000- and 4,000-foot peaks that crowded the skyline on both sides of the narrow fiord. As I came around a point where the mountains almost pinched off the end of the sound, a sightseeing steel-hulled catamaran suddenly appeared from around the bend. As it approached, I heard the captain announce to the passengers crowded on deck that "the yellow kayak off to the port side is on a solo circumnavigation of the South Island." After the exposure and the solitude of the outer coast, it was strange to hear the skipper's words echoing across the water, explaining who I was and what I was attempting to do. The *Commander* was stationed in Deep Cove at the very back of Doubtful Sound, where the New Zealand power authorities had built a hydroelectric generating station. A dirt road connected the power station to Lake Manapouri and the "outside" world, providing a unique access to the unspoiled reaches of the sound. Tourists could take a ferry across the lake, hop on a bus, explore the upper reaches of Doubtful Sound by boat, and be back on the far side of the Southern Alps by evening. In contrast to coming in from the open sea, touring by ferry may not have been as intimate as seeing the sound from the seat of a kayak, but it was definitely a lot safer. Meri had told me about the *Commander* and she had obviously let the skipper know that I would eventually find my way into Doubtful Sound. I waved to the tourists on deck as the *Commander* closed to within 100 yards and then roared into full power as it set off on its tour.

For three days I explored the inner reaches of the sound and the even narrower fingers of Hall's Arm, Crooked Arm, and First Arm, which struck off the main fiord like twisted jointed fingers of deep blue. I stayed in close to the shore, tucking under overhanging branches of manuka trees and gliding effortlessly over the shallows as well as the sudden black drop-offs. I let my body rest from the heavy strain of paddling the outer coast and often just sat with the paddle across the cockpit rim, my feet off the foot pegs and my eyes closed as I catnapped in the boat. Around each turn of the coastline was another sky-piercing tower of mountain, with waterfalls trickling in silver ribbons through the vertical greenery. After so many weeks of wind and the near-constant noise of waves and surf, the silence and calm of the inner sounds slowly soaked into me and released some of the tension that the outer coast had been building.

On the morning of February 17 I left Crooked Arm and headed for Thompson Sound, which ran behind Secretary Island. I could have gone on the outside of Secretary, but I wasn't ready yet for the open water. I was still basking in the calm that had so far been all too rare on the trip. Sheets of silken clouds hung suspended over the sound and reached into the lower elevations and drainages of the mountains on both Secretary Island and the mainland. The sound stretched northward between the two coastlines like some kind of fairy-tale passage into a magical land. I couldn't remember a morning so silent and still beneath patches of blue sky and slowly drifting layers of light cloud. Maybe the weather that I had hoped for was finally arriving, the stable weather of the summer, which was almost over. With the stable weather moving in, I remembered what Paul had told me about the typical summer winds: "The winds will be calm until around 11:00 A.M.; then you'll get a fairly strong southerly that will build till early evening, then die back down."

On my first day back on the open water, the winds did exactly as Paul had predicted. I left the protection of Thompson Sound and moved quickly north, paddling past Nancy Sound just as the winds began to build. Four miles up the rugged mountainous coast, Charles Sound opened up, with its mile-wide schism cutting deep into the mountains. I paddled 2 miles into the sound, then returned to the open water before the winds would make getting out of the sound a real workout.

True to Paul's advice, by early afternoon the winds were blowing steadily at 20 knots, with frequent gusts to 25. The seas went from smooth-faced 6-foot swells to gradually more and more whitecaps, which stretched as far as I could see. The increase was slow and predictable, giving me time to settle into the rhythm and the more challenging paddling of the afternoon. The seas built into regular lines of 6- and 8-footers, surfing the boat down breakers with a glaring white brilliance that had me sprinting and leaning forward as I tried to get the most distance out of each surfing wave. The rides were fast and joyfully noisy as the waves broke behind, surfed me along, then rumbled past as they outraced the boat. This was ocean kayaking at its best: racing with the winds along a mountainous coastline and knowing that every

5 to 10 miles there was a guaranteed safe haven of a sound to pull into. After too many weeks of battling the winds and waves, I was finally reaping the rewards of running with the energy of the Tasman Sea.

Islet Point, to the north of Charles Sound, slid past as I kept the bow pointed straight down the following seas and let the big swells race me northward. Between the surfing waves I would twist in the seat of the boat, trailing the paddle on the surface of the sea for support and gazing at the wild beauty of the ocean. When a large wave lifted me 8 or 10 feet high, I could see a mile or more of huge rollers, with streaks of breakers moving up from the South Pacific. From the tops of the mountains all the way out to the endless horizon, there wasn't a cloud in the sky. The Roaring Forties was living up to its name once again, this time with a high-pressure system that made paddling in the heavy seas a joy instead of a terrifying experience.

With the compass barely moving off its northward heading and the boat speeding at 6 to 7 knots down the face of the swells, the headlands on my chart slid by faster than I could keep track of them. Islet, Nugget, and McKerr Point appeared off the bow, then melted into lesser headlands as I came broadside and then swept passed them. A few minutes later the southeast-facing, narrow opening of Caswell Sound opened up as I came even with its mouth. From a mile offshore it looked as though the swells were nearly blocking the entrance with explosions of white water leaping high onto the rocks.

Unlike so many other times on the trip, I ended this day feeling as if I hadn't expended any energy at all. The sea and the wind did all the work as I sat in the cockpit, edging the boat and using a stern rudder to keep the bow racing north. By late afternoon, after a leisurely morning start, my day ended with an idyllic campsite in Two Thumb Bay, a perfect crescent of sand protected by its own curvature and some outlying rocks that allowed me to land without any threat of getting rolled. A sparkling, shallow river wound its way out of the mountains and emptied through a twisting channel of shifting sands and driftwood thrown up by winter storms. On the south end of the beach, a small stream poured over a moss-covered cliff, spreading itself wide and falling in silver ribbons into a pool of smooth-faced boulders.

I set the tent up, tied the boat to the south side of it, and wandered over to the cliff face, hopping from rock to rock for no reason other than the play it provided. At the edge of the pool, I stripped off my clothes, left them in a pile on the rocks, and stepped under the shower of cool falling waters. The western sun warmed my skin as the fresh water washed the salt from my beard and gently pummeled my shoulders. Splashing, tingling, tannic-stained waters rushed off the cliff ledges and shelves and fell in soft, steady murmurings into the pool. I stayed under the cascade until I was too cold to stand it, stood out in the hot sun until the goose bumps disappeared, then stepped back under the falls again. Later I sat in the tent, quietly watching and listening to the evening as well as my breathing and thoughts. When the journal entries were finished, I turned the page and let the pen find the words for the evening.

Long Twilight

Soft blue sky
The gentle notes of a small waterfall
The growl of distant surf
Jagged islets
Silhouetted black on a peach horizon
Alone on the edge of the world

Dusk surrenders to night
Full moon rising
Shimmering yellow on waves
Southern Cross glittering
Perfect geometry of the sky

Chapter 11

GIFTS FROM THE SEA

When we remember we are all mad,
the mysteries disappear and life stands explained.
—*Mark Twain*

SOMETIMES WHEN THE SEAS ARE CALM, or even when the swells are big but there isn't any wind to drive the crests into breakers, my mind goes on "walk about," an Australian Aboriginal term, which, for me, seems to fit the division of the mind and the body. While the body is engaged and on autopilot, the mind wanders away, occasionally checking back in when a wave catches the eye but then just as quickly drifting off again and finding what it needs to work on in its own way. It is a time when both the mind and the body are free to stretch and explore independent of the other. It can be a time of great physical and psychological release—the taut springs of both sides of me slowly uncoiling, relaxing, and working out the kinks in stiff muscles and the twists and turns of the mind. And sometimes something happens that brings the two worlds back together in a way that is as mysterious and unfathomable as the sea itself.

I was 20 miles north of Two Thumb Bay and paddling a mile offshore beneath the same clear, blue skies that had escorted me for the past few days. The winds, for some blessed reason, hadn't built as they typically had in the past, so there weren't any threats that my mind had to lock onto. My mind was off on its own, one minute registering the physical sensuousness of the sun and the slow rise and fall of the thick swells, and the next minute wandering off to a place of expanding thoughts of home, friends, and emotions. The miles, the minutes, and the swells slipped past as the morning sun climbed higher and warmed the paddling shirt stretched across my shoulders. I was supremely happy and quietly aware of how fortunate I was to be alive and to be exactly where I was, paddling along one of the more remote coastlines on earth and feeling completely at peace with the world. An albatross swooped by to check me out, and dozens of shearwaters flew circles around the boat while the mountains slowly changed shape as I crept past their masses.

Somewhere in the silent solitude of that inner and outer calm, a doubt slipped into my thoughts, and for some strange but necessary reason, it began to grow.

The very comfort and security that I felt on the edge of this wild and remote coast focused an inner lens on the other side of my life, the one I would return to when the trip had come full circle. As I paddled along feeling so much a part of the ocean realm I was immersed in, it dawned on me, as it had many times before, how utterly fantastic my life was and, at the same time, how absolutely ill prepared I was for life. Here I was content, comfortable, and alive in the fullest sense of the word, yet when I thought of the end of the journey, I realized how frightening that prospect was. The singular and absolute focus that my life on the trip depended upon was so very different than the fracturing multitasks that modern, fast-paced life demanded.

The more I allowed my mind to get wrapped into the worries of the future, the more I got worked up by my own insecurities. I thought how I didn't have a degree, or even a résumé, that I could hand to a potential employer; I didn't have any formal training, no piece of paper or proof of anything that I had accomplished in life. All that I had learned was self-taught, and though I could turn my hand to a number of skills I was the classic "jack-of-all-trades, master of none." If I were to write of my skills, I could include the dubious value of being able to roll a fully loaded boat in 10-foot surf, set up a tent in driving winds and rain, and survive on some pretty terrible-tasting food for weeks on end. Yes, I could build a simple house, wire and plumb it, insulate and sheet rock it, but those were all skills that required a strong, healthy body. With nothing to dislodge the arrow of my thoughts, it continued to burrow in deeper and closer to the real target of my worries, the time when my body would no longer allow me to travel and explore and to make a simple living with my hands and back. At age sixty-five or seventy where would I be, and how in the world was I going to support myself? When friends and family would be collecting pensions and Social Security, what was I going to be doing? I had neither. The more I thought about it, the more distressed I became. It was insane to let my mind so completely take me away from the glory of the paddling moment, but that was what had happened. I was no longer in the boat with body and mind; I was split in two, my body doing what it needed to do in moving the boat forward, and my mind confronting something I had no answer for—the unknowns of the future. I was forgetting one of the most valuable lessons I had learned through 15,000 miles of paddling: Don't worry about what's 5 miles ahead of the bow; stay focused on a 10-yard circle around the boat and just move that circle forward one paddle stroke at a time. I was very good at applying that lesson on the oceans of the world, but not very good at applying it to the rest of my life.

As if to refocus my attention and bring me back to the moment, a red shape caught my eye on the surface of the sea 20 yards in front and to the right of the bow. Whatever it was, it disappeared behind a swell for several seconds, then bobbed back into view, and again disappeared as its own weight pulled it just below the surface of the sea. By the time I spotted it for the third time, I was already turning the boat sharply toward it when I saw another red shape bobbing up and down in the crystal-clear, sun-pierced swells.

Apples! Two apples—less than 3 feet apart—almost directly in line with my course a mile offshore?

I coasted to within inches of the first one, floating stem up, and plucked it from the sea, glistening red and shiny. A half stroke on the left side of the boat brought me even with the second one, which I scooped up and dropped beside the first one, now rolling gently across the neoprene spray deck. There wasn't a boat within sight and none that I had seen since the *Commander*, deep in Doubtful Sound four or five days earlier. Nothing else floated on the sea—no debris, no flotsam, and no wreckage. There weren't any hiking tracks at this end of the park and not even any jet contrails overhead. There couldn't have been too many places in the world that were as empty as that corner of New Zealand, washed and battered by the Tasman Sea. Yet I had just picked two red, perfectly shaped apples bobbing side by side out of its currents. Suddenly my worries of the future were replaced by disbelief and the rich aroma of the apples rolling around on the spray deck. After weeks of smelling nothing but the sea—seaweed-covered rocks, the fish that I caught and filleted for my dinner, and the smell of the ozone from broken waves—my sense of smell, my sense of sight, and every cell in my brain was suddenly registering *apples!*

I was suddenly rich, at least for the moment. Now all I had to do was to decide what to do with my unexpected wealth, which one to bite into first and devour in a gluttonous feeding frenzy. A swell rolled the boat over on its edge, and both apples shot toward the rim of the cockpit. I let go of the paddle with one hand, jerked my right knee up under the deck of the boat to bring it level, and grabbed the apples before they dropped overboard. I hadn't had fresh fruit in more than three weeks, and there was no way I was going to lose what had just been handed me from the ocean. Where they came from I didn't know, but where they were going I did. I popped the day hatch behind the cockpit and wedged one of the apples in beside the VHF and the soft bundle of the tent. For the next five minutes I let the other one roll around as I got the boat underway and thought about whether I should eat it or save it for later.

Every once in a while I would pick the apple up, polish it on my shirt, and sniff the skin, drawing the sweet aroma deep into the bottom of my lungs; then I would place it back on the spray deck, momentarily balanced on its knobby base. The apple was perfectly formed, not a blemish or bruise and the stem as straight as if it was just picked from a tree. I imagined how it must taste—mouthwatering, sweet and juicy, with just the right amount of tartness.

For five minutes I fought the urge to just grab it and sink my teeth into its red roundness. And then it happened . . . the apple started to roll off the starboard side. I dropped the paddle and grabbed the apple as it hit the cockpit rim and bounced into the air. In one smooth twist of the wrist, I spun the stem onto the inside of my thumb, raised it to my mouth, and took a huge bite out of it.

The skin popped and snapped as I bit in and tasted a miniexplosion of white, crunchy, sweet fruit filled with juices that dribbled out of the corners of my mouth. I could hear my teeth crunching into every slow, purposeful precious bite as I chewed that first chunk until it was nothing but pulp. I was a mile offshore in 6- and 8-foot swells, looking at 3,000-foot mountain peaks and eating the world's best apple plucked from the currents of the Tasman Sea. I raised the paddle in my left hand and the apple in my right and yelled, "Yes-s-s-s!!!" I didn't know where the apples had come from, and I still wasn't sure what I would be doing when and if I reached the age of seventy or eighty, but suddenly everything was back in balance. The apples were a gift, a certain sign that I was on the right course in life and that I would find what I needed along its path. I just had to have faith and follow my heart.

I ate the rest of that apple as slowly and thoroughly as any had ever been eaten, right down to where the seed pocket and the stem joined, and then sucked the last hint of juice out of the core. When there was nothing left but seeds and woody stem, I launched the remains in a celebratory arc as high overhead as I could throw it, then watched as it plopped back into the sea. I licked my fingers clean, picked up the paddle, and swung into the first strokes of getting the boat underway again. At that moment I was as high as anybody on earth could have been.

Finding the apples seemed to be an omen of good luck for the rest of the way north to Milford Sound. Each day dawned with a cool, deep-blue clarity that slowly warmed as the sun crept over the jagged skyline and touched the sea. The sun was rising a full two hours later than it had at the summer solstice, but it seemed the fall weather was far more stable than the summer weather, which had never really developed. By mid-morning the chill was out of the air, and there were two or three more hours of easy paddling before the winds started kicking up. Later in the afternoons, when the swells broke and overtook the boat in glaring rumblings, there still wasn't the dread of the power and volume of earlier swells in the trip. Autumn seemed to have mellowed both the sea and the winds.

I explored several of the sounds along the way—tucking into George Sound, paddling the length of Bligh Sound, and poking into Sutherland Sound and Poison Bay. Gradually the outer-coast scenery was changing from the heavily wooded green of the southern sounds to the more vertical (if that was possible) and angular rock that was visible above treeline. Ten miles south of Milford I could see for the first time a snowcapped peak reaching high above the rounded summits of the surrounding mountains.

In the bliss of sunshine and following swells, towering mountains and glistening snow in the distance, I thought how the worst of the trip must now be over. I had weathered too many gales to bother trying to count, had gotten knocked over a half dozen times in the surf, and had been forced to paddle too often at close to my maximum limits. I was ready for a gentle, peaceful autumn to finish off the remaining 600 miles of the trip. Perhaps, like the rest of life, it was a good thing that I could not see into the future—even the very near future, of less than a week away.

Chapter 12

Fortune pays you sometimes for the intensity
of her favors by the shortness of their duration.
She soon tires of carrying any one long
on her shoulders.

—*Baltasar Gracián y Morales*

"ARE YOU THE MAN PADDLING AROUND the South Island?" a bushy-dark-haired fellow, dressed in yellow rain gear, shouted over the noise of the winds, which were driving the seas into steep 3-foot breakers. He was hanging onto the cabin struts of an aluminum workboat that had just overtaken me 2 miles inside of Milford Sound. A tall blonde-haired guy, who looked like a bearded Viking, was spinning the boat's wheel and backing down on the throttle as the following seas surfed their boat dangerously close to me.

The wind was throwing spray off the tops of the waves and plastering the paddle jacket against my back. One minute the boat was surfing down the face of a wave, flying beneath the 5,000-foot granite peaks, and the next it was wallowing in the troughs. The waves were too erratic and the winds too strong to just sit in one place and not paddle. I slowed my pace, kept the bow pointed downwind to minimized windage, and shouted back, "I am."

A wave lifted the stern of my boat and shot me forward away from the skiff. It may have appeared rude, but it was too much work to try to back paddle out of the surfing. I let the wave take the boat on a long, bow-burying surf ride and heard the outboard kick in as it followed me. Fifty yards downwind, my boat slid off the back of the wave, and the skiff powered up alongside again. The bushy-haired guy leaned over the rail and shouted, "Kevin Beaumont told me about you. I do contract filming for NZ-1, the national television station out of Christchurch." The two boats were side by side, and the skiff blocked some of the noise of the wind. "My name's Dave McCarlie, and this is Jim Huntington." He gestured at the fellow at the wheel, "And that's Nick Aitchison trying not to get sick."

Dave and Jim seemed to be perfectly at home in the rough seas, the battered and dented aluminum hull looking very much like a workboat that the two of them knew well. Nick was apparently out for the ride and looked as though he'd rather be on land as the skiff was thrown side to side, then surfed forward in the choppy seas.

David continued, "Kevin thought you'd be coming into Milford pretty soon, but he didn't know exactly when. We were out filming some diving, but if you don't mind I'd like to get some shots of you in these waves."

The last thing I expected was to have a film crew escorting me into Milford, but Dave assured me all I had to do was keep paddling and he and Jim would get the footage they needed.

Jim backed the skiff away and gave me the room I needed to maneuver. For the next fifteen minutes, they jockeyed around and behind me as they tried to capture the scale of the seas and the sheer cliffs that dwarfed the kayak.

When Dave was satisfied with his filming, Jim eased back alongside for an "on-the-water interview." I had been interviewed dozens of times on past journeys but never in 3-foot waves, bouncing alongside another boat in high winds. After the past two weeks of solitude, and literally living on the edge of the world, I was suddenly looking up at a microphone and television camera and wondering how in the heck everything of the last half hour had come about. In a wacky way I thought the whole thing was comically absurd. My world for the past several weeks had been governed by the winds, the waves, the weather, and the gut-level feelings and skills that had guided me and kept me alive. At times I had been so focused on just surviving that I had almost forgotten that any other world even existed. Now I was face to face with that other world—and the two million people who would watch the interview with this bearded guy in a yellow kayak surfing into Milford.

In a strange way I felt half removed from the moment, looking down from 100 feet and just watching the filming and interviewing process. As Dave asked the leading questions, I tried to sound as though I did this kind of interview every day and, at the same time, tried not to get rolled over as my attention was split between the camera and the paddling. The one thing I do recall saying in the interview was how I thought the worst of the trip was over. If ever there were words that would come back to haunt me, those words certainly would.

For three days I relaxed in Milford Sound, staying in a Department of Conservation cabin where Jim was also staying. In addition to being half owner in the skiff with Dave and being his hunting, filming, and diving partner, Jim was also a builder and was in Milford working on a hangar for one of the primary helicopter touring businesses. He offered the cabin as a place where I could rest, eat regular meals, and actually have a hot shower whenever I wanted. A real bed with clean sheets and a genuine pillow, instead of rolled up clothes, were the perfect ingredients for several ten-hour comatose-like nights of rest.

In Te Anau I phoned Kevin and Dawn Beaumont, who drove an hour and a half on the twisting mountain road into Milford and brought in another twenty pounds of food for the next leg of the trip. From Milford it would be more than 200 miles to Hokitika, where I could fully resupply the boat. In between the two ports was a coastline that offered two guaranteed safe landings; everything else was going to be a matter of timing the swells and running the surf. Part of the reason for coming into Milford was not only to restock the boat, but also to take a break from the constant din of the surf and prepare mentally for this next section of coast.

The three days of sitting and resting and just taking it easy felt like an interminable amount of time away from the open sea. I knew I needed the rest, but after the second day I was more than ready to get back to the quiet and simple focus of paddling. Milford Sound was stunning in its quiet glory of early morning and late evening, but during the day it was mobbed by hundreds of tourists getting on or off buses, tour boats, sightseeing planes, and helicopters. If the weather had been better on the outside, I would have returned to the sea a day earlier, but a full southerly gale made any passage north impossible. I packed the boat with the new supply of food and waited for the weather to "come right" as the locals say. On the evening of the third day, I walked down to the fishing dock and spoke with one of the fishermen about the weather. A gale was still blowing out of the south but was supposed to calm down by morning. He knew about my trip from Meri and suggested I stop by first thing the next morning to get an updated forecast.

The following morning's forecast was as close to being ideal as I could have asked for. The gale had blown itself out, and the marine forecast was for southwest winds at 15 knots with a 6-foot southerly swell, perfect conditions for the 20-mile paddle to my destination of Martins Bay. I had paddled many 30- and 35-mile days in similar conditions and knew I could easily do the distance, especially with the winds and swell at my back. It would be an easy paddle and one where I could save my energy for the long mileage that I would have to do later in the week. I called Kevin and asked him to pass word on to Meri that I was heading off.

On the morning of February 22, I set off as the sun was edging over the crest of the peaks surrounding the headwaters of Milford Sound. The heavy rains of the last few days had stopped, and the clouds were rapidly breaking up, revealing larger and larger patches of deep-blue sky and sparkling waterfalls streaming off the cliffs. If the weather held, I would be in the safety of Martins Bay in five hours.

The 9-mile paddle out of Milford was just long enough to stretch out the paddling muscles and get back into the mind-set of slowly moving the boat forward beneath the massive scale of the mountains. Beyond the mouth of the sound, whitecaps were already covering most of the sea, and the swell was all of the predicted 6 feet but running smooth and well spaced. I turned the bow north and watched the compass slowly swing in its liquid-filled sphere until it settled out on roughly thirty degrees. The bearing was more of a pleasant distraction than a necessity because the air was crystal clear and I could see Yates Point 6 miles down the coast. It was a perfect day to be offshore.

In the hour and a half that it took to reach Yates Point, the winds had built well beyond the predicted 15 knots, and I was beginning to wonder about the forecast. The gusts were already grabbing the high paddle, and the swells, which were running closer to 8 feet, were thick with the volume of a distant, powerful storm. What had begun as a perfect day to make the run for Martins Bay was steadily deteriorating into conditions that I didn't trust. Obviously the forecast was wrong, but if the conditions held, I could still make the bay and land on the southern shore, well protected by the curve of the bay. Turning back into the wind and seeking the shelter of Milford was out of the question; the winds were already too strong, and the tops of the swells were breaking in longer and wider cascades of white foam. The only way out of the weather was to run with it and hope it didn't continue to build.

An hour north of Yates Point the seas had built to some of the biggest I had seen so far on the trip. Massive swells overtook the boat and moments later exploded on the rocks and the short, steep gravel beaches below the cliffs. The winds had driven the whitecaps into continuous breakers that poured off the crests of the swells and repeatedly overtook the boat. In another half hour the winds continued to climb in an alarming way—not in the gradual, almost unnoticeable, way that winds tend to build but in dramatic and powerful gusts that grew into a steady scream past my ears.

Martins Bay was still 6 or 7 miles to the north, and I had no way of knowing how high the winds were going to go.

As the breakers swept over the stern and buried the back half of the boat, I pointed the bow downwind, kept paddling, and weighed my options. Option one, turning back, wasn't even worth thinking about. Option two, trying to land through the 10-foot surf exploding on the steep gravel beaches, wasn't much better. The problem was that the beaches were really nothing more than eroded pockets of sand between fingers of rock. There was no way that I could run the violence of the dumping surf, without getting knocked over at least once. From the back of the breaking surf, I wouldn't be able to see any rocks until I was right on top of them—if I was still upright. I shoved aside the thought of hitting a rock while upside down and considered the third option, continuing to Martins Bay. If I went for the bay, the winds could go up to 40 or 50 knots as they had already done too many times on the trip. Years earlier I had been in 50-knot winds where there hadn't been any fetch for the winds to build the seas. I had barely been able to hang onto the paddle and stay upright. I couldn't imagine trying to paddle with 10-foot breakers overtaking the boat, plus the power of near-storm-force winds. The option to continue on to Martins Bay would be just as high a gamble as attempting to land through the surf.

Moments crawled by and still the boat surfed, barely in control, down the face of the waves. I was spending almost as much time back-paddling to keep the boat from cartwheeling end over end as I was paddling forward. The winds and the waves, which had been an asset two hours earlier, were now steamrolling over me with mind-numbing noise. There was no way I was going to make it to Martins Bay in those conditions.

From the crest of an unbroken swell, I caught a glimpse of beach behind a house-sized rock surrounded by smaller rocks. The following trough sucked the boat backward and blocked out any view except the back of the roller I had just been on. Two or three more swells rolled under me, and each time I caught another glimpse of what looked like a semiprotected small beach behind the rock. To the north and south of the rock were steep beaches where the swells curled onto the gravel and sand in huge, dumping breakers. There wouldn't be a chance of landing there. Behind the rocks the swells broke in several large sets, but at least they looked relatively small by the time they hit the beach. Over several cycles of crest-to-trough views, I saw a route past the rocks and into the smaller, but more chaotic, waves beyond.

Between sets I slipped the front of the spray deck off, grabbed the helmet, and quickly snapped the deck back in place. If I could get through the outer breakers, I could time the smaller waves and hopefully land between the sets. The first thing was to get through the outer breakers.

Any wave more than 8 feet is nearly impossible to surf in a loaded kayak. When waves get that big, they are usually racing over the bottom at speeds of 10 to 15 knots, far too fast for a kayak to stay in front of and not get either pitchpoled end over end or simply thrown to one side and overrun by the wall of collapsing blue-green water. The key isn't in trying to surf the wave but in locking onto the mental image of rolling back up when the inevitable knockdown occurs.

The most difficult part of a surf landing is sitting just beyond the surf zone, watching it erupt in white fury, and knowing that the only way to safety is through its terrifying power. The wind still howls, and the swells still overtake the boat as you sit there, holding it steady and trying to contain the fear that wants to flare into panic. It is an awful gut-twisting paradox to be in the relative safety of deep but huge seas and know that there are no options but to enter the surf zone. You can't stay where you are, and you can't get to true safety without purposefully pulling yourself straight into conditions that, in any other situation, would be sheer madness.

In this thundering world of collapsing seas and whistling winds, one tries to assess the risks and to come up with a plan in the face of danger or fear. That's what surviving is all about. To know fear and to listen to its voice is wise and healthy, but there is also the hazard of freezing in fear and allowing conditions to completely overwhelm and control us. Fear turns to indecision. It feeds upon and multiplies itself until confusion overwhelms logic and locks us into a downward spiral. Any skills we may have had to handle the threat are swept away, and we are left to survive or perish by little more than luck.

For long minutes I sat and watched and tried to see again the route that had convinced me to attempt to run the breakers. I let several large swells roll under me, watched them disintegrate in flying spray, and then made a snap decision that started the paddle blades spinning. Once the boat was underway and moving toward a slot of dark-blue water between the rocks, my mind was racing, calculating distances and time: How far back was the next wave? Was I being swept too close to the rock? Where the wave in front of me broke once, it would break again, and that's where I would get rolled. I kept spinning my head, searching the lines of rollers overtaking me, trying to register how steep they were and predicting when they would crest, hang for a second or two, and then fold.

Twenty yards in front and slightly to the left, a wave peaked and roared into its collapse. An instant later the other end of the wave to the right went off with the same chest-shaking thunder. I pivoted halfway around in the seat to check on the next set and saw a swell blocking out the horizon. There was no point in trying to outrun or outmaneuver it. I lay as far back on the rear deck as I could to keep the bow from diving and then felt the stern rise sharply onto its face.

Seconds later I was upside down, not even registering what happened but feeling the boat getting pounded and buried by the crashing wave. The boat was across the front of the wave, the pressure from the racing water pushing my upper body sideways and, at the same time, jerking my shoulders, arms, and head in different directions. Twice the boat almost righted itself, the rolling hydraulics of the inner wave lifting my body and beginning to turn the boat on its axis back toward the surface. Another force crashed and slammed the boat back under. The pressure changed from my side to my back, pinning my helmet onto the spray deck while the boat spun and was surfed backward, still upside down and still on the face of the wave. The overturned hull continued to spin and get thrown forward of the breaker as its buoyancy tried to outrace the wall of water. With every change of direction, the hydraulics would seize my upper body, which was acting like an anchor to the overturned hull, and try to rip it free from the boat. I locked my thighs under the cockpit rim, jammed my feet against the foot pegs, and wedged myself against the backrest of the seat. If I could just hang on long enough for the drag of my body to overcome the power of the wave, the wave would wash over me and I could roll up on the back side of it.

The large bladed paddles that were such a help on the surface now worked like demons on my shoulders, providing too much surface area for the wave to act on. The paddle corkscrewed my upper body across the rear deck and almost pulled me out of the cockpit. I opened my left hand and hung onto the shaft with my right as the paddle spun and whipped around my head and shoulders like a broken helicopter rotor. From the waist up I had to relax as much as possible to minimize any muscle strain. From the waist down I was locked in as tightly as my legs and feet could brace inside the boat.

Cold seawater burned the lining of my nose and shot painfully into my ear canal as the roar of the wave replaced the high pitch of the winds. Beneath the overturned boat and amid the pummeling, the noise, and the physical strain of trying to hang on, I waited for what felt like an eternity for the wave to let me go. As the wave slammed and spun the boat, I began the slow inward journey of the mind.

One voice began shouting, "Bail! Swim! You're out of air!"

Another voice whispered strongly back, "Wait. Hang in there! The cycle. The cycle. It'll come."

The voices continued their arguing as my mind's eye saw the yellow bottom of the boat ricocheting off the water as it was hurled in front of the wave, the black shaft and blades of the paddle appearing and vanishing as the boat spun around.

Ten seconds passed. Fifteen seconds, and still the wave held the boat. Time started burning holes in my lungs and weakening the will to stay in the cockpit.

"Bail. Get out."

The voice wouldn't go away. The urge to breathe came in small involuntary spasms in my chest and throat. I spit out seawater that had filled my mouth, clamped my teeth together, and swallowed hard.

"Stay with it. Go deep. Go deep."

The voice of reason was still there, urging me to hang on for maybe another five more seconds. The cycle of storm to calm was coming. Now was not the time to bail.

Mentally I turned inside. I went deeper into a physical place at the center of my chest and stayed there, stayed with the burn in my lungs and tried to block out the voice that was now screaming in my ears. Somehow through that inner focus I bought another few precious seconds while the wave began to pass over the boat and release it to the following trough. The roar of the wave weakened, and the thrashing from side to side slowly grew less violent.

I pulled in the paddle with my right hand, found the shaft with my left, and forced it into the setup position for a roll—parallel and held tightly against the right side of the boat. When most of the noise of the wave subsided, I unwound into my roll, pivoting the left blade ninety degrees out to the side and pulling straight down. The boat rolled swiftly back around, seawater pouring out of my helmet and streaming over my face as I exhaled, spitting water and sucking in desperate gasps of pure, sweet air. I was inside the first line of surf but was now heading straight out to sea and looking through the sting of salt water at the next wave already white and rumbling in.

The voice started again, "Ten seconds. Ten seconds. Turn the boat. *Turn the boat!!*"

While I raced to spin the boat around, I hyperventilated, clearing my lungs of carbon dioxide and flooding it with as much clean air as I could. The second wave was only marginally smaller than the first, but I was in shallower water. When it hit, it would roll me again.

When the second wave hit, I didn't even try to surf it or to stay upright for the few seconds that I may have been able to. I got a few last gasps of air and was over before I had the boat completely turned toward the beach. Ten seconds of air and I was back in the same violent, submerged tumbling as before. The only thing different was that I didn't have the strength to hang on as long. There was the same drumming and thrashing, the same release of the upper body and the locking of the lower, and the same voices, one more insistent than before, and the other weaker and less certain in its resolve to stay focused and to wait for the cycle. And then there was another voice, just one word that I couldn't silence, "Rocks."

And that started it, the image of the boat careening straight for one of the rocks I had seen seconds before when I was upright. Panic started to take over. I waited for the impact, the bone-smashing blow and the blackness that would follow. Thoughts of getting clear of the boat raced through my mind. I needed to get out—get my head up so that I could see what was coming— get air. I reached for the grab loop on the spray deck, felt the soft, 2-inch-wide webbing in my fingers and the place where it was sewn over itself at the end of its loop. One pull and I would be free from the roar and confusion inside the wave. One pull and I would be swimming instead of being dragged upside down. The urge to rip off the deck and "wet exit" was driving me to do what I knew I shouldn't—swim free of the boat.

I had to break away, not from the boat but from the mental urgency to give up and just fling myself out into the wave. Being out of the boat wasn't any safer than staying in it. And if I stayed with the overturned hull, I'd at least have a chance of hitting the roll again and maybe getting to the beach in one piece. I let go of the grab loop and locked onto the commitment to stay in the cockpit until I ran completely out of air or the wave let me go. I hunched my shoulders, pulled my head in tighter, and retreated back into that physical and mental place of limbo while the wave took the boat through the rocks. Seconds crept by. Time became an onslaught of noise and hydraulic arms that tore and battered and twisted my body while my eyes squinted as tightly as my throat, and I waited. Waited.

When the wave finally started to quiet, I surfaced through the mental layers of protection and survival and reached for the paddle shaft. The blade sliced out, grabbed the surface of the water, and I was back around, spitting and gasping air as before, with the sea again pouring out of my helmet and into my eyes. This time I was well inside the last line of big surf and looking straight ahead at the waves dumping on the gravel beach 50 yards away. Broken waves and 4- and 5-foot swells that had slipped over the shallows turned the sea into a confused mess of clashing breakers, but at least the power of the outer surf had been broken. I shifted the boat laterally, avoiding some small breakers and sizing up the beach for the best place to drive the bow onto the gravel. If I timed it just right, I could jump out between the confused sets and pull the boat clear of the surf.

I closed the distance to the beach to less than 20 yards, waited for a 4-footer to overtake me and break, and then sprinted in. Halfway in I glanced over my shoulder and saw that I had misjudged the set. A 5- or 6-foot swell was closing in and was going to break just as the bow hit the beach. If I tried to turn around, the wave would hit me broadside and drive me upside down onto the small rocks and gravel. The only thing to do was to pull the spray deck off as the boat hit the beach and jump clear of it—just let the wave take the boat.

When the keel knifed into the marble-sized gravel, I was already half out of the cockpit, with one knee pulled up and both hands on the rim behind me to give me a good position from which to launch myself. I cleared the boat just as the wave crashed onto the rear deck, flipped the boat into the air and plowed it into the gravel. The retreating wave then dragged the water- and gravel-filled hull back off the beach and into the next breaker, which repeated the same thrashing. As the boat rolled and dug into the gravel for the second time, I pulled the Velcro paddle leash off my wrist, threw the paddle high onto the beach, and ran for the toggle on the bow of the boat. Just as I got a hand on it, the wave sucked the boat back into the surf again. There was no way I could hang onto a hundred and sixty pounds of sliding energy plus the weight of the flooded cockpit. I let it go and watched as it was swallowed by the next wave, thrown onto the beach again, and then dragged back out into deep water, where it started to drift away.

Everything I needed to survive was in the overturned yellow hull. I got rid of the life jacket so that I could dive under the boat if it was thrown in my direction and ran into the surf. As soon as I got within reach of the boat, a wave launched it toward me like a drift log. I jumped clear of it and was knocked off my feet by the wave. Twice more I got a hand on it but couldn't stand in the undertow and pull it toward the beach at the same time. I ducked once under the waves as the boat shot over me and glanced off my arms, which were wrapped over my helmet. By some miracle a wave finally threw it and me far enough up the beach that I was able to grab the bow, dig my feet into the gravel, and hold it long enough for the wave to retreat. Before the next set came in, I rolled the boat over, emptied most of the water, and dragged it out of reach of the surf.

What was so strange was that even after getting rolled twice and having to swim for the boat, I was exhausted physically but very calm mentally. Out of sheer necessity, as soon as each roll had been executed, the trauma had been shoved aside and I had locked onto the next threat. On a lesser scale I had been doing the same thing for the past three months: dealing directly with conflicts and hardship, accepting them for what they were as part of the whole, and dismissing them as soon as the threat was over.

There hadn't been any time to really think about what had happened; there had only been the necessity to act quickly and do what needed to be done. Now as I stood on the beach and regained my strength, I was still in that survival mode, dealing with the present, assessing the situation, and coming up with a plan for the next step. The wind still howled, and the waves thundered ashore with the same deafening roar, but my mind had already shifted from the sea to the line of trees above the beach. I needed to get out of the wind and set up a camp.

I had been alternately looking up the beach for an obvious break in the bush, then out to the surf and rocks through which I had just been washed. After several minutes of rest, I looked down at the bow and noticed for the first time that the compass had been ripped out of its housing forward of the front hatch. Four screw holes marked where the compass had been mounted to the empty recessed fitting. The loss of the compass registered with the same feeling of regret, yet acceptance, as when my flashlight had abruptly quit working the previous week. It had been a disappointment, but as soon as it was obvious that the flashlight was finished, I hadn't wasted time or energy worrying about it; I would simply get along without it. Now I had to make that same adjustment as I looked down on the screw holes and the filaments of fiberglass pulled from the deck. I had a fiberglass repair kit with resin and cloth with which I could repair the holes. I hadn't really used the compass for anything other than a distraction on the long hours offshore, sometimes just watching it slowly pivot as the boat had rolled side to side. I would miss it, but compared with what could have happened in the surf, it was a minor loss.

I left the boat where it sat and went to retrieve the water bag that had flushed out of the cockpit and washed up farther down the beach. On the way back to the boat, I picked up the paddle, consciously shook the sand from the blades, and thought how lucky I was not to have gotten hurt in the landing.

It wasn't until I was within a dozen feet of the boat that I froze in shocked disbelief at what had been right in front of me ever since pulling the boat out of the surf. Half of the fiberglass cockpit rim was *gone*—ripped off the deck of the boat and leaving fibers and shattered gel coat where the black rim should have been. At first the loss didn't completely register. This boat, which hadn't had a serious scratch in its entire hull, was now suddenly missing half the rim that held the spray deck in place. I looked from the remains of the cockpit down around the hull beneath the seat and saw more smashed-in gel coat and the exposed weave of fiberglass cloth, torn and filled with sand and gravel. The more I looked at the boat, the more the damage became grossly evident. The boat was a complete wreck! Beneath the seat was a jagged tear that ran all the way up to where the rim should have been. Another tear ran across the other side and down again so that only a 4-inch-wide strip of undamaged glass tied the front half of the boat to the rear half. I lifted the bow, and the hull folded a few inches in front of the seat like a giant hinge. Along the forward deck the fiberglass seam that held the deck to the hull was ripped open for 4 feet. I lifted the deck like a clamshell then knelt beside the boat and looked inside. The front bulkhead was torn halfway out, and water was draining from the forward compartment where my sleeping bag and fleece clothing were stored.

Every place I looked there were cracks and holes in the fiberglass. I popped the hatch off the rear compartment and saw water pooling between the food bags. In the middle hatch where the tent, stove, and more importantly, the radio were packed tightly against one another, everything looked dry and intact. I turned the rubber knob on the radio, and the large black numbers immediately appeared on the small illuminated screen. Thankfully that was one piece of equipment that was still in working order.

The more I looked at the boat, the more I realized there wasn't any way I could repair it. The damage was structural and so extensive that the small repair kit I had on board was useless. After inspecting the boat again, a sense of resignation completely overwhelmed me, then quickly changed to a surprising calm and surrender. After 1,000 miles of paddling and dealing with adverse weather and seas, the power of the surf had not only broken the boat but it had just broken my will to continue. I stood and looked at the boat and then said, "Well that's it. I quit."

In an instant the trip was over. I was done with it and could forget about the whole damn thing. There was a certain peace and acceptance in saying it out loud. The words echoed in my head until I spoke them again, "I quit."

I left the crippled hull on the sand and walked up to the woods to look for shelter from the winds.

In an hour I had the tent set up under the protection of some low-hung manuka trees on the edge of the beach. My clothes, sleeping bag, food, and an assortment of bags and gear were spread out, drying on the rocks and driftwood out of the winds. I had dragged the boat above the high-tide mark and left it at an odd angle, dropped where it lay as if discarded and uncared for. Out on the exposed beach, the winds carried the spray off the tops of the waves and made walking in a straight line almost impossible. I walked down to the edge of the sea, stood just above the reach of the waves, and gazed out at the raging surf. An endless march of huge swells powered into the offshore rock, throwing great volumes of white water into the cloudless sky. Closer in, between swells, rocks appeared, like black pilings randomly scattered through the surf. How I had missed them while I was upside down was a miracle. I watched the sea for a few minutes and then returned to my camp out of the wind.

Later that evening the wind and surf began dropping as quickly as they had built. Just before dusk a fishing boat passed a mile offshore, plowing south into the swell toward Yates Point. I thought of trying to raise them on the radio but just watched the boat getting smaller and finally disappearing in the swells. Although I had decided the trip was over, I needed time to just let the realization sink in. I needed to get off the beach somehow, but more than that, I needed time to think—or perhaps not to think but rather just sit with the piles of gear and the wrecked boat for a day.

My sleep that night was filled with dreams: boats and paddlers drifting in with everyone certain of where they were going while I was lost, paddling down a river that led farther and farther from the sea. The river went through a city, beneath overpasses, and beside warehouses where I couldn't camp. There was no greenery, no life in the concrete, only the channeled river that swept me onward. Eventually the river made a huge U-turn and emptied back into the sea where it had begun.

I woke from the dream at 2:00 A.M., confused and, for some reason, going through rescue options and the first vague thoughts of continuing. I didn't want to continue. I wanted to walk off the plane in Seattle into the arms of friends. I curled into a ball and tried to force myself back to sleep. A half hour later I was still awake. I got up and walked the beach—a beautiful, crystal-clear night with the Milky Way arched overhead in twinkling wonder, no wind and the surf continuing to quiet. By dawn the sea would be tauntingly calm. As if I had been tricked by some sirens, I felt like a foolish, small man defeated by the sea, which now chuckled and rolled harmlessly onto the beach. In that stillness of the night, a shadow of possibly continuing began to surface. Was it ego? Was it pride or foolishness? Was it just my stubborn nature to refuse defeat? Maybe it was all of those things, and maybe it was something deeper that I didn't yet understand. Under the stream of stars that filled the sky and defied time, I let the possibility of continuing quietly sit inside of me. Perhaps the dawn would have the answer.

Chapter 13

RESCUE AND REPAIRS

*Sometimes it's better to grit your teeth
and get on with it.*

—*Ellen MacArthur*

*Youngest person to complete around the
world Vendee Globe sailing race*

IN IRELAND THE ISLANDERS OF THE PAST LIVED OFF the wreckage of ships thrown onto the rocks: barrels of food, timbers, rigging, and steel. All were salvaged and seen as a blessing from the sea, one ship's terror and demise feeding and sustaining the shore bound. One day the sea is savage and violent, the next so calm and forgiving. Once again it is a cycle: the cycle of storm to calm; the cycle of fighting and surrender, of resisting and of finding harmony.

The morning after wrecking the boat, I weighed my options of rescue. Walking out was almost out of the question. Three- and four-thousand-foot-high mountains stood in a jumbled mass of peaks between Milford Sound and me. Trying to find my way through the jungle-thick lower elevations and over the passes would take days. Walking the coastline, with the sheer cliffs falling into the surf, looked just as foreboding and foolish. A slip off the rocks and into the surf could be deadly. Besides, I couldn't carry enough food and gear with me to make either trek a viable option. The only other options were rescue either from the sea or the air, and that depended on the radio. I had tried several times to reach Fiordland Maritime Rescue, but after each transmission, the radio was stone silent. The mountains that blocked any easy passage out also blocked any radio frequencies. Unless I saw a boat offshore, the radio was useless. In the meantime I had to occupy my mind and come up with another way of signaling for help.

Two hundred yards down the beach from my tent I found a tangled heap of rope that the sea had thrown upon the rocks and sand. I heaved and dragged the mass of sun-stiffened and salt-encrusted rope to a log beside the tent and cut off the buoy on one end. Now at least I had a starting place to unravel the mess of twisted and contorted knots. I pushed the first 6 inches of gnarled rope back through a series of loops, following the path of the rope deeper into the labyrinth and getting drawn into the task of making sense of the storm-tossed tangle. Slowly the loose end of the rope began to grow longer and straighter as I pushed, pulled, untwisted, and stretched its length. A half hour passed, and my fingers began to ache from the work. I looked at the waist-high mass in front of me and at the 30 feet of straightened line leading out of it like a snake crawling from its den. I was making headway, drawing from this waste of the sea something of value, something I could use. I wiggled my hips deeper into the sand and set back to work. The boat, the shattered fiberglass, the remote beach, and the defeat of the sea all faded as I followed the lines and gradually loosened the knots of tension, of storm violence tangled in the rope and in my mind. I let my fingers and wrists do the work while my mind found its own way through the tricks and twists of the task.

An hour later the heap of rope lay neatly coiled in overlapping circles of order and form beside the log. Out of the storm's chaos had come something that gave me a direction and a plan: I was going to build a signal tower.

Fifty yards from the tent was an old, rusted crayfishing pot, with its netting rotted and its steel frame mostly buried in the sand. The pot would be the base for the tower. I searched the beach and eventually found two straight tree limbs, which I dragged back to the tent site. I lashed the two limbs together and tied my yellow paddling jacket and red sleeping-bag stuff sack to one end. Four logs dragged into a rough circle were the anchor points for the pole jammed into the craypot. The 200 feet of rope I had untangled ran from the logs to a point 8 feet up the pole and held it upright, like a finger jutting into the sky. The yellow jacket and red stuff sack hung limp in the still winds, but at least there was a splash of color that could be seen from the sea or the air. The tower was useless unless a boat or plane passed close by, but at least it had given me an immediate focus. If the tower didn't work, I could gather a bunch of driftwood, soak it with the stove fuel, and toss the rubber hatch covers on the fire to create a plume of smoke. I had plenty of food, a stream to get water from, and now a signal tower. There was a certain satisfaction in stepping back and seeing what I had erected on the tiny beach: a signal of life between the rocks and the sea.

Throughout the remainder of the day, I watched the sea from the sand-fly haven of the tent, four times racing out to the edge of the beach when I spotted fishing boats a half mile to 3 miles out. Each time I turned the radio on and watched the battery indicator slowly grow smaller as I radioed, "Fishing vessel, fishing vessel, fishing vessel. This is Sea Kayaker One, Sea Kayaker One, on channel one six; Over." While I stood waiting and hoping for a reply, the sand-flies landed by the hundreds and sank their devilish teeth into any exposed skin. I swatted and wiped them off in streaks of black and smeared blood and watched the fishing boats continue steaming across the horizon, oblivious to both the radio and the signal tower. By late afternoon another two boats had cruised past, and a small plane out of the direction of Milford practically flew right over my position. By the time I raced from the tent and tried the radio, the plane's engine noise was rapidly fading to the north. I retreated back into the tent, zipped the mesh opening closed, and spent twenty minutes killing the swarms that had entered the tent as I dove through the doorway.

At 5:00 P.M. I had almost given up on a rescue for the day. I was getting the stove and pots organized for my dinner when I happened to look out on the overcast horizon. Seven or eight miles offshore and heading north was a cruise ship! I launched myself out of the tent and began madly slapping and smearing sand flies as I pressed the transmit key and called: "Cruise ship, cruise ship, cruise ship heading north out of Milford. This is Sea Kayaker One, Sea Kayaker One. Over."

A heavily accented voice came back almost immediately: "Sea Kayaker One, dis es de *Marco Polo*. Over."

I quickly explained that I had crash-landed on the beach directly to the east of their position, that I had no way of getting off the beach in the damaged kayak, and that I needed a helicopter evacuation. The German-accented voice came back with an almost comical reply, "Vell, I am sorry, but ve do not have a helicopter."

I looked at the battery indicator on the radio and saw it was down to 10 percent and dipping to zero each time I keyed the mike. I had used the last of the spare batteries and now had to explain that I didn't need their helicopter but just needed them to patch word through to Fiordland Maritime Rescue that I was in need of an evacuation. Just as I was about to begin the long transmission, Fiordland Maritime abruptly broke in. They must have been monitoring the radio frequency that the *Marco Polo* was using. I had tried multiple times to raise them on the same frequency but had been unable to. Now suddenly it sounded as if they were 10 yards behind me rather than 50 miles over the mountains. It didn't matter why I couldn't raise them before; I had little power left in the batteries and had to let them know my position.

"Sea Kayaker One, what is your situation?"

I explained quickly what had happened and that I thought I was about 10 or 12 miles north of the entrance to Milford Sound. I also told them I had plenty of food and water, that I wasn't hurt, and there wasn't any emergency.

"Roger, Sea Kayaker One. We'll see if we can get a helicopter out of Milford. Stand by. Over."

Stand by? I was afraid to move from my position for fear of losing radio contact, but there was no way I could just stand there and let the sand flies suck the last of my blood. I started running in a large circle up and down the beach and thinking how I should have grabbed a shirt and long pants before calling the cruise ship. If I made a dash for the tent, I might miss Fiordland Maritime's call. I continued to run around in circles as another half hour went by before the radio suddenly crackled back to life.

"Sea Kayaker One, this is Fiordland Maritime. Are you still there?"

Was I still there? Where was I going to go? I was half naked, trying to outrun a growing swarm of flying teeth on a remote New Zealand beach. I wasn't going anywhere except in a circle. I was out of breath and almost laughing as I replied, "Roger, Fiordland, I'm still here."

"Roger, Sea Kayaker One. We have contact with Milford. Stand by."

Fifteen minutes passed, then another half hour. I looked at the signal tower each time I did another lap with my trailing cloud of sand flies. If the chopper came, they would need a clear place to land. I ran over to a level stretch of beach and threw some small limbs and clumps of seaweed farther up the beach. As soon as the rescue center let me know the chopper was in the air, I could start breaking the camp down and be packed by the time it arrived. I was going through the sequence of things I would have to do when all of a sudden the whining scream of turbines filled the air, and from behind the headland to the south of my camp, a glistening blue helicopter came straight up the beach toward me. The machine flared and hovered over the tower, then turned slowly like a huge mechanical dragonfly, its tail facing the sea. I could see the pilot scanning the area, glancing at me, then slowly raising the chopper and coming in for a gentle landing on the cleared section of beach. Debris and sand flew out in a circle around the landing zone as the pilot settled the machine on its skids and slowed the rotors and turbine scream of the engines. My ride had arrived.

Through the bug-eye curve of the helicopter window, I recognized Jeff Shanks, the pilot whose hangar Jim had been building in Milford. Jeff was a quiet guy with a very dry, sarcastic sense of humor. He had a physique and an air about him that spoke of absolute confidence and professionalism. Beside him was his copilot, nicknamed Snow, who looked as though he belonged on a rugby team—short, powerfully built, and always smiling. They both climbed out of the chopper in matching blue coveralls, leaving the chopper spinning its rotors and clearing the last of any twigs and seaweed from the beach. As they approached the tent where I waited out of the rotor wash, Jeff stopped and looked at the busted-up boat, gave it a little nudge with the toe of his boot, then continued up to the tent. With a smile and shake of his head he said, "Ye didn't get very far, mate."

There was no point in arguing the obvious. I let the comment go.

In minutes the campsite was broken down, with everything stowed in the rear compartment of the chopper. Jeff and Snow had lashed the boat to the left strut as I pulled down the signal tower and reclaimed my paddle jacket and stuff sack. Before I climbed in through the back left of the chopper, Jeff shouted in my ear above the noise of the idling engines, "No guarantees on the boat staying in one piece." I nodded, looked over the boat one last time, and climbed in. Snow handed a set of headphones over his shoulder and pointed to the place behind me where I should plug the jack in.

Fifteen minutes after they had screamed over my campsite, we were airborne and flying against the face of the coastal mountains 1,000 feet above the waves. Outside the window the mountains seemed close enough to reach out and touch, the trees somehow clinging to the mountainside between areas of bare rock. Jeff flew at a steady altitude, in tight and hugging the mountain's contours as though they formed a race track with the inside lane the fastest route to the finish. Trees, rocks, and cliff flashed by too close and too fast for me to register. I pressed my forehead against the window and looked down at my shattered boat vibrating itself to pieces in the downdraft of the rotors. Through my thoughts and the noise of the engines, Snow's voice came over the headphones and seemed to speak from the center of my skull, "What happened?"

What happened? When? Where? My mind was going as fast as the chopper. It was all happening too fast—the evacuation of the beach site, the speed, and the flight against the mountain face that made the chopper feel so tiny. I had forgotten about wrecking the boat, forgotten about the surf. I was hanging onto the edge of the seat with white-tipped fingers and suddenly conscious of my stomach and thigh muscles tensed and locked. Below, the waves crashed white and snaked along a coastline that I didn't recognize but knew I had paddled past just two days earlier. What happened? How could I explain that a wave had picked up the boat and thrown it onto the gravel and rocks? I adjusted the high-tech microphone on its slim plastic arm so that it rested in front of my lips. Through the headphones my voice sounded strange as I explained something about a bad forecast, big waves, and swimming for the boat. Jeff made a comment about being damn lucky. I nodded and checked on the boat again, whose upper deck was slamming into the hull.

The chopper vibrated and shook, shifted and swayed side to side in the mountain air currents. The tail swung one way and Jeff calmly compensated, as he looked nonchalantly out his side window at the sea below. Both of his hands and feet were constantly on the move, unconsciously adjusting, tweaking, and gently pulling on levers. He was surfing, playing at 1,000 feet with the same ease that I surfed the waves. I wanted to ask him to either slow down or just take us a little farther away from the cliffs. Big surf was scary, but it suddenly seemed like child's play compared to this.

Beyond the view of gauges and levers and the curve of the Plexiglas window, the mouth of Milford Sound suddenly opened up in front of us. Jeff banked the chopper into a stomach-churning turn, and minutes later the docks and visitor center at the head of the sound came into view. As we flew in closer, Jeff suddenly changed course, banking the chopper again and flying straight toward a waterfall that cascaded hundreds of feet off a cliff face. I watched the falls grow larger and more defined through the front window, waiting for Jeff to either pull up, come around, or just plain stop the suicidal run toward the rock wall. If this little showmanship of flying skill was for my benefit, I had already seen plenty. I just wanted out of the chopper and to feel solid land under my feet.

Jeff finally slowed the chopper when the waterfall completely filled the front view of the cockpit. I sat staring past Snow and Jeff's shoulders in sweaty panic as he inched the helicopter even closer to the falls and the cliff. Sheets of spray covered the windows and obliterated any vision of the rock walls in front and to either side of us. The tips of the rotors disappeared, and I waited for the whiplash crash and spin of the chopper as it hit the cliffs. A steady drip of water fell from overhead and hit my right shoulder while Jeff very calmly maneuvered sideways, tilting and swinging the machine into the spray, apparently to wash off any salt water and sand from the beach landing. When he was satisfied, he gently backed the chopper away, then powered into a reverse turn that just about finished me off in the back seat. Minutes later the skids touched down on the macadam in front of the hangar. The rotors stopped spinning, and, for the first time in too long, I could hear my own heart beat. The chopper ride had been more traumatic for me than the entire surf episode. Snow opened the rear door, and as my feet touched the ground, I noticed my legs shaking.

With the bags of gear and the boat safely stowed in the corner of the hangar, there was one more bit of business to take care of, paying for the flight out. Jeff was in his office filling out some paperwork when I walked in.

"Well, Jeff, what do I owe you for the flight?" I asked.

He looked at me as if I had sand in my head from the surf landing and said, "You don't pay me, the police will. They called for the flight. I'll bill 'em. That's their policy."

Whether that was their policy or not, I didn't agree with it. I was a guest in New Zealand and had been prepared to pay for the flight as soon as I realized it was the only way off the beach. "Do you take a credit card?" I asked.

"You don't pay me, mate. The police will." He impatiently repeated.

When he realized I wasn't leaving until I had paid the $600 bill, he relented and told me he'd explain it to the police.

I caught a ride into Te Anau with Jeff, who was hitting more than 100 kilometers an hour on turns I wouldn't have driven at 60. He drove his car as relaxed and light-handed as he flew his helicopter. It seemed that he knew only one speed—*fast*—as he slipped from one twisted turn into the next and never once touched the brakes. After traveling at 4 miles an hour for almost three months, my senses couldn't keep up with the impulse overload of speed, the shifting images, and the sudden weight changes as the car sped along the mountain road. By the time we arrived at Kevin and Dawn's house, time and place no longer made any sense to me. A few hours earlier I had been on an isolated beach with my busted-up boat and my camp set up in the shelter of native New Zealand bush. Now as Kevin and Dawn welcomed me with hugs and questions of concern, I looked around and saw a normal modern home with overstuffed chairs, magazines, a TV, and a child's toys, plus an Easter basket filled with jellybeans and chocolate-covered bunnies. Everything of value to me was back at Jeff's hangar: my tent, stove, sleeping bag, battered boat, and faithful paddles. As I stood in Kevin and Dawn's kitchen, they told me how the previous night's national news had featured the film clip of my interview with Dave. While two million Kiwis thought I was still making my way north along the west coast, I was standing in my friend's kitchen, uncertain of anything but the cup of tea Dawn had brewed for me. The cup was hot in my hands, and the sweet aroma filled my nostrils.

I was quickly coming down from the high that had sustained me for the past two days. If I looked at anything for longer than a few seconds, my eyes would slip into a stare and my mind would go blank. Dawn could see my exhaustion and led the way to the spare bedroom, then showed me where the shower was.

As hot water drummed against my skin and ran in rivulets down my body, I closed my eyes and leaned against the shower wall, swaying slightly from side to side and registering the feel of tile against my back and the smooth surface of the tub beneath my feet. Fatigue blended images of rolling seas, endless blue skies, and mountains rising straight above lines of white surf. Hot water, steam, and the smell of soap brought me back to the present. While the shower washed the salt of the Tasman Sea from my beard and skin, conflicting thoughts of continuing or giving up on the attempt slipped in and out of my mind. I toweled off and tried to force the thoughts away, not wanting to think of anything—about continuing or quitting or even wondering what happened to all my gear, which I was normally so meticulous about. For the moment all I wanted was sleep, which came seconds after I lay my head on the crisp, clean pillow.

Chapter 14

REBUILDING THE BOAT
AND THE DREAM

Vitality shows in not only the ability to persist
but the ability to start over.

—*F. Scott Fitzgerald*

SOMETIME IN THE MIDDLE OF THE NIGHT, THE SILENCE of the darkened room awakened me. I opened my eyes and vaguely made out the right angles of the walls meeting the ceiling over the bed, defined planes that met with precision and purpose. I shut my eyes and tried to go back to sleep, but seconds later I was again looking up at the shadows. In the soft darkness my mind searched for something to focus on and immediately honed in on the boat. I could see the forward deck split from the hull, half the cockpit cowling missing, and the ragged torn holes in the sides and bottom. Normally the boat would have been inches away, tied to the tent as an anchor against the winds. Now it lay on its side in the corner of Jeff's hangar surrounded by the gear that would normally be organized in the compartments. Without the boat tied to the tent, without the smooth curve of the tent ceiling overhead, and, without the sound of the sea, as disturbing and irritating as it was, I was adrift in the stillness of Kevin and Dawn's home. The coastal environment that I had known for a thousand intimate miles haunted me. The exposure, the constant motion of the sea, the endless horizons, and the mantra of paddle blades reaching and pulling had been replaced by a soft bed and walls that muffled the sounds of the night and trapped the movement of air. The physical journey had ended with the abrupt lifting of the helicopter off the beach—rotor blades swirling sand, seaweed, and twigs—while out of the chopper window the sea still rolled on and reminded me of the remaining 700 miles of coast that stretched to the north.

The arrival of the chopper had left little time for the mental and emotional part of the journey to sort itself out. That emotional attachment had awakened me and stirred to life the fragments of the journey, my mind trying to piece together the broken boat and thoughts of continuing.

◆ ◆ ◆

The decision to continue or not began the next morning with a series of phone calls to find someone who could look at the boat and determine if it was repairable. I called Paul Caffyn and told him what had happened. He had been behind this trip from its conception and knew the highs and lows of long journeys. He had also had his share of mishaps, had broken boats up in the surf, and knew how relentless and seemingly possessed the sea could be. Paul offered me one of his spare expedition boats if I couldn't get mine repaired, then gave me the number of Graham Sisson, a kayak builder near the north tip of the island who might know someone local who could look at my boat.

The next call was to Graham, who had seen the news release and not only gave me the name of an excellent fiberglass man but also offered one of his company's expedition kayaks at cost. He would ship it to me as soon as I wanted it. Like Paul, he didn't want the trip to end simply for the want of a boat. I thanked him and told him I needed time to see if I could get my boat repaired, but I would hold his offer as a backup.

As soon as I hung up with Graham, the local police called and asked if they could pass on Kevin and Dawn's number to a kayak-shop manager who wanted to talk to me. Dawn gave them permission, and minutes later I was talking with Steve Council in Christchurch, who had also seen the news and then the follow-up report of the wreck, which apparently had been on the previous night's news. Steve was calling to offer another boat at cost. All I had to say was yes, and he would ship it straight to Te Anau. If I wanted, I could be back on the water the next day and heading out of Milford Sound again.

The cumulative effect of the trip and the events of the last three days had left me not only physically but also emotionally spent. After three offers of boats in less than fifteen minutes, I was numb, speechless, and moved to tears. Seconds ticked by until I could trust my voice not to crack with the emotions that were overwhelming me. The generosity and sincere help from Kevin and Dawn, and the offer of boats from Paul, Graham, and now Steve was the first realization of how closely the Kiwis were following the trip. I was an emotional wreck from the strain of the last three months and didn't know what to say to these people, who had no stake in the expedition other than the desire to see me finish, if that was what I wanted. I needed time, time to sort out my options and emotions and to see if the boat was even repairable. There were still 400 miles of heavy surf to deal with, and if I was going to continue, I wanted to be in a boat that I knew. I had chosen the *Explorer* for the design aspects that made it maneuverable in heavy seas. I thanked Steve for his offer, then asked him, as I had Paul and Graham, to give me a few days to sort out my options.

After I hung up the phone with Steve, I thought of Paddy Dillon, who had driven me into Dunedin to find a new set of tent poles; of John Kirk Anderson, the reporter from the *Christchurch Press;* of Tony Limburg, who had greeted me in Dunedin with a cup of tea at his boat ramp; of Inis and Helen in Timaru; of Jeff at The Lodge; and David and Ray aboard the *Oraki.* There was also Meri and Ian down in Bluff, and Edwina and Paddy in Gore Bay. I had arrived in New Zealand knowing absolutely no one, and now, though I may have been paddling solo, I was far from alone. The caring and the prayers of my family and friends back home, along with all the many wonderful people I had met along the way, were the energy that had made the trip possible. I was not the only one swept into the passion of this trip; it seemed the trip affected everyone who came in contact with it. Everyone wanted to contribute to the dream—to the absurdity and the wild wonderful possibility of it. My decision to quit when I was on the beach had been a necessary mental break from the strain and fatigue that had culminated with the boat breaking up in the surf landing. I had needed to quit, to back away from the intensity and focus of the journey even if it was only for two days. I needed to hear my own voice say the words "I quit." Now in the midst of phone calls and offers of assistance, another voice was whispering, "Maybe it isn't over"—derailed but not over.

I made two more phone calls, one to Al Zob, who needed to know about the wreck and the delay so that he could update the Web site. The other call was to my parents. I wanted them to hear what had happened directly from me rather than through the reports that would certainly follow Al's update. The response I got from both my mother and father was what I expected. I told them exactly what had happened, assured them that I hadn't so much as gotten scraped up in the ordeal, and waited for the question that I knew was coming.

"Are you going to continue, Chris?" my mom asked. The question was direct, without any judgment or pressure. Was I going to continue?

I heard the question and the silence that hung for long seconds afterward. I tried to hear some hint of emotion in her words. I knew my dad was on the other phone just waiting and listening. There was only silence.

I finally replied, "Yes, I am. I'm working on getting the boat repaired, and there've been offers for new boats if I want them. It's going to take a while to get things organized but, yes, I'm going to give it another try."

It wasn't until I spoke those words that I was certain of continuing, but once the words were out of my mouth, I was suddenly focused again. The trip was back on track.

The next day Kevin drove me back into Milford to retrieve the boat and gear. Dawn then drove me two hours south to the repair shop, where I met John Lowery, a furniture maker and fiberglass boatbuilder. He prodded, poked, and quietly looked at the damaged boat and the gravel packed into the split seams of the deck and hull. He stepped back from the sawhorses, where the boat sat twisted and sagging, and told me if I could get him a new cockpit rim, he could fix it. That evening I called Great River Outfitters in Michigan, the kayak company who imported my boat into the United States from Wales. They had a cockpit rim hanging on the shop wall and would send it express mail to John's shop.

One day drifted into the next as the pieces of the boat and the trip were gradually realigned and put back together. The hardest thing to endure was the time away from the sea and the hours spent walking around Te Anau while the sun shone and the marine forecast continued to call for mild, settled weather. Kevin and Dawn pulled another chair up to the dining-room table and treated me like a member of their family. I got caught up on sleep, ate well, and tried to wait patiently for the repairs to be completed.

Ten days after getting flown off the beach, I borrowed Kevin's truck and drove back to John's shop. The boat sat on the same sawhorses as before, but now the new cockpit rim was epoxied in place, and clear resin patches showed where the torn fabric had been cut out and replaced with multiple layers of new fiberglass. I turned the boat over and sighted down the worn keel strip to see if the hull was still straight. Somehow John had managed to realign the boat so that it looked as straight as when it was new. The only question was whether the repairs would hold together in the surf landings that lay ahead.

Chapter 15

It isn't the mountains that wear you out,
it's the grain of sand in your shoe.
—Unknown

BEFORE LEAVING KEVIN AND DAWN, I went through all my gear and discarded anything that wasn't absolutely essential. The extra cooking pot that nested inside a larger one was put to one side, as was the knife and fork. I kept one pot and one spoon for my meals. Two extra fleece shirts were added to the pile that would stay behind. Twenty rolls of exposed film, the fishing gear, the flashlight that had failed earlier, and a small land camera that had also failed were laid on top of the shirts. An extra pair of socks, waterproof oversocks, and the nail clippers were added to the growing pile after the initial purging. A small pocketknife would take the place of the clippers, and I would put up with cold feet for the next few weeks of the trip.

The weight of the culled gear didn't matter as much as knowing how my mind works and how I need to eliminate everything but the nonessentials when I am pushed to the limit, either by intention or by circumstances. By clearing the boat of every extra ounce of gear, I was also clearing my mind, ridding the boat of anything that didn't directly contribute to the attainment of the goal and narrowing an already defined focus. Wrecking the boat in the surf had almost broken my resolve to continue; in fact I *had* quit, at least for a few hours while my body and brain processed the options. Quitting was important, but so, too, was regaining the momentum—making the decision to continue, culling the gear, checking the repaired boat for leaks, oiling the O-rings on the stove, and slowly pulling the gear together again for another attempt. The lost time would be dealt with by a phone call to the airlines to change my departure flight. All I really wanted was to sit in the cockpit of that patched kayak and point its bow back toward my goal of circumnavigating the South Island. It was that simple. How the repaired boat would hold up in the surf was something I would find out after the first landing. Beyond studying the patches for any signs of weakness and standing on the over-turned hull of the boat, there was no way to replicate the hydraulics and the twisting and pounding that the boat would have to endure. With the last of the gear sorted in bags and a fresh supply of food for the next leg of the trip, I was ready to get back to paddling.

Four days later, after waiting for a low-pressure system to move through, I was back in Milford Sound. The heavy rains and winds had cleared the air and left dozens of waterfalls streaming off the faces of the mountains and catching the sunshine in their long plummets to the valley floor. It was a perfect day to once again set off from Milford.

By late afternoon the boat was packed, and I was paddling past the fishing boats tied to the piers and then out to the open waters of the sound. After two weeks of not paddling, the boat felt heavy, and my back muscles strained as I slowly got it up to speed. I watched the waters streaming past the slight indentation of the hull where John Lowery had cut away the shattered fiberglass and rebuilt the side of the boat. The water rippled a little as it ran over the repair, but the boat seemed to track as well as ever. The new cockpit rim that he had fiberglassed in was identical to the old one, and it held the spray deck firmly stretched over its opening. Slowly I began to gain confidence in the boat's strength and performance as I edged it first one way and then the other to see how it carved through the water. Everything seemed normal, but until I ran the first inevitable line of surf, I wouldn't know for sure. I pulled the bow more in line with a small bay a few miles along the north shore of the sound and settled into the rhythm of paddling. I had no intention of going far, certainly not out to the mouth of the sound, where the seas were still running big from the previous day's winds. What I needed was a short paddle to see how the boat felt; then I would set up a camp and try to regain the mental focus that the two-week break had blurred.

The forecast for the following day's paddle was identical to the one when I had wrecked the boat: southwest winds at 15 knots and a 6-foot southerly swell. I paddled out of the mouth of Milford Sound and headed once again for Martins Bay. Within an hour the winds began the same rapid increase as the day of the wreck, and the waves once again started to surf the boat and break in long, running rumbles of white. This time there was no hesitation in debating what to do. I recognized a nearby headland on the map as John O'Groats and immediately turned the bow toward a small beach to the south of it. Fifty yards outside the surf zone I pulled the helmet and life jacket on and tried to psych myself into believing I could run the multiple lines of surf without smashing the boat again. Three or four 8-footers rolled under me and turned my stomach in an acid tumble of nerves. Testing the integrity of the hull and my ability to focus again in the surf was going to be a trial by fire.

I should have waited for the smaller sets to establish a pattern, but the roar of the surf and the memories of wrecking the boat had completely spooked me. Rather than sitting in the winds and watching the sets, I dug in with the paddles and committed too early to the surf zone. By the time I looked behind me, a big set was rolling in, and it was too late to change course. The wave hit the boat with the same power as too many times before and immediately knocked me over. Long seconds ticked by with the same twisting, pummeling, and pounding of the boat as I hung beneath the overturned hull. Once again I was upside down and racing toward the rocks with nothing to do but hunch tightly in the seat and wait for the long seconds to pass.

As soon as the wave began to release the boat, I set up and rolled just as the next wave overran the boat. The wave surfed the boat for a few yards, then spun it sideways—still upright on its face—and raced it toward two rocks that barely broke the surface 20 yards away. There wasn't enough time or distance to roll over and hope the drag of my body would slow the boat enough for the wave to pass. If I rolled, I'd certainly hit the rocks with my body. If I stayed upright, the boat was going to hit one of the rocks solidly just aft of my feet. I raised my right knee as far as I dared, lifting the edge of the boat out of the water, and again waited. The wave rumbled and bounced the boat violently in front of it, my left paddle thrust into the broken water and holding the boat upright. Ten, then fifteen yards of buffer vanished in seconds, as I waited for the impact that was inevitable. By some miracle a surge in the wave lifted the boat at the precise second of impact and threw it over the rock, which flashed inches under my feet. The wave slowly lost its power and left me shaking in 2-footers that surfed me onto the gravel.

Later that evening I wrote in the journal:

I sit in the tent doorway and listen to the awful roar of the surf. I can't imagine 400 miles of this kind of paddling. I am afraid to even write these words—as if to write them I may already be admitting defeat; yet I know I can't continue to come through surf this size and not either get hurt or again wreck the boat. I don't want to quit, but I have to be reasonable.

The next morning I launched with the helmet and life jacket snugged tightly in place as I made my way through the "soup" of the inner surf. Two- and three-foot waves lifted the bow and broke noisily behind me on the gravel as I sat studying the outer break. From 2.5 feet above the water, the waves that had appeared moderate from the steep beach now looked huge and blocked out the narrow channel that I had spotted before climbing into the boat.

I watched until a small set rolled in, then sprinted to get the boat up to speed, paddling like a madman for a slot where I thought the channel was. When the first wave hit, it lifted the bow sharply toward the sky, threw it backward and immediately knocked me over. I came back around spitting and blowing water out of my mouth and nose and digging in with the paddle blades again, trying to get the boat back up to speed before the next wave. Twice more the bow buried into the oncoming waves, each time losing hard-won progress and all forward momentum. My shoulder joints felt as though they were ripping apart from the sprinting and the sudden bracing that kept the boat from going over each time a wave hit. One last wave peaked sharply, but the boat was up to full speed and cut through the transparent knife-edge of its crest, fully airborne as the wave folded behind me. The boat sailed all too briefly through the air, then slammed down with enough force to fold my body over the front deck. Thoughts of the repairs raced through my mind and were just as quickly discarded as the next roller approached.

Not until I was in deep water could I finally rest from the exertion of the surf. I sat on the smooth, rolling surface of the sea and felt my legs and arms go weak from the adrenaline meltdown. This wasn't the way that I had wanted to start the trip again.

An hour after coming through the surf, I saw the rock up ahead where I had wrecked the boat. I had bought detailed topographical maps of the coast while waiting for the boat to be repaired and now knew the rock had a name, Lion Rock. The closer I got to it, the tenser I became.

Lion Rock was just as I had remembered it: a wave-battered, multifaced pillar rising 30 feet above the breaking seas. Behind the rock was Ruby Beach. From the top of the swells and when the timing of the breakers was just right, I could see the gravel rising innocently to the edge of the dense green bush at the base of the mountains. As I came abreast of the rock, my mind involuntarily started slipping into the sequence of events leading up to the wreck, remembering the mounting tension of those moments of trying to decide what to do and feeling the quickening of my breathing and heartbeat, as I had searched the back of the breakers for an answer.

I let the boat glide to a stop amid the swells and sat watching the waves wrap themselves around the rock and then roll onto the boulders and gravel where I had pulled the boat from the surf. I could see where the tent had been set up and where the chopper had landed and then lifted me off the beach. I needed to look at the wreck site and see it for what it was, a place of emotional and physical trauma where the trip had almost ended, but also as a place of unique and remarkable beauty. If I set the emotions of the wreck aside for a moment, Lion Rock and Ruby Beach were stunningly beautiful; the blue of the sea smashed onto the faces of the rock, flinging sheets of white into the air. In its raw, natural beauty, there was nothing more glorious.

I sat for those few moments, and gradually the muscles in my chest began to relax. I took several deep breaths and looked up and down the mountainous coastline. The rocks and the breaking waves offered nothing in the way of a safe landing, but I wasn't looking for a landing. I was looking at the fortunes of a king, gazing in awe at such a magnificent rugged coastline. The sight and sound of the surf were still intimidating, and the emotions of the wreck site were still spinning around inside me, but it was time to move on, to get back into the rhythm of the paddling. As Lion Rock slowly fell behind me, I began to rebuild the momentum of the 1,000 miles that lay behind and the 700 that lay in front of me.

By the time I reached Martins Bay, the wind was on the increase, and thick, dark clouds were rolling in from the south. The 6-foot southerly swells of the morning had slowly built to 8-footers, a result of the low-pressure system that had brought the overcast skies and higher winds. I could have camped on the south end of the bay, where a hook of land sheltered a small pocket beach from the surf, but in a northerly wind the beach would be a trap. Somewhere across the 4 miles of bay was the mouth of the Hollyford River. If I could locate the mouth from the backside of the 8-footers, I could run the surf over the bar and get into the quiet, protected waters of the river. I left the shelter of the south side of the bay hoping to find the river and a reprieve from the exposure of the outer coast.

From 200 yards offshore the sand-laden swells completely blocked out any view of the beach. The river mouth appeared to be at the far northerly end of the bay, where the land suddenly rose to high bluffs, but there was no way to get close enough to see the channel without entering the surf line. As I sat debating what to do, the winds tore off the tops of the breakers and filled the air with drifting sheets of spray. With the winds approaching gale force and the leaden skies adding to the stress, my thoughts started to collide in indecision. Do I attempt a landing? Maybe the river mouth is farther north? Maybe I better just head back to the south edge of the bay.

I kept searching the surf zone for a way through its lines of brown, churning breakers, aware of the massive swells that rolled in from behind and to my right. My right paddle blade was on the surface of the water, sweeping forward and aft and giving my inner ear a reference point for balance. I was seconds away from gambling on an attempt to land—reaching forward with that right blade for the first strokes of charging the surf line and driving the boat towards the dunes. I took several tentative strokes toward the outer break just as a large swell lifted me high into the air, dropped me sharply back into its trough, and then raced onward to a colossal explosion. The noise and power of the wave shocked me back to reality. There was no way I was going to get through 8-foot dumping surf without getting hurt—badly. I quickly backed away, turned the boat into the winds, and started the long, slow work of returning to the south end of the bay.

After finally landing through 3-foot surf, I spent an hour wandering through the scrub and sand dunes looking for a hut that Jeff Shanks told me he had seen from the air. I didn't find the hut but stumbled upon the bow, then the stern, of a wrecked fishing boat 100 yards inland from the roar of the sea. The more I wandered around looking for the hut, the more evidence of the old wreck I found: a section of the pilothouse, part of the oak keel, and delaminated sections of painted plywood, all scattered by the obvious but unimaginable strength of a winter storm. Each piece of the boat was another sobering reality of the power of the sea.

That night I awoke at 1:00 A.M. to the ever-present rumble of the surf. I wrapped a fleece jacket around my ears to block out the noise but still couldn't get back to sleep. I tossed and turned and, for some reason, kept rehearsing the close call at John O'Groats—racing sideways towards the rocks, preparing for the impact, and then miraculously getting washed over them. I could feel the muscle strain and the boat slamming and bouncing in front of the wave. The more I tried to push it out of my mind, the more it kept surfacing.

The demands of the trip were taking a toll, the surf and the exposure of the west coast filling the nights as well as the days. This was not sea kayaking as I had defined it in the past. This was ocean paddling, where there wasn't any room for error or misjudgment. And because of that exposure, when the winds did die down and the swells weren't huge and breaking, there was a greater joy just in being there and in pulling the boat past the mountains and on deeper into the journey. The risks were higher but so, too, were the rewards and the sense of satisfaction of engaging with something so vast and wild as the Tasman Sea.

Chapter 16

We do not receive wisdom, we must discover it
for ourselves, after a journey through the
wilderness which no one else can make for us,
which no one can spare us, for our wisdom
is the point of view from which we come
at last to regard the world.
　　　　　　　—*Marcel Proust*

I HAD FORGOTTEN WHO FIRST TOLD ME ABOUT BEANSPROUT; his name just kept coming up when people learned I was heading north of Milford Sound along the coast. Most stories I heard about him, this hermit who had been living in an old miner's cabin at the mouth of the Gorge River for the last twenty years, were almost legendary. The stories were mostly hearsay, with few details and fewer people who had actually met Beansprout. No one that I talked to had ever been to his home and for good reason: It was a three-day hike to the nearest road, with three major river crossings in between. How Robert Long had become known as Beansprout, no one seemed to know. They just knew he was now married with two small children and still living in the same cabin tucked into the bush at the river's mouth.

The abrupt cut in the coastal mountains and the house-sized offshore rock clearly marked the mouth of the Gorge River. With a stiff wind at my back and 6-footers surfing the boat along, it had taken less than four hours to paddle the 20 miles from Martins Bay. I arrived just as the winds were becoming more of a worry than an asset to the day's paddling. As I lined the bow up with the narrow river pouring into the surf I could see the roofline of a tiny cabin above wildly swaying branches of flax, which hid the cabin from full view.

The run through the surf and over the river bar was as close to perfection as any landing could have been. A clear, green, 4-foot wave lifted the stern and raced the boat over the bar and the large smooth boulders of the outer break. Sunlight glinted off the front deck as the bow split the water and the boat raced into the shallows of the river. The wave gradually weakened, slowing the boat, but holding it on a straight course into a tannic-stained pool bordered on the north by a steep cliff and on the south by a cobble-and-coarse-sand beach. In the calm of the gorge, I let the boat drift to a stop against the sand and stepped out in ankle-deep water.

It wasn't hard to see how the Gorge River had gotten its name. A stone's throw upstream the slowly turning pool of quiet water narrowed between dense bush and thick-limbed trees. The brown current, flecked with white foam, poured from behind a 300-foot-high wall of moss- and bush-covered rock. The river seemed to run out of the very rock of the coastal mountains, gathering its strength in the still pool before pouring over the river bar and into the lines of surf.

In front of the boat, a well-worn path led from the beach and fist-sized cobbles and then disappeared into the underbrush of the riverbank. I dragged the boat above the highest line of seaweed and followed the path up through the damp of low-hanging branches and grass-covered stones. The trail twisted, then rose slightly higher to an open garden area fenced off with hanging fish net. Through shoulder-high vegetation, the back of a cabin appeared off to the left, as the noise of the wind and the surf reached through the trees. The gentle curve of the trail led around to the front of the tiny cabin, which sat with its back wall nestled into the native bush and its windows and low door facing the sea less than 30 yards away. The developing southerly gale lifted sea spray above the flax bushes and carried it into the overgrown yard as I walked up and knocked on the front door.

I heard the creak of floorboards seconds before the door opened outward. A tall, thin man with shaggy hair, a graying beard, and wearing several worn layers of shirts and sweaters and calf-high black rubber boots filled the narrow doorway. He stood very still, showing no sign of emotion on his face that someone should appear out of nowhere and knock upon his door. I introduced myself, then explained that I was paddling a sea kayak around the South Island and had sought the protection of the river from the increasing gale. What struck me immediately were his eyes, which were the most intense pale blue that I had ever seen. Those eyes looked at me briefly and then found a place out on the horizon where the sea met the sky and simply stayed there, as if he was waiting for something to appear.

"Where did you start?" he asked.

"Picton. On December 5th," I answered.

He nodded and kept looking out on the sea with the same intense, yet peaceful, stare. He never seemed to blink. He just stared and seemed to wait for thoughts or something more to come to him.

After listening to the surf and the wind, he asked, "Would you like to come in?"

The tiny, low-ceilinged room was cluttered as only a workspace can be. A bench of salvaged boards stood nailed to one wall. Tin cans and glass jars filled with nails, screws, and bolts were tucked between wall studs, while tools hung from rusty nails above the bench. A grinding wheel was bolted to one end of the bench. Bits of greenstone lay around its base as if I had interrupted the polishing of the semiprecious stone. Beside the greenstone was a piece of whalebone that had begun to take the shape of a traditional Maori fishing hook.

Against the back wall, a stride away, was a three-legged easel with an oil painting of a fishing boat at anchor, its fine straight lines of rigging and deep-red and black hull contrasting with the thick texture and muted colors that the artist had chosen for the choppy water in which the boat rested. A rocky sea stack in the foreground balanced the light strokes of soft yellows in the painted sky. Whoever painted the canvas knew the sea as only one who has spent time watching its subtleties of color and shifting moods.

The gray-bearded fellow led me over tilting and uneven floorboards through another narrow doorway and into the main room of the cabin. Around a rustic table in the middle of the room, a boy of eight years and a girl slightly younger sat writing with crayons and colored pencils. A woman was moving from a low woodstove to the table, checking on whatever was in the pot and whatever it was the children's assignment seemed to be.

Children's paintings cluttered the lower walls, while higher up, the letters of the alphabet—*A* is for Anteater, *B* is for Bellbird—flowed along the upper reaches of the rough-planked wall. A single large bed built into one corner was rumpled with a nestlike heap of twisted and tossed blankets. A child's black rubber boots lay where they had been kicked off at the base of the bed as if the feet of the owner were in a hurry to wiggle beneath the weight of the blankets. Four windows of varying sizes looked out on the sea, framing its blue and white rollers in neat squares. The cabin had a feeling of additions and salvaged unpainted wood that met at warm, interesting angles and held a collection of stories and adventures within its walls. The kids must have heard the history of the old miner's cabin on nights when the winds howled and the rains pelted against the windows—stories that I, too, wanted to hear.

As we came through the doorway, the two children and the woman looked up, the little girl moving slightly closer to her brother at the table.

"This man is paddling a sea kayak around the South Island." The introductions then followed.

"This is my wife, Catherine, my son, Christan, and daughter, Robin. My name's Robert Long. People call me Beansprout," he explained.

Catherine smiled a warm, shy welcome and softly asked where I had camped the previous night. I told her Martins Bay and saw Christan's eyes light up with familiarity. He whispered to his mother, "He came from Martins Bay."

Robin, his little sister, didn't move a muscle but watched with huge eyes from the far side of the table as I answered the questions her father and mother asked about my route around the island. Christan kept looking at his mother as if to confirm what he was hearing, then asked me in a soft voice, "Where's your boat now?"

"Oh it's down in the river mouth, pulled up next to the net I saw on the rocks," I explained.

"Can we go see it?" he asked.

"Maybe we should let Chris get into some dry clothes first," Catherine suggested. "He can move his gear into the hunting cabin for the night; then we can go down and have a look at his boat."

Beansprout led the way back outside, with Catherine and the children very quietly following and not making any eye contact with me. We followed Beansprout along a faint trail to the south side of their home, where another tiny cabin sat low and almost overgrown in native bush. Christan raced ahead and held the screen door open as Beansprout explained that the DOC maintained the hut and let hunters use it as a base for deer hunting. Inside were bunk beds, a sink with gravity-fed water, and a woodstove—minus the stovepipe. Even with the winds whistling through the corrugated-tin-roof eaves and the noise of the surf just yards away, the cabin still felt luxurious—four stout walls that wouldn't shudder in the wind and a real bed on which to unroll my sleeping bag.

I walked back to the boat along the now-familiar trail and gathered what I would need for the night: dry clothes, the journal, camera, and sleeping bag. After I changed into the soft warmth of fleece, Christan showed up at the cabin and asked if we could now see the kayak. When I said yes, he ran off to collect his family. A few minutes later we walked single file down through the bush and onto the beach, where everyone but Christan stood a few yards back and just looked at the yellow kayak resting on the gray of the cobbles.

"What's that?" Christan asked, pointing to the forward rubber hatch cover.

"That's where I keep all my clothes and camping equipment. Everything stays dry, even if I get knocked over and have to do an Eskimo roll."

"Have you gotten rolled over?" Catherine asked.

"Oh yeah," I chuckled. "The count is up to eight or maybe nine times so far. From here to Farewell Spit there aren't many sheltered landings, so I'm sure there'll be more rolls."

"How do you do an Eskimo. . . thing?" Christan asked.

I picked up the paddle and tried to demonstrate being upside down and sweeping the paddle out to one side, then pulling down on it and twisting my hips at the same time. What I did so naturally underwater felt strange and disorienting on the beach. Like so much of the trip, the roll, once removed from the context of the wave hydraulics and the survival of the sea, felt awkward and contrived. There was no threat on the land, no coiled muscle of the sea, and no body hanging upside down in its grasp. How could I demonstrate, let alone explain, something that was so foreign to others yet so familiar to me? I handed the paddle to Beansprout, as if the paddle could explain what I could not. Beansprout held it the way one might hold a bird's egg: aware of how little it weighed yet how much life was within its apparent fragile shell. He passed the paddle to Catherine. The same look of wonder registered on her face before she gently lowered the paddle to Christan, who stood waiting his turn. He turned the blades as if paddling in slow motion, not impressed with the lack of weight or fine engineering but rather watching the blades as they spun slowly overhead, then down past his knees and over the rocks of the beach. For a moment he was circumnavigating the South Island—arms high and hands spread wide on the paddle shaft. The blades turned, and he was part of them.

Before the tips of the blades could strike the rocks at Christan's feet, Catherine gently took the paddle and handed it back to me. When someone hands me my own paddle, it somehow feels different, as if I feel for the first time the balance and grace of it. I took the blade and gently tucked it into the cockpit, where the winds couldn't carry it off.

Later that evening after I had written in my journal, I knocked on their cabin door and Beansprout led me into the main room, where dinner was waiting. A hunter had been flown in by helicopter the previous week and had shot a deer, leaving a hindquarter for the family. Catherine had boiled the strong-tasting meat with some spuds and then allowed it to cool. We sat around the table, the children crowding in close to their parents as we ate slowly, and I answered the questions that were so familiar to me. These conversations I have had on all my trips follow a pattern. The questions begin with distant, well-known headlands and dangerous capes or reefs, then gradually come in closer to the points that are just a few miles away. "How was the south coast? Puysegur Point? Fiordland?" And in closer. . . "What was the sea like coming around Long Reef Point?" I answered the questions of distance paddled in a day, of where I got my food and water, and how I found places to camp. In exchange for their food and their company, I told them of my past trips, of my life as a writer, a carpenter, and an idealist looking in life for something more than what was right on the surface.

As the western sky softened with the last light of day turning deep blue, then purple, and finally that shade of evening when color is almost an imagined thing, the depth of our conversation shifted from my journey to a deeper, more personal level—a shift toward the intimacy of life's journey.

A trust had developed in the sharing of food and the telling of my story. Now it was time for Beansprout's story—a tale of growing up in a well-to-do family in Australia, of starting medical school, and of being drawn into something that was more a part of his family's desires than his own. There were a lot of details that were left out, details that I didn't question because that would have interrupted the story and broken the wandering thoughts of the teller.

In the late seventies Beansprout had "dropped out" not only of medical school but also out of whatever passed for normal society and had come to New Zealand and eventually to the abandoned miner's cabin at Gorge River. As he told his story, I watched, or rather was captivated, by his eyes—those eyes that had greeted me with such unreadable depth of pale-blue intensity. In this lean, aging man, who so tenderly touched his son's hair with large weathered hands, I saw a gentleness and intense focus of someone aware of the storms and calms of life's cycles.

Beansprout told how he started painting when he came out to the coast— painting the shorelines, the offshore rocks, the fishing boats, and the sea. He would carry his art inland, following the coastline to the rivers farther north, which led back through the mountains and to civilization. The income from his paintings was enough to buy him the necessities he needed back at Gorge River. He began carving and polishing the native greenstone, which the Maoris had sought from certain rivers along the west coast. He knew where to find the rare rock, which looked so ordinary until it was sawn with a harder rock, polished smooth, and wetted by the sea to reveal a green so pure and soothing in its depth. To his oil painting and greenstone work, he added whalebone carving, taking the bone from dead whales and creating polished replicas of Maori art. He made repairs to the long-abandoned cabin, put in a garden, and took his living from the sea—from the fish that he caught offshore in a small dinghy when the seas allowed and from his inspired artwork, which the seascape and nature provided. There could hardly be another soul that knew the solitude and the beauty of the sea as Beansprout did. He appeared to be a man who had found his place on the earth.

I listened to his stories sitting on a wooden crate that must have been found along the shore—sitting, listening, and eating strips of venison with my fingers. The night settled in with its darkness, and the sound of the surf rumbled beyond the wood-framed windows as I sat and looked across the table at this family living so close to the sea and to one another. While the fire burned and the children slept, I listened as Catherine told how ten years earlier she had hiked the remote and rugged west coast and had met Beansprout. She filled in some of the details that explained the practical side of living in such an isolated place.

Every four or five months, when the family needed supplies or when there was enough artwork to carry out, they would all hike north along the beach, then inland along the same route that Beansprout had been using since moving to the Gorge River. If the rivers were low, they would ford them and continue on; if not, they would use cached tents and stashed food as a base and wait for them to recede. When the artwork was sold, supplies would be purchased, and a helicopter or plane would fly them back over the coastal mountains and land on the grass runway that ran parallel and just yards from the surf. Children's books, art supplies, the basics of flour, sugar and salt, seeds for the garden, mail, and items of repair for the house would be unloaded, and the plane would leave them to the solitude and peace of their cabin home.

Catherine told how at times she missed her family. They had flown out to the cabin site several times over the years, but it was difficult not having extended family close by. In an emergency, and during Catherine's pregnancies, a solar-powered VHF radio and the fortune of a passing fishing boat were their only links to the outside world. She explained with a quiet laugh how one year they had gotten Christmas mail in July.

For all its inconveniences there seemed to be an acceptance in both Beansprout's voice and Catherine's of the risks and sacrifices of living such an isolated life. They had both made a choice of where and how to live their lives and how to raise their children beside the sea. From the simple comforts and warmth of their home, they seemed content in those choices.

As I was packing up my gear the next morning, Christan came to my cabin door and asked if I wanted to see his helicopter. I wasn't sure what he meant but followed him to the side of the garden where he stood proudly with his sister beside a perfectly scaled model of a driftwood helicopter. Curved pieces of soft gray weathered limbs formed the cockpit area, while straighter limbs reached back and formed the tail of the chopper. An old instrument panel from a boat wreck sat tipped at an angle in front of the pilot's seat. Driftwood skids held the sculpture off the ground, while the main rotor was a board balanced and nailed just behind and above the cockpit. Christan showed me how the rear rotor would spin if the wind off the sea were strong enough. He then climbed into the pilot's seat, slipped on a pair of old red ear protectors, which served as headphones, and posed for a picture with his sister shyly looking over his shoulder. All it took for the driftwood creation to fly was the imagination and dreams of a young boy pulling back on the stick in front of the seat and lifting off into the winds.

Chapter 17

A mind that is stretched by new experience
can never go back to its old dimensions.
—*Oliver Wendell Holmes*

THERE ARE IMAGES AND MEMORIES IN MY MIND that time cannot erase or blur. And in my mind I have a picture of Beansprout and his family standing in a close circle at the mouth of the Gorge River, where it pours into the lines of white surf. As I turn in the seat of the kayak and wave from the safety of deep water, Beansprout is easily identifiable by his height and his layers of dark sweaters. Catherine is beside him, shorter and bundled in a coat and hat against the cold east wind that streams out of the gorge like the river itself. And the children, Christan and Robin, are there, Robin holding onto her mother's leg for warmth and closeness and Christan standing slightly to one side, already showing his father's genes of independence. I lift the paddle in my farewell salute to their kindness and hospitality, and we wave across the barrier of surf lines.

My visit with the Long family was brief, as were most of my meetings with people along my route. Those whom I had met were people who lived closely with the dynamics of the sea, both its beauty and its savagery. Perhaps it was this common denominator of nature's strengths and shifting moods that marked our connections with a rare openness. We were no less vulnerable to the ravages of the sea than any other life along its shores; and as if in acknowledgment of that, there was a quiet, almost urgent honesty that cut away triviality and didn't waste time on judgments or values. In some ways we were all dependent on one another: the traveler seeking the protection of quiet waters and human connection, and the people ashore sharing vicariously the traveler's tales and adventures. One fed the other, and all awaited the calming of the storm surge and the inevitable parting of company. The winds dictated the hour of that parting. Final farewells were called out. New friends waved from the shore. And the paddle blade sliced into the sea, which connected as well as separated lives.

◆ ◆ ◆

One day's paddle north of the Long homestead I sat watching the shore dump near the mouth of the Cascade River. A north breeze barely stirred the surface of the sea while 4- to 6-footers rolled smoothly, then folded onto the steep sands of the beach. The forecast was for northerly gales, which would make an attempt to get around Jackson Head, another 15 miles north, risky if the winds did pick up. All I needed was another four hours and I could be in the shelter of Jackson Bay, eating fish and chips where the coastal road ended at the fishing pier. Four hours seems such a short amount of time, but time on the sea isn't measured in minutes; it's measured in spent energy and in what one reads in the clouds. With a team of strong paddlers, I may have opted to take the risk and to go for the shelter of Jackson Bay, but I didn't have the strength of a team. Caution was the better part of valor, and I decided to run the surf and wait for a more favorable forecast.

I strapped the helmet on, started in, and immediately got tossed over on the outer break. I was beginning to rate the rolls by how long I was upside down waiting for the cycle of wave to trough. The Cascade River roll was number eleven but was almost gentle compared with some of the other rolls. I came quickly back around and finished the landing, with the keel grinding into the soft sand of the beach.

That night after setting up camp, I sat on an eroded edge of the dunes with a pot of pasta warming my hands. In front of me the sun was setting behind a dark band of cloud, while behind me, over the slow twist and turn of the Cascade River, the hills rolled in purple and black contours that reached farther inland to sharper snowcapped peaks. Over the sea a crescent moon hung above the ranks of waves that mounded up in the shallows and unzipped from right to left in raspy white lines.

I finished dinner, left the pot sitting near a drift log, and walked the length of the beach to the north, where it abruptly ended against the cliff of Cascade Head. Penguin tracks appeared above the reach of the scouring waves and ran in a straight snowshoelike shuffle toward the safety of the dune grasses. Fragile seashells lay where the sea or wind had left them, their concave hollows partly filled with the finest of sands. I picked up one, walked 50 yards and found another that would nest perfectly into the first. I carried them for 200 yards, then, for some reason, set them on the end of a half-buried log whose bark had long been peeled away by time and whose wood grain was silvered with salt and wind. Near the base of the cliff, a small trickle of water ran off the rock, hit the sand with a splatter, and fanned out in a seeping melt toward the sea. There was not a single footprint, or bottle, or piece of lumber marked with the square cut of man's touch on the beach. There were only the tracks of penguins and seals and the wave-tossed waste of shells and seaweed and gray weathered limbs lying in the sand. I turned around and walked with the wind at my back, following and sometimes purposefully stepping in the bare footprint of my own track for no reason other than to minimize my mark on the beach.

Two days later I walked the same beach, drops of rainwater mixing with the salt on my skin and dripping into the corners of my mouth. My hands were cold, and the rain jacket was plastered against my chest as I walked into the wind. The northerly had arrived and with it, a sea that looked possessed, angry, and fatally cold in its ceaseless hammering of the beach. I had missed my chance to get off the beach the previous day when the surf would have allowed it. Now great rollers—thick shadows of colorless weight—rose out of the blackened sea and steepened as they approached the outer break. The rollers hesitated for a second, lost their transparent tops to the cold winds, and then collapsed in massive tubes that added to the din of a mile of heavy surf. I stopped and studied the surf from different angles, looking for a way through it and trying to imagine what it would be like on the outside. After three days of waiting, I was impatient and knew the foolishness of even thinking of trying to get out. Yet still I looked for a route through the lines.

When it was time for the marine weather report, I switched on the VHF and listened to the reports of rising barometer readings to the south. The clockwise spinning of the low-pressure system sitting over the island was weakening. The north winds would now die out as a high-pressure system built over the south Tasman Sea and the winds would calm.

By early afternoon on the following day, the winds had dropped to barely a whisper, and the swells were down to 4-footers. I launched through three lines of surf, slicing through the crests of two and easily riding over the third. Once in deep water and a half mile from land, there was no sound of the surf, only the smooth rise and fall of swells. A half hour later I was paddling beneath the forest-topped cliffs of Cascade Head and looking up at three glistening waterfalls pouring their volume of storm waters over the ledges. The sea sparkled and shone beneath a clear sky, and the gulls and shearwaters, which had been absent for three days, suddenly reappeared, flying circles around me as I paddled along the cliffs leading to Jackson Head.

A quarter mile south of Jackson Head a yacht with the lines of a fishing trawler overtook me as it powered and rolled into the northerly swell. She split the seas with a full high bow, and even from a distance her engines growled the low, throaty rumble of diesel. She swung wide of the rocks, taking the swells broadside and rolling with the keel weight and design of an offshore vessel. We both came around the headland in identical radius arcs, the yacht staying well offshore in deep water and me amid the shallows and rocks directly beneath the headland. We arrived in the shelter of the bay at the same time, the two boats gliding effortlessly past red and black mooring buoys clustered around the commercial fishing pier.

By the time I pulled my boat above the high-tide mark and walked into the Cray Pot, the trailer-sized restaurant near the pier, the occupants of the yacht were seated and ordering their dinner. Smells of deep-fried fish and grilled steak greeted me as I walked in and felt the heat of the kitchen flood over my skin. I slid into a chair, felt the softness of the cushioned seat, and the routered edge of the table under my forearms. A knife, fork, and spoon rested very neatly on a folded white napkin, which sat on the right edge of a laminated map highlighting things to see and do along the west coast of the South Island. Snippets of conversation floated from the kitchen. A young woman poked her head in through an outside kitchen door and explained how she wouldn't be working next Saturday because she was going to see her grandmother. Other bits of conversation—something about Milford Sound—drifted from the table with the four yachtsmen, two men and two women. It was all very exciting and almost too much of an impulse overload for me to adjust to. I could still taste the salt on my lips and feel the rise and fall of the boat from rounding the headland. I noticed how dry the backs of my hands were from the constant exposure to the sea and the sun and my feet were wet and cold. I suddenly felt very tired as I settled into the curve of the seat and let the heat soak into me.

After a heaping plate of fish and chips, I stood up just as the crew from the yacht were getting ready to leave. One of the fellows asked, "Were you the guy in the kayak coming around Jackson Head an hour ago?"

I told him I was but that I was surprised they had seen me in among the rocks.

"We spotted you just south of the headland and watched you tuck in close. You're not the guy that's paddling around the South Island, are you?"

"Actually I am," I answered.

"Well, I'll be damned. The fishermen in Milford told us to keep an eye out for you. And then Meri asked if we had seen anything of you."

The fellow introduced himself as Ian, owner and skipper of the *Sapphire*, a 43-foot converted fishing boat out of Auckland. He then explained, "We've been in Milford waiting for this break to make a run for Greymouth. If the bar's OK, we'll tuck in there; if not, we'll go for Westport. I tell ye I fish a few dozen pots off the North Island, but these winds and waters down here are a whole different story. Once you're on the outside, there's no place to run to if things get bad. The guys here really work for their money."

Ian then introduced me to his wife and the other couple, but within seconds I could not recall their names. My mind had made a leap toward Greymouth as soon as Ian had mentioned the river bar. The crew began recalling various sounds and headlands and how they had spent one or two nights in certain anchorages waiting for the weather to "come right." I listened for a few minutes, then felt myself growing impatient as the stories began to linger with their monthlong visit in Fiordland. I thought it was just fatigue that I was feeling but then noticed how irritable and tense I was becoming. The longer the conversation continued the more impatient I became. I wanted to just relax and enjoy the company of these folks who had seen and visited many of the same waters as I had, yet I couldn't. Once my brain had picked up on the mention of Greymouth and the river bar, I was back on the water, figuring distances and times to various points north—200 miles at 4 miles an hour with maybe a sheltered landing in Okarito and possibly another in Hokitika. Two hundred—seven or eight days if the weather held. If the surf didn't lie down, how many surf landings? And if another front moved in, how many additional days? Even while I was conscious of the conversation, and also the fidgeting and shifting of my weight from one foot to the other, I was also aware of how abnormal my own behavior felt. I wanted to be present to the conversation, but my mind and the nervous energy in my body were already back in the boat and pulling for sheltered water while the winds were calm.

"We're going to get an early start in the morning. It's a good twelve- or fourteen-hour run to Greymouth, depending on the seas."

Ian's comment brought me back to the present. My mind was being selective, registering only those details from the conversation that were critical to the remainder of the west-coast trip. Everything else was a blur of words.

With a push of the throttle, the *Sapphire* would be up to its cruising speed of 12 knots. Fourteen hours to Greymouth, and if the bar wasn't breaking white across the river mouth, they would be in the shelter of the inner harbor. I suddenly wanted to get back to the boat, set up the tent, and pore over the topographical maps, stepping off distances and looking for any indentations in the nearly straight coast for possible sheltered landings.

I asked Ian if he could send word to Meri that I was safe and heading north out of Jackson Bay. I then bid everyone a safe trip, stepped into the cool of the evening, and listened to the quiet of the bay—the stillness that was so wonderfully empty and calming, a place that allowed my mind to slow down and refocus. The quiet night and the simple awareness of the sound of my footsteps on the gravel was such a contrast to the excitement and the sensory overload of the small restaurant and the conversation I had had with Ian and the crew of the *Sapphire*. The soft crunch of gravel made me realize how intensely singular the last couple of months had been, how I had lived with the slow, deliberate work of pulling the boat forward for hours, days, weeks, and months at a time with few distractions from my goal.

The crew's stories of a month's vacation in Fiordland, the 200 miles to Greymouth in fourteen hours, the mention of Westport and of Auckland 1,000 miles to the north, and the concerns for their safe passage in a 43-foot, diesel-powered yacht was too much for me. It was too surreal and out of any context that I could understand. In a selfish way I wanted to tell them what it felt like to be upside down in the heart of a 10-foot wave and racing toward rocks in the surf zone. I wanted to tell them what it felt like to wait for an impact that never came, to roll back up and get hit seconds later with the same wildness of brute force. I wanted to tell them this but would never have found the words standing beside a table in a restaurant. And perhaps even if I found the words, I doubt if I would have spoken them because of the intimacy of that terror and the place where I had retreated in order to deal with it. I didn't fully understand it myself. How could I explain it to others? I also wanted to tell them of the paradox of a rainbow arching high overhead as a rogue wave swept me high into a stormy sky and made me feel so fragile yet so pumped full of life. Yet once again the timing and the words were not there.

I found the boat in the last light of day exactly as I had left it, resting gracefully on a mound of crumbled bits of shells that the waves had plowed onto the highest bank of the beach. Despite my worries the patches seemed to be holding well, and none of the hatches was leaking a drop of water. A tingle of wavelets was barely audible and the air was awash with the iron smell of low tide and decaying seaweed. I leveled a place in the shells with a piece of driftwood and set the tent up so that the door faced north looking across the bay that I would paddle in the morning. I liked this life, the satisfaction of deliberate and purposeful actions guided by a connection to the intertidal zone. It was like living with one foot in the water and one on land, holding one life beside the other in a balance of perspective. I zipped the mesh netting shut but left the tent flap open so that I could watch the sea disappear into inky blackness.

For the first time since leaving Picton on December 5, the stable weather and calm winds, which I had gambled on and prayed for since the beginning of the trip, finally arrived. A massive high-pressure system developed over the South Island and deflected the weaker lows coming up from the Antarctic. I set off from Jackson Bay beneath a cloudless soft blue sky, with the bow slicing sweetly into a flat sea. The 20-mile crossing from Jackson Bay to Haast should have taken four and a half hours. Halfway across, when I could just barely make out the telephone poles on the far side, the insistent beeping of the alarm on my watch suddenly went off. I pushed all the buttons, shook it, and knocked it on the edge of the boat but all to no avail. Triple 888s were displayed on the watch face, and nothing I did altered the numbers. I finally pulled it off and stuffed it under the contents of the hatch behind the seat. For the next five minutes, the alarm begged its last attentive pleas through the hull into the depths of the ocean.

I stopped in Haast to resupply the boat and to meet the owner of the little grocery store beside the highway. Beansprout had asked me to stop and let Ian know that everything at Gorge River was fine. He had mentioned that Ian was originally from the Orkney Islands in northern Scotland and how over the years they had become friends.

As I walked into his store, Ian stood leaning on the short counter, with thick powerful forearms and hands. When I introduced myself and explained where I had come from, he greeted me with an accent as thick as his ample girth, "Ach, yer a hard man if yev' paddled a canoe up the west coast."

I told him that I had spent an evening with Beansprout and Catherine and how I was impressed with the hike out they faced every five months or so.

Ian shook his head a little and said, "Ah, walk out they do. The whole family. An' Beansprout has bin doin' it fer twenty-odd years. Now there's a man fer ye. Eyes like I've niver seen before. They jest look right through ye, they do. I went to his wedding. He was barefoot, he was. That long hair and those eyes—he looked like Jesus the man himself."

I liked Ian immediately. His accent brought back memories of living in

Scotland during my navy days, and I wanted to know how he came to live so far from his homeland and if he ever went back to the Orkneys.

"Ach, I came out here in '63 for a visit an' stayed to hunt deer for five years. They were thick as could be then. 'Twas a good place to live, and I decided to stay. We used to go back every few years but not so much anymore. 'Tis home now."

I explained that I was heading for Greymouth and asked where the next town north along the coast was and how far inland I would have to hike to restock the boat.

"Ye'd be wise to stock up here. 'Tis a week's camel ride inta Fox Glacier," he answered.

Ian was about to lock up the shop for the day when I had walked in but didn't hurry me as I walked the four aisles and found enough dried fruit, cereal, powdered milk, and pasta to last me another week. He then followed me across the road and down a narrow break in the dunes to where the boat sat above high tide. He looked over the boat with few words but a careful eye on its width and length—the hatches into which the food disappeared, and the repairs that showed the evening light through the translucent fiberglass patches. I answered his questions about the repairs, explaining briefly that the boat had gotten damaged in large surf just north of Milford. He didn't say anything but continued to look the boat over and occasionally shake his head in silence. The evening light was low and cast the shadow of a bleached white driftwood snag across the golden sands. Ian extended a huge hand in a warm handshake. "Yev' come a long way in that wee boat of yers. But from here north there isn't more than a handful of places ta land 'til Greymouth. Ye mind the bar if yer thinkin' of going in there. They jest lost a fishin' boat out of Halfmoon Bay last week; fella thought he could make it and got rolled as he come in. Skipper and mate drowned. 'Tisn't the first time this summer it's happened. Ye best be careful."

I thanked Ian for his advice and for keeping the store open late for me, then watched as he turned and followed our tracks back toward the grass-topped dunes. I kicked my sandals off next to the boat as I looked out on a peach-colored sunset. For the second time in as many days, I had been warned about the river bar at Greymouth. Thoughts of the bar slipped in through the quiet of the evening and began to fill my mind. If I allowed it, the worry of the river bar 150 miles away could steal the moment of the sunset, and it would be lost. I inhaled deeply and breathed in the soft pinks and yellow of the western clouds. The small surf, the warm sands, and the sun-

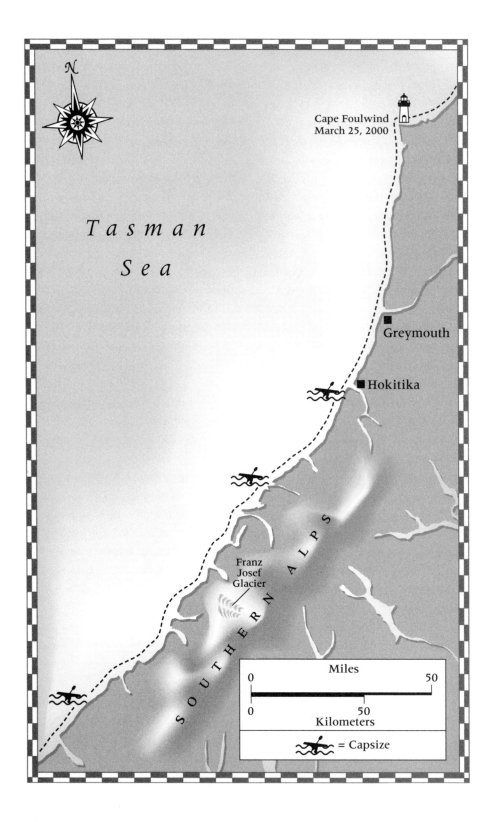

N

Tasman

Sea

Cape Foulwind
March 25, 2000

Greymouth

Hokitika

SOUTHERN ALPS

Franz
Josef
Glacier

Miles
0   50

0   50
Kilometers

~ = Capsize

set settled my mind, and I whispered a prayer to bring me back to the present: "Just this moment, just this moment."

For five days the winds remained calm while low, broad swells continued to roll in from a storm far beyond the horizon. The calm seas allowed me to push hard, covering 30 to 40 miles in a day and arriving at the next camping beach hoping to run the surf without getting rolled. Sometimes it worked; sometimes it didn't. Either way, clothes would be stripped off and hung on the driftwood while the tent was set up and the sun dried the salt on my skin.

One day followed the next with the morning's dew dripping off the tent as I stowed it away with the first sun rays warming my hands. I would load the boat, drag it to the edge of the highest reach of the waves, and try to launch with the fingers of the waves floating the bow while the stern lay cradled in the sand and gravel. Like the surf landing, some launchings went well, the last reach of the waves pulling the boat off the beach and a full paddle stroke meeting the first line of surf. As I cleared the last line of breakers and landed with a whack on the far side, I would be smiling ear to ear—the pleasure of a small victory on the ocean.

Other launchings were far more awkward and exhausting; the boat would float off the beach but immediately get hit by a wave that turned it broadside and washed it back ashore. A second or third attempt would be made by jumping out of the boat, pulling the stern so that the bow was again perpendicular to the oncoming waves, and jumping back into the cockpit. Knuckles would push against the sand and gravel while thighs would pull up against the weight of the boat, trying to lift it off the sand as the next wave approached. At the last instant the paddle resting across the cockpit would be grabbed and the first stroke of the blade grinding into the sand would be taken. Finally in deeper water a wave would hit the bow at a blunt angle and throw the boat backward and over at a near capsize. Sometimes there wasn't enough strength or will to keep the boat from going over; it wasn't worth the effort to stay upright, and I would let the momentum of the hit roll the boat rather than risk a shoulder injury. One way or the other I would arrive on the deepwater side of the surf, and the day would begin. The miles would slip past as each stroke moved the boat another 3 or 4 feet forward in the 1,700-mile journey.

I stayed well offshore, crossing the braided mouths of the rivers that drained the western slopes of the Southern Alps. The Paringa, the Mahitahi, the Makawhio, and a score of smaller rivers emptied their clouded waters into the blue of the Tasman and in turn absorbed the power of its swells, which shifted the sands at their river mouths. Across the blue fathoms of deep water and the aqua green of shoals, the Fox Glacier hung glistening in the sunlight and looked close enough for me to land and run up to. The only thing that blocked the way was the surf. As long as the winds remained calm, I stayed offshore and avoided the shallows near the river mouths and off points like Otorokua to the north of the Cook River. Here the sea gave plenty of warning of its strength and intentions as the swells steepened and turned translucent green in their final rush over the light-colored sands.

Five days after leaving Jackson Bay, I landed on the north edge of the village of Hokitika. The swells had been building all day, and the normally clear sky was brushed with the classic high, wispy clouds that warned of an approaching frontal system. The idea of a hot meal in town and a shower and bed at the local youth hostel sounded like a perfect way to hide from the coming storm. Five minutes after pulling the boat into the dune grass and rolling it over with the paddle tucked inside the cockpit, I was walking on a sidewalk and once again thinking how sudden and strange it felt to be in a town. Cars swept by with a whoosh of tires and the whine of shifting transmissions while overhead the power lines swayed and moaned with the increasing wind. I found a Back Packers hostel within sound of the surf and checked in for the night.

On this stormy, wet night, the communal living room was packed with hikers, bicyclers, and climbers from all over the world: Germans, Brits, Kiwis, an Italian mountain climber who had just summited Mount Cook, and an American from Boothbay, Maine. The atmosphere was warm and relaxed as the travelers sat in front of the central fireplace and shared traveling tips, trail maps, and bus schedules. Maps were pulled out as language difficulties were sorted and overcome. The Italian was leaving first thing in the morning to catch a bus to Christchurch and then go home to Italy to climb a peak in the Alps. An English woman who had been hitchhiking all over the South Island and wanted to go to the Franz Josef Glacier was teaming up with a German woman. Such is the life in youth hostels all over the world, a melting pot of nationalities and personalities on the move with adventure.

I sat on the overstuffed and sagging couch with the fellow from Maine and learned that he had worked as a seasonal ranger in Olympic National Park, which is less than 20 miles from my home. He had been in New Zealand for a month, busing and hitching around the island. In three days he would be back in Maine. He told me about his travels, then asked about mine. I told him of the journey so far and the distance yet to travel—of closing in on the last few hundred miles back to Picton. As we talked, the television in the corner flickered its blue-light images of the national news: A fisherman had been swept off the rocks near Chaslin's Mistake, an area that I remembered paddling past just east of Bluff; another report was of a search called off after four days for two others swept away by the sea on the east coast. The fellow from Maine had been listening to the news with me and told me again of the boat capsize at Greymouth and how two months earlier there had been another at the same river bar. I thought it odd for a land traveler to be so aware of the sea, but as he explained, he was from a coastal village and knew something of the moods and unpredictability of the sea. The news moved on to a commercial. He wandered into the kitchen for a while but came back into the living room before heading off to one of the bunk rooms. He held out his hand and said, "Have a safe trip. I suppose it's more than luck but . . . good luck!"

His words and the television reports haunted me as the rain splattered against the windows with each blast of wind. When everyone had turned in for the night I sat on the sofa and wrote in my journal.

I think I am shaken by the stories of these deaths on the sea because of how vulnerable I am as I paddle. I know by the pounding of my heart, the acid taste of fear in my stomach, and the cotton-mouth dryness in my throat what it's like to be close to death. In the midst of those moments of fighting for one's life, one does not have the luxury of measured philosophical thoughts. It is only after surviving that perhaps we have the slightest hint of how close we were. And how much more would it have taken? An unseen rock in the surf? A series of capsizes off some headland where the rebounding waves are no smaller and certainly no less forgiving than those that the boat barely climbs over? It all comes down to the feeble efforts, strength, and skill with which one faces the sea—all of which at times can feel so helplessly inadequate. When the sea is whipped and driven into a frenzy by winds and storm swells, I am afraid of it as I am of no other form of nature. There is nothing so cruel and unforgiving. . . . Some days I welcome the experience of being enveloped by the magnificence and the glory of the ocean. Other days I run from its fury and pray for a safe refuge. It is this fear—the tightness of chest muscles, the weakness that comes after the adrenaline, the stinging of salt water in the eyes and sinuses, the raspy breath, and the slight shaking of the hands—this emotional, physical, nauseating fear reminds me and holds me ashore on days when the sea is something far greater than I am.

The journal was my sounding board, a place where I could put my thoughts into words if for no other reason than to try and understand the passion I felt for the sea. The same question that had surfaced back on the east coast was still there: Why? Why, if this thing was so huge and uncaring and bone-shakingly frightening at times, why did I return to it? When I read the words that my own hand had printed in the pages of the journal, this life on the sea, which at times seemed so difficult and vulnerable, seemed not to make sense. And yet, I continued to return to it, perhaps because the sea demanded so much, but it also fed me in a way that no other lifestyle had. In its demands there was no masking the fragility of human life, yet in those extremes there was also a beauty that surpassed anything I had experienced. And in that intimacy of extremes, I had found the fullness and acceptance of who I was and how I fit into a very complicated and busy world, a world where I had, at times, felt overwhelmed and pulled far from the things that engaged my soul and mind. The ever-changing, ravaging, and seductive sea forces one to acknowledge how tenuous and rich are the moments of a heartbeat, the flight of an albatross, and the arc of a rainbow.

I closed the journal, not certain of, but closer to, understanding the power that the sea had over me. Maybe it was enough just to acknowledge the power of the sea and the value I placed in exploring my relationship with it. Maybe I didn't have to understand it any more deeply than that.

Morning brought slashing rains on the windows of the kitchen and the smell of coffee wafting through the hostel. Everyone was up early, and folks readied themselves with rain gear and brightly colored packs leaning against the front hallway walls. Farewells were called out as, one by one, most of the visitors headed off for their next destination. I walked back to the beach to check on the boat and look out on the sea, which had been calm for so many days.

The winds had returned and swept into the vacuum that the drifting high-pressure system had vacated. The low was coming out of the southwest and filling the air with energy that would have been terrifying had I been out in it. Breakers rode the backs of black rollers, the teeth of the waves set in gnashing brilliance against the sheen of colorless swells. I stood in the rain and wind and felt the damp drafts find their way through layers of fleece and Gore-Tex until my skin was tight with goose bumps and my muscles quivered with the cold. This was a day better spent within the comfort of walls and glass. The sea would wait, or rather I would wait for the sea to calm and allow me to press on.

I spent the day writing letters and sending e-mails from the library and eating in the cafes of the village. By evening the dark skies, which had offered little light and warmth during the day, were brightening with lighter shades of gray and rapidly shifting low clouds. The cycle of storm to calm was moving through fast. A following high was due to blow in during the night, bringing with it another spell of calm but cold air. I called Paul Caffyn, who lived just 20 miles away north of Greymouth, to make a plan to meet with him either in Greymouth or some other place of easy landing. The phone rang twice, and Paul answered. "Hello, Paul, this is Chris."

"G'day, mate. I was thinking ye must be getting close. Where are ye?"

I explained that I was in Hokitika and just waiting for the winds and sea to calm before heading off again. "I've been hearing stories about the river bar, and I need to know if you think I can get over it tomorrow. The winds are supposed to die out, and I want to move as soon as I can. What do you think?"

Paul's voice was certain and almost emotionless as he said, "Well, it doesn't matter what the bar looks like right now. It can change by the hour. If it's breaking, there's no way you'll get over it. We've had three boats go over this summer." There was a pause, as if he were thinking of a plan. Then he said, "Tell ye what I'll do, Chris—what time do ye think you'll be off the river mouth?"

I thought fast and figured the miles and the paddling time to Greymouth.

"If I leave first thing, I should be there by noon."

"Right then. I'll be in my car on the seawall. If ye see my lights flashing, come in. If they're on steady, don't try it. Keep going up to Cape Elizabeth, 4 miles farther. Swing wide around the cape; then tuck in close. There's bluff all along the south end of the bay, but there's a beach where we surf, and ye should be able to land there. Ye'll be fine, mate."

Paul's plan and optimism helped with the anxiety that had been building ever since Jackson Bay. At least there was an apparent safe landing if the river bar closed the landing at Greymouth. I hung up the phone feeling slightly better but still anxious about the next day.

The morning dawned bitter cold and clear, with an offshore breeze bending the tops of the frozen dune grasses. The boat was covered in skim ice, and the hatches were as stiff as my fingers as I packed away the sleeping bag, journal, and camera. I pulled the boat to the edge of the waves washing onto the gravel and climbed in as the sun glared off the white of the breakers. A wave pulled the boat free of the sand and immediately into the path of the oncoming surf. Three large waves hit the boat in succession: The first one slowed the boat, the second stopped it in its wake, and the third threw me over as it surfed me backward. It was a fitting way to start what was to be a challenging day.

By the time I was in deep water, I was more than warmed up by the work of getting out beyond the lines of surf. I stowed the helmet, checked that the spares hadn't gotten dislodged in the surf, and then turned the bow north. A shroud of sparkling silver mist hung over the land in the direction of Greymouth while the boat rode innocently up and over the moderate-sized swells. It was a perfect fall morning—the crisp, rain-washed air rapidly warming as the sun rose higher while the offshore breeze dropped to hardly a breath.

An hour into the day the sea was like glass; the smooth volume of the swell was almost imperceptible because of its long, slow rise. On one of my frequent "radar" checks, I happened to look back just as a 5-foot blue shark made an investigative pass near the stern. The shadowy outline below the fin closed to within a few feet, then suddenly slashed away and disappeared. A half hour later another fin and tail appeared off the bow, slowly swimming on a parallel course to the south. The shark passed within 20 feet but didn't seem the least bit interested in coming any closer. I watched the slow sweep of its tail as it moved gracefully past, then slipped below the surface and vanished. The image of the controlled power, grace, and beauty of both sharks stayed with me for the next hour as the swells steadily grew and I approached the cluster of houses near the mouth of the Grey River.

A mile south of Greymouth the clarity of the Tasman clouded with swirls of brown freshwater floating with branches, leaves, and forest debris from the previous night's rains. The river disgorged its flooded waters into the swells, which had thickened in the three hours it had taken me to paddle from Hokitika. From the crests of the swells, I could see a three-story building on the seawall that disappeared each time I sank into the troughs. I was an hour earlier than I had told Paul and overly cautious about approaching even the outer break, which roared with the noise of a jet engine. I couldn't actually see the entrance to the river from the backside of the waves, nor could I see any car lights, but the size of the swell was reason enough to forget about entering the river. I didn't know it, but Paul was on the pier and watching with a pair of binoculars as I sat debating what to do. I must not have been lined up with the steady beam of his lights, or I would have clearly seen his signal to continue to Cape Elizabeth. He told me later how he watched me sit for several minutes in the crest-to-trough cycles, then continue to paddle past the river mouth heading north.

The closer I got to the cape, the more uncomfortable I became with the size and volume of the westerly swells. They were obviously from a powerful offshore storm whose winds I never felt but whose energy was radiating outward from its distant center. The rolling mountains of water met the vertical red-and-tan cliffs of Cape Elizabeth, exploded in glaring white, then rebounded with reflected and confused patterns. I moved farther offshore to avoid the chaos of rebounding waves and hoped that once I was around the eroded rocks and sea stack of the cape, there would be some refuge.

As I paddled well clear of the cape, then turned slightly in behind it, I tried to remember what Paul had told me about the "safe landing" on the south end of the bay. In front of me there were nothing but the backs of huge swells rolling deep blue, then exploding in short, thunderous, sand-filled bursts as they folded over hidden shoals. I couldn't see the beach a mile away, much less concentrate on anything but a vague angle toward the end of the bluffs where the land opened into a broad valley. I worked the boat laterally through the multiple lines of 10-footers, watching the sets roll in, changing course, back-paddling in dry-throated hesitation, then sprinting from one spot of deep blue to the next. Amid the sensory overload and the near panic as waves closed out less than 30 yards away, I forced myself to take deep breaths, filling my lungs and calming my nerves, which were strung as tight as piano wires.

The waves to avoid were the ones that transformed themselves like demons from blue rollers into steep, hanging walls of dirty-brown death. I swiveled from side to side, madly tracking two or three close breakers while moving the boat first to the left, then forward, then quickly back again to the right to avoid a breaker that suddenly appeared out of nowhere. Waves that broke and narrowly missed the boat had to be forgotten as soon as the threat was gone. There were only two things to lock onto: controlling the fear and sticking with the commitment that it took to thread my way through the mile of breakers. Everything else was blocked out. Life was reduced to living in seconds of intensity, of bracing into near misses, and of gauging wave speed and heights and moving accordingly.

Somehow each breaker was dealt with, and the regular lines of shore surf slowly drew closer. I was so focused on the waves all around me that it wasn't until I had closed to within 100 yards of the beach that I looked up and saw Paul and two women hooting and hollering and shooting pictures as

I surfed the final 3-footers. Paul waded into the last of the waves, grabbed the bow, and guided it onto the sand. As I jumped out of the boat, he gave me a huge bear hug and exclaimed with unabashed excitement, "Brilliant run, mate! Ye did it just right. Brilliant. Welcome to Rapahoe."

Paul then introduced me to his neighbor Linda, and Marie—a caver, climber, and ski instructor from France who was visiting him. We had a noisy meeting on the beach. Paul and the women described the view they had of my "brilliant" maneuvering through the lines of huge surf, while I was still strung out on the adrenaline and the astonished rush of somehow not getting pummeled in the lines of breakers. After the excitement of the landing abated, we unloaded the hundred pounds of gear from the boat, strapped the boat to Paul's roof rack, and headed to his house, fifteen minutes away.

For the next two days, Paul treated me like a brother. He drove me into Greymouth and showed me the infamous river bar that closed white across the narrow confines of the seawalls; he then ran me around for groceries, mail, and repair material for the keel strip on my boat. I ate well, slept in the same cubbyhole of the loft that I had slept in prior to the trip, and pored over charts and maps that Paul loaned me for the remaining 175 miles to Farewell Spit, the top of the island and the end of any surf worries. We spent several hours pulling off what was left of the worn keel strip and replacing it with a 2-inch-wide band of impregnated fiberglass tape. During dinner Paul told me stories of his expeditions: his circumnavigation of Australia, his near hero worship by the Japanese people for his solo circumnavigation of Japan, and his various epics around all three islands of New Zealand, as well as other trips he had done in Greenland and Alaska. Listening to his tales was something akin to sitting at the feet of a master and just trying to imagine what he had seen in his lifetime of paddling.

At the end of the second day, the surf had dropped to 4-footers, I was well rested and fed, and my gear was patched up and ready for the last leg of the west coast. The forecast was favorable, and Paul wisely suggested I get moving while another high sat over the island.

At breakfast the next morning, Paul started rummaging through his cupboards and collecting food for me as I finished off a full plate of eggs, sausage, bacon, toast, and tea. He found a box of granola bars, some cookies, half a loaf of bread, and some cheese, which was all piled onto the kitchen table. Later, as I was loading the truck with my gear he came out with a salami, a banana, and a can of beer that he insisted I take as well. Paul had already done so much for me in the way of pretrip planning, offering one of his beloved kayaks when mine was smashed in two, and opening his tiny ocean-side home to me so that I could regroup for the last stages of the trip. Now it seemed he couldn't do enough for me as I loaded the last of the gear into the truck.

A half hour later he helped carry the loaded boat over the exposed sands of low tide while Linda and Marie took photos in the bitter-cold offshore breeze. After the hatches were sealed and double-checked for the last time, we all said goodbye with shivering hugs. Goodbyes are always hard for me. The generosity and caring of strangers or, in this case, new friends, tugs at my emotions and makes the parting difficult. Calls of "farewell," "good luck," and "stay safe" reached across the shallows as the blades cut into the sea and pulled the boat away from the land.

Chapter 18

SAFE   HAVEN   AND   CALM   WATERS

Silence, like a poultice,
comes to heal the blows of sound.
—Oliver Wendell Holmes

THE WEATHER GODS MUST HAVE TAKEN PITY on me as I closed the final miles to Farewell Spit. The westerly swell had lost most of its thick volume, and the wind stayed in the southern quadrant, surfing me along on perfectly spaced 2- and 3-foot-wind waves that licked at the tops of a 6-foot westerly swell. I slipped past Cape Foulwind, well offshore and safe from the boomers that exploded on its outer shoals and rocks. Every mile, every fifteen minutes of calm wind and following seas brought me that much closer to the quiet waters behind Farewell Spit.

A touch of fall was in the air, with the days quickly growing shorter and cooler. I had to wear more clothes inside the summer-weight sleeping bag, and I relished the long hours of sleep my body and mind so badly needed. I had long dreamed of paddling this west coast, and now, as that dream drew closer to its final days, I had mixed feelings about leaving it and paddling the last miles along the north coast and back into Picton. Even as I narrowed my focus on Farewell Spit, I knew that once I was "over the top," I was going to miss everything I associated with the west coast: the exposure, the remoteness, and the evenings when I sat beside the tent and watched the sun burn its orange ball of fire into the straight line of the horizon. I had poured myself into this last 800 miles because that was what this part of the trip demanded. And in the course of that energy-depleting adventure, I had learned about the volatile nature of its seas, its winds, and the mountains that boldly rose out of its seas. Memories of Jeff, David, and Ray and my shore support team were mixed with images of penguins and dolphins and individual camps tucked into the shelter of the bush. Within these flashes of memory were also the emotions of looking up at monstrous waves and straining to pull the boat out of the path of reef breaks and lines of surf. So much had happened in the course of the last two and a half months that the west coast felt like a book I needed to read again, as if its first reading were just an introduction. Each day had brought with it a new revelation and discovery along the route.

On March 29, I was 20 miles south of Cape Farewell and paddling under a clear sky. My thoughts were on the sheltered waters that lay less than two day's paddling to the north. I was almost home free. Little did I know that I had one more adventure to finish off the west-coast portion of the trip, and as it turned out, it was a very pleasant and different kind of adventure from any I was accustomed to.

I was nearly out of water and needing a break from the day's paddling when I spotted a farmhouse on the bluff overlooking the mouth of the Paturau River. I decided to run the small surf into the river and walk up to the house and hopefully fill my water bag. A low, 3-foot swell was running with an occasional larger set, but the shore break looked almost friendly after so many crash landings of the past. I didn't bother pulling on the helmet or the life jacket, which I had tied to the rear deck; instead, I very lazily started in toward the river mouth.

Unbeknownst to me, my arrival was being watched by the wife of the manager of the sheep station, where I was hoping to get water. A neighboring farmer had called and told her he had spotted a kayaker paddling north along the coast. This neighbor must have put two and two together and figured I might be heading for the river. As I started my approach toward shore, the woman had just walked down from the bluff with her three-year-old son. As she watched from 50 feet away, I nonchalantly paddled over the river bar just as a 5-footer lifted the stern and cartwheeled the boat end over end in front of her.

The "endo" caught me completely off guard, to say the least. It was one of those moments that developed quickly and then stalled just long enough for me to think about what was going to happen next. The bow nosed into the shallows of the river, stuck into the sandy bottom, and stalled. Almost 18 feet of sea kayak was standing on its nose for just a few seconds before the wave finished pushing it over in a lovely arc that landed me once again, upside down. The knockdown count had just hit sixteen, and it was a classic.

I did my Eskimo roll, finished paddling up the river, and landed with water still coming out of my nose and ears in front of the woman. "Hi," I said.

The woman was in her early thirties, wholesome and friendly looking, but with a look of shock on her face. With genuine concern in her voice she

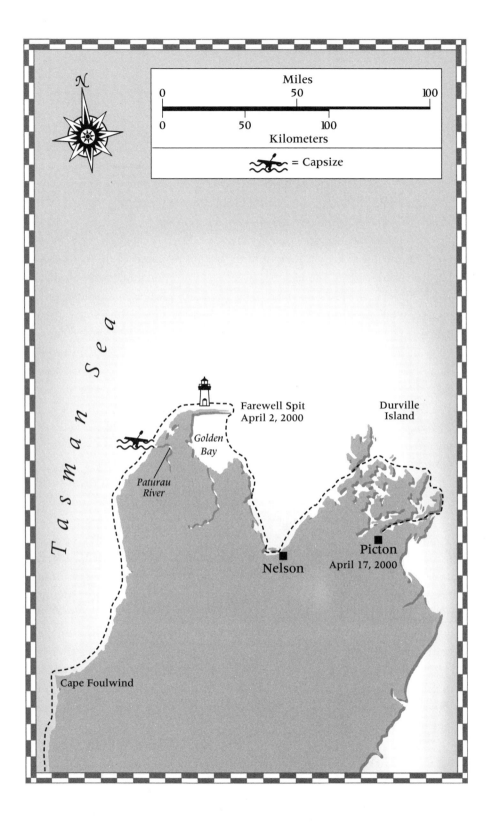

N

Miles
0   50   100

0   50   100
Kilometers

⬤≋ = Capsize

T a s m a n   S e a

Farewell Spit
April 2, 2000

Durville
Island

*Golden
Bay*

*Paturau
River*

Picton
April 17, 2000

Nelson

Cape Foulwind

asked, "Would you like a cup of tea?"

I laughed heartily and shook the last of the water from my ears and said, "A cup of tea would be really great. Thank you."

After a brief introduction and an explanation that what she had just witnessed was not the normal way a kayaker comes ashore, I followed Kate McEwen up the trail to the farmhouse. Over a cup of black tea with lots of sugar and cream I met her husband, Dave, a typical Kiwi bloke if there ever was one. He was friendly in a direct, rough sort of way and was dressed like many of the farmers, carpenters, plumbers, and equipment operators I had met on my bike trip. High-top leather boots and shorts were what the working-class men wore to work. I learned that he and Kate were the station managers of the 1,500-acre sheep and cattle station. The station was owned by an American businesswoman who left most of the decisions of breeding, fencing, reseeding, and maintenance to Dave. While he ran the station, Kate kept the books and figures straight and looked after their two children. They told me about life on the remote station, where the nearest town was almost two hours away. They asked about my trip—where and when I had started and what the southern part of the coast had been like. I told them the stories of my trip, and as we finished off the last of the tea, Dave asked if I had ever gone "mustering." I told him I hadn't.

"Well mate, ye can't paddle all the way around the South Island without mustering a few sheep. I've got to move 1,800 of last year's ewes this afternoon. Ye kin join in if you want."

I thought about it for a couple of seconds and then decided I was close enough to sheltered water that I was finally able to relax and take a day off. "Just tell me what to do," I replied.

Fifteen minutes later I was hanging off the back of a 4-wheeler, bouncing down a dirt track, while Jack, Blue, Bess, Sue, and Clyde yelped, barked, and ran inches away from the fat, knobby tires that threw clods of dirt into the air. The dogs were a mix of breeds—some long and lanky, others shorter but still lightly built and eager to run. All of them had bright sharp eyes that kept track of the bike and the other dogs bounding and careening into one another as they raced along beside us.

The farm track cut across the top of one field, down into a deep wash, and up the far side, where we could look for miles down the coast toward Cape Farewell. Dave got off the bike and opened a gate leading to the higher paddocks of the station.

"Soon as we're through, jump off and close that again, will ye?"

Before the bike had completely stopped, I jumped off and swung the gate partially closed, waiting for the last dog to catch up and come through the gate. Something on another ridge had caught the dog's eye. His ears were perked up, and his pink tongue was hanging out the side of his mouth in a doggy grin.

"Clyde!" Dave called out.

The brown rangy dog kept staring out across the ravine.

"*Clyde!* Damn it. *Get in behind!*" Dave yelled again.

The dog glanced at the bike, looked across the ravine again, and then reluctantly trotted through the gate, tail wagging and happy to see the other dogs and Dave, who was impatiently waiting for him.

Another quarter mile of flying dust, with me bouncing off the rear of the seat, brought us to where the thistle and rocks crowded out the last of the track. Dave shut the bike off, and we took to the steep hills on foot.

"What we'll do is pull the ewes off the tops first, then get 'em movin' through that cut over there." Dave pointed to a distant hill that dropped off into a steep gully. Ridges and towers of eroded rock stood like fortress gates, with sheep trails winding their way through them. A thousand feet above us, white specks grazed on a steep-sided mountain laced with the same meandering trails.

"If we can get the bloody hounds to do their work, we'll be home for supper."

Dave stopped in the thick scrub and gazed with squinted eyes toward the top of the ridges. "These hills are mostly limestone. All kinds of drop-offs, caves, and holes you can't see till yer on top of 'em—or fallin' into 'em."

The dogs were starting to scatter, and Dave calmly called out, "Get in behind."

The command came in a low voice, which most of the dogs immediately responded to. A black-and-white collie mix came and sat leaning against my leg. The others, except for Clyde, stood obediently right behind Dave, tails up and eyes shifting from Dave to the white dots on the hill above. Clyde was on his back having a good stretch and back scratch on some coarse stubble of grass.

"*Clyde! In behind!*"

As Clyde joined the others, Dave muttered, "He's lovable but hopeless."

When all the dogs were tucked in close behind Dave, he gave a one-word, soft command. "Jack."

An older dog, who looked like a mix of terrier and shepherd, took off for the top of the hill at a full-out run. The others sat or stood quivering with excitement.

"Where, Jack; where, Jack," Dave called out to the bounding dog, who was getting smaller and smaller against the rising backdrop of green. Jack moved to the right of the sheep and kept running, lunging upward with a rangy gate.

"Where, Jack. Where, Jack." The commands were getting louder as Dave guided the dog farther to the right to sweep around a loose cluster of sheep. Jack dropped into a ravine and then reappeared on the far side but ran straight into a tangle of thistle, brambles, and boulders on the other side. We could see him hunting for a way around it, running from side to side, head in the air and looking up toward the sheep, then occasionally looking back down the mountain toward Dave.

"Go *back up,* Jack. Go *back up,* Jack," Dave called out with his hands cupped around his mouth and emphasized back up. "He's confused—can't see the sheep above him," he explained. "Go *back up,* Jack."

Jack finally found a way through the maze of rock and brush and swept up the right flank of the dozen sheep.

"*Walk,* Jack." I was beginning to pay attention to the emphasis on each command word. The dog slowed from his run to a half crouch and slowly moved toward the sheep.

"It's too hot to push 'em this early. Jack's a Heading dog like Blue. He'll turn the lead sheep back toward us and get 'em moving in the right direction. Soon as we get a few more gathered, we'll send Bess or Sue up. They're Huntaways; they'll push 'em—keep barking and keep 'em moving from behind while Jack and Blue guide 'em from the front."

"What's Clyde?" I asked.

"He's supposed to be a Landish, something in between the others. But I don't think he knows it." Dave sounded a little dubious. "We'll give him a chance to prove himself a bit later."

While Jack brought his group of sheep down the mountain and steadily picked up more along the way, Dave sent Blue off in another direction to pull in another group of thirty or so animals. Commands of "Where, Blue" or "Where, Jack" moved the dogs to the right, whereas commands of "Come here, Jack or "Come here, Blue" moved the dogs to the left. When the sheep started to race in panic, Dave called out to both dogs, "Sit Jack. Sit Blue." Both dogs immediately dropped to the ground and stared intently at the flock as it slowed and then returned to grazing. After a half hour of calling out commands and sending the Huntaways out to help drive the growing lines of sheep, Dave and I walked over another ridge, where more sheep were grazing in scattered groups. Jack and Blue would funnel the first group into this second, larger flock, and Sue and Bess would slowly drive the mass of bobbing wooly heads steadily lower and around the shoulder of the mountain. Dave spotted a group of ten sheep that were getting left behind on a distant ridge. All the dogs, except Clyde, were out working the other flank of the mountain. Almost reluctantly he said, "Well let's see what Clyde'll do."

At the mention of his name, Clyde sat up from his nap and, with Dave's command, took off like an overeager adolescent. He bolted into a ravine and up the other side, his huge paws digging into the steep hillside and throwing bits of grass and dirt behind him. Dave let him climb for a few minutes and then gave him his first command to move left. For a while Clyde obeyed Dave's shouted commands, moving steadily higher and higher toward the sheep that he couldn't see above him. But as soon as he caught sight of the dozen or so sheep, everything "turned to custard," as the Kiwis are found of saying. Clyde ran straight into the middle of the small flock and split it in two, sending some in a panic down toward the main flock and the others racing higher up the mountain.

"*Clyde! Sit!*" Dave yelled when he saw what Clyde was doing.

"*Clyde! Sit!*"

Clyde just kept pushing the sheep first one way and then the other, overjoyed at finally being called upon to help with the mustering. Even from 500 feet below, it was easy to see that he was having the time of his life.

"*Ye damn mongrel, Clyde. Sit. Sit, Clyde.*" Any self-control in Dave's voice was lost. He may as well have been yelling at the mountain as Clyde raced with unbound excitement below, above, and to either side of the scattering sheep. Somewhere in his hyper-juvenile mind, there must have remained the instinct to herd the panicking sheep. The problem was they wouldn't hold still long enough for him to decide which way he should go with them. In the end he finally decided that straight up was the best direction.

When Dave saw him turn the six sheep for the summit, I thought he was going to have a stroke. The language that came out of his mouth was the most creative and colorfully abusive language that I had ever heard. "*Ah, ye #$%*! mongrel. Ye half-brained #^ℓ³* idiot. Sit, Clyde!! Sit!!*" The expletives and abuse echoed across the hills and valleys as Dave tried every command he knew to halt Clyde's run for the summit.

Finally in desperation he yelled, "*If I had my gun I'd shoot ye, ye worthless son of a #$%^!!*" But Clyde didn't hear a word of Dave's commands. He had disappeared over the top of the mountain, bounding after his panicked little flock.

While 1,800 head of ewes obediently wound their way through the rocks, ledges, and tufts of the hills down to the lower paddocks, Dave and I hiked the brutally steep mountain looking for Clyde. Every once in a while we would hear his deep bass voice and then a surprised yelp as if he might have fallen into a sinkhole or took a tumble down a ledge. Minutes later his bark was off in another direction; he was no doubt pushing the sheep over another ridge. When we finally found him, he was sitting sphinxlike, exhausted, and obviously pleased with himself. In front of him were six sheep that were wedged into a funnel of limestone ridges that dropped precipitously off a 10-foot cliff. Clyde had finally herded them to a standstill. Dave's rage seemed to have spent itself on the hour climb through the brush and over the rocks. Between deep breaths he just shook his head in disgust as if this were not the first time Clyde had fouled things up. Clyde, for his part, moved a little farther away but kept his ears and eyes on the sheep that he now considered his.

By late in the afternoon, I had learned that "mustering" was a lot more than moving a bunch of sheep from one paddock to the next. It was a careful orchestration of matching the skills of different dogs to whatever the task or challenge might have been. The dogs were sent out in pairs and then periodically pulled in for a rest while another pair took over. Dave watched the sheep for any signs of limping or stress from the pace of being moved over the rough terrain.

As we stood on the ridge overlooking the lower paddock, the 1,800 sheep flowed in three orderly lines that converged at the paddock entrance. I understood what Dave meant when he said, "One good dog is worth three men." The dogs had worked hard and were clearly tired from the miles they had climbed and run. Amid the constant bleating and occasional dry coughing of the sheep, the dogs walked flat-footed and then eagerly sat as soon as Dave gave them the command. Even Clyde was staying out of trouble as he slowly followed us down toward the open gate. At one point he sidled up to Dave's leg. Dave must have forgotten his earlier threats and frustration. He roughed up Clyde's head in a loving way and said, "Yer absolutely useless, Clyde, but I guess we'll have to keep ye." It was hard to stay mad at such a happy and enthusiastic hound.

Three days after leaving Dave and Kate, I tried to remember the strain of climbing a 1,000-foot mountain in my sandals. The bleating of sheep and the sweet smell of wool had been washed away in the winds, a southerly gale that lifted the sands and swept them like dry-ice vapor over the sand flats.

My visit to the sheep station felt as surreal as my disappearing footprints as I circled the tent again, head down, as if in a blizzard. The wind-driven sands lashed the backs of my hands and the tops of my feet and pelted like sleet against my rain hood. I finished piling driftwood logs on the corner stakes of the tent and then retreated into the zippered comfort of the straining nylon. Once again it was time to sit and wait.

I was camped on the extreme end of Farewell Spit, where the highest point in 20 miles was the lone sand dune that the tent was backed up against. Two hundred yards to the west was the last surf of the Tasman Sea, breaking in ten-second intervals. The tent doorway sat facing east, looking across the protected waters of Golden Bay—at least when the tide was in. When the tide was out, there was nothing but sand flats, miles of barren ocean bottom that held pools of wind-driven shallows. It didn't seem possible that the west coast should end so abruptly with this narrow finger of sand holding the surf at a distance. The completion of the west coast felt anticlimactic—very welcomed, yet at the same time too sudden. As fine sands blew between the tent and the rain fly and filtered through the mesh top of the tent, I tried to remember the moment of rounding the bottom of the island 600 miles to the south.

Puysegur Point had been that beginning, the headland where my transit—and all northerly transits of the west coast—begin. For countless millions it may as well not even exist; its prominence is hardly significant compared with the struggle and concerns of many of the world's six billion people. But for any crew or individual transiting the west coast, Puysegur is a milestone, a place of decision to abort the attempt or to press on. They have already calculated the tides and are aware of the winds and the lack of shelter along the approach. They are also aware of the greater risks that lie beyond Puysegur's cliffs. For to not be aware is foolhardy. Yet anyone who slips past those cliffs and carries on northward, enduring and exalting in the challenges of the passage, may well emerge from the experience with a different perspective, not in the sense of achieving anything of great notoriety but rather in the awareness of how one's life is a blessing, and if there is anything insignificant on the earth, it is the heartbeat of time in which we spend our lives.

As I looked back, I realized how both Puysegur Point and Farewell Spit contained the extremes of ocean paddling. Puysegur was where the wind and seas rushed out of the sub-Antarctic and, for the first time, met the resistance of land. It was a place filled with the drama of anticipation, doubt, awe, and commitment. I had approached it cautiously yet deliberately, knowing it was the starting gate through which the flood of adventure swept me.

If Puysegur was the beginning, then Farewell Spit, so aptly named, was the finish and its antithesis. Its very form was an acknowledgement of the winds and waves that so patiently wore away at the rock farther south, grinding its stubborn resistance into golden sands that were deposited by time and tide around the northern tip of the island.

The two points that define the west coast of New Zealand—along with all the named and nameless islets and headlands—may not be known to millions or even billions of people on this earth, but they are still significant. Perhaps in the course of exploring something as wild as the west coast, there was a connection to the whole of the world just in the reverence one experiences. In that northward passage I had gained not only a greater respect for the sea but also a greater awareness of the hours of my life. Beside its mountainous shores and on its beaches, where cycles of storms had deposited bleached and broken limbs like piles of dried bones, I had richly spent a segment of my allotted time on earth: two and a half months that I could well account for. The west coast felt like a metaphor for life, that amid the journey there were forces at work sculpting, weathering, and moving me onward to some distant and definite point of departure. Along the way there had been extremes of both beauty and difficulty, the one balancing the other. As I waited for the winds to calm, I was aware of the muscle and mental fatigue, but equally aware of the satisfaction of having lived fully and passionately my west-coast quest.

Halfway across Golden Bay a lone male orca surfaced 50 yards from the bow. The 5-foot scimitar of dorsal fin sliced out of the sea, followed by the glistening back of the whale. We passed one another 7 miles from the nearest land; the whale was heading on a westerly course while I pulled for the east. The orca stayed on the surface for several deep breaths and then slipped into the depths of the sea, its dorsal fin slowly receding and then disappearing. Seconds later the only sign of the whale's passing was a slight disturbance where the tail thrusts gently boiled the surface. I sat in the middle of Golden Bay and waited, hoping to catch a final glimpse of the whale as it headed for the Tasman Sea. But that was the last I saw of it. Our journeys had intersected just for that moment. It seemed appropriate that the brief encounter should happen in the middle of my final crossing of the journey. The last miles of the crossing melted away as thoughts of the orca and the silence of still waters slowly enveloped me.

The closer I drew to the shores of Abel Tasman National Park the more obvious it became that I was entering a world far different from the one on the far side of Farewell Spit. The relaxed cadence of glistening paddle blades greeted me as I approached Awara Head, my first landfall on the north coast. Farther around into Anchorage Bay, dozens of kayaks floated on the aqua-green water or were pulled into coves of white sand, bordered by lush green forests. There was almost a subtropical, holiday atmosphere in the air as couples in T-shirts and shorts lounged beside their kayaks, waiting for the water taxis to ferry them back to where their journey had begun. Another couple in a double kayak had a yellow-and-green sail set and were lazily enjoying the afternoon breeze.

Because of the hundreds of kayakers who paddle in Abel Tasman National Park, the Department of Conservation doesn't allow random camping. Everything is organized to handle the international travelers who come to paddle and enjoy the dolphins, the warm water, and the picturesque bays. By early afternoon I landed and dragged my battered boat up beside a dozen other kayaks and registered for a tent site at one of the mandatory campgrounds. The field was recently mowed, and there were picnic tables and fire pits at each site. There were flush toilets, hot showers, and an outside spigot where campers filled their cooking pots and washed their dishes. The water ran from the spigot into a drain set into the mowed grass; the pressurized water disappeared back into the ground, which I found odd.

I chose a campsite and set up the tent on the thick shorn grass. Later that evening I sat looking at my map and listening to the laughter and fragmented conversations as my neighbors talked into the night. The smell of wood fires and someone wearing RD, the bug repellent most campers used against the sand flies, found its way into the tent. The communal campground was my first introduction back to civilization.

The map I had used for the last 1,600 miles of my trip (the same map I had used on my bicycle trip throughout the South Island six years earlier) was now almost in tatters. On each page of the booklet-style map was the blue route I had followed on my mountain bike, as well as the notes and mileage markers I had penned from the kayak journey. The map was water stained, with mildew spores where the staples held the pages together. I turned to the page that showed Nelson on the upper-lefthand corner and the fingers and bays of Marlborough Sounds reaching toward the North Island on the right corner. On that one page were not only the final four days of the trip but also its beginning. Between the damp pages, which were frayed at their corners, were four and a half months of paddling: the people, the miles, the storms and calms, the highs and the lows. It was all there. The adventure was almost over, coming full circle back to the place where the gear had had the odor of newness about it and my beard had not yet begun to grow.

I left Abel Tasman behind and paddled the rim of Tasman Bay, which brought me into villages and past hillsides with houses of glass looking out across the water. An occasional jet floated out of the distant sky as it made its approach over the city of Nelson. Like a glistening aluminum albatross, it seemed to float into a banking turn and then glide lower and disappear from view over the hills. Seconds later the roar of its reversing engines announced its arrival.

My own arrival was slower. There was more time to adjust to the convergence of airways, roads, shipping channels, and overhead power lines that fed the needs of a population I had not seen in 800 miles. The closer I paddled at 4 miles an hour, the farther I was removed from the wilds that had been my life for a brief privileged time. It was inevitable and certainly my choice to return to the "outside world," but it was also a challenge to hold onto the memories that lay within the worn gear, the printed words of my journal, and the unspoken emotions layered like fine sediments within my heart. It would take more time than remained of the journey, and a greater distance from it, to sort out what the trip meant for me. But there would be time for that later.

The final tides of the Tasman swept me through Frenchmen's Pass and out around the bone thin fingers of Clay Point, Alligator Head, and Jackson Head. As I entered Queen Charlotte Sound, a fishing boat out of Picton plowed into the low swell, its captain waving from the spray-covered windows as his boat rolled in the swells and continued out to open water. The wind and swells that the fishing boat pushed into were at my back, ushering me toward the journey's end.

On April 17, 2000, I took the final strokes of the South Island journey and let the boat glide, then grind itself gently onto a coarse-sand beach. With those last liquid strokes and sudden, undeniable grounding, I was back where I had started four and a half months earlier. The same fishing and ferry vessels were tied to the same docks, and there was the same mirror reflection of green hills and small houses on Picton's inner harbor. A family of four—a young mother pushing a baby carriage and a dad holding the outstretched hand of a little boy—walked along the edge of the parking lot where the blacktop ended and the land dropped steeply to the water's edge. They didn't take any notice of me but continued their leisurely stroll toward a steel pedestrian bridge that arched gracefully into the blue sky over the tops of masts and piers, connecting the quiet marina to the bustle of the village.

I got out of the boat, pulled it a little higher so that a third of it rested on the sand, then slowly straightened and stood beside the boat, looking at the translucent fiberglass patches. I pulled the two-piece graphite paddle apart, slid it gently into the cockpit, and like so many times before, gradually began the transition from sea paddler to land dweller. I pulled the spray deck down over my waist, stepped out of it, and tossed it onto the seat of the kayak— black neoprene on black fiberglass. It looked as new as the first time I had stretched it over the cockpit rim and drummed a staccato rhythm on its skin. The yellow paddle jacket was next, with its powdery lines of dried salt in the crook of each elbow and where the worn fabric folded against itself in front of the shoulders. The jacket came off over my head, a Houdini act of contortions that left it bunched on my wrists, where the latex seals had to be stretched to release my hands. The jacket was like a second skin that I no longer had need of—a skin that had shed months of breaking seas and salt spray thrown against it in lashing winds, a skin that I now peeled off inside out, like a snake's skin left hanging on rough-edged stones.

I needed to strip off all the gear and leave it sitting in the cockpit of the boat and then look at it from a distance. It was the only way I would begin to understand what this journey had meant to me, how it had shattered all preconceptions I had had prior to setting off, and how it had both filled me with an exhilaration of its ocean wilderness and had nearly buried me in its terror. The paddling journey was finished, but the inner journey wasn't.

I pulled the backpack from the front hatch and put the things I valued most in its damp green nylon: the journal, the camera, twenty rolls of exposed film, and my passport and wallet. I was going to celebrate with a hot shower and then splurge on a restaurant meal of the biggest plate of pasta I could buy.

As I turned away from the boat, I had the same feelings of freedom that I had at the end of each of my past sea journeys. The freedom came from peeling off all the protective clothing and gear that I had relied upon for the last 1,700 miles. It also came from leaving the weight of the boat resting alone on the sand and knowing that for a little while at least, I didn't have to think about it or worry where to camp, or what the wisps of clouds in the western sky meant, on what time the tides were going to shift. Yesterday all of that was essential to my survival. Today, suddenly, none of it was. The longed-for

Epilogue

MONTHS AFTER THE SOUTH ISLAND CIRCUMNAVIGATION, I chanced upon meeting John Moore, who had paddled around Great Britain with two women in 1984. He had since married Dawn, one of the team members, and now teaches at an outdoor education center in Britain. As we talked of expeditions and our Great Britain circumnavigations, he shared with me a story that stung my eyes with a flood of unexpected emotions.

John and Dawn had been watching a television program on the 2000 Vendee Globe, a solo, nonstop yacht race around the world. One moment in the documentary showed the press anxiously waiting for twenty-four-year old British sailor Ellen MacArthur's yacht to come alongside for the final docking, just after she had finished second in this toughest sailing race in the world. Cameras and microphones were pointed in her direction as she stepped through the lifelines of her boat and then down to the dock. Ellen ignored the press and walked to the bow of her boat and tearfully kissed its hull. John told me how he had looked over at his wife and, through his own tears, saw that she too was crying. Something in Ellen's actions had hit a tender nerve. In that moment of Ellen completing a circle that no one could possibly understand, John and Dawn were swept with the memories of utter relief, triumph of spirit, and the countless minutiae as well as overwhelming challenges they had faced on their own trip.

Later there were some in the media who commented that Ellen's actions may have been for the benefit of the cameras. As John recounted the story and talked of his and Dawn's emotions, tears filled my own eyes. I didn't attempt to hide them from this man whom I barely knew but with whom I shared an understanding of the relentless powers of the sea.

I have since thought of that meeting and how restful it was to finally talk with someone who knew the underlying lure, trauma, magnificence, heartbreak, and glory of a long journey upon the sea. And I have thought also of the media's comments on Ellen's actions and I have compared the two—one person's understanding and other people's misinterpretation.

There comes a time when it does not matter that tears are misinterpreted, or that there are not words to speak. It only matters that you know you have risked it all on some thread of a dream, and by luck or skill, or a combination of both, you stand there for a moment and know you have never been so alive and so certain of at least one thing in life: That one thing is that you have lived passionately—some would say recklessly—in the pursuit of your dream. Once you have lived as such, it is purely yours to understand and to relive and to know that you have given it your very best. In all the uncertainty of life, we should all know a moment as pure and as real as this.

Appendix

L O G I S T I C S

Length of trip:	Approximately 1,700 miles
Time span:	December 5, 1999–April 17, 2000
Cost:	Approximately $5,000

E Q U I P M E N T   U S E D

Boat:	Nigel Dennis Explorer; 17.5 feet x 22 inches; fiberglass, no rudder or skeg; three-hatch configuration; keyhole cockpit
Paddles:	Werner graphite Molokai; 215 centimeters
Spray deck:	Kevlar Snap Dragon with implosion bar
Dry suit:	Gore-Tex Kokatat Meridian
Life jacket:	Kokatat Outfit
Tent:	Mountain Hardware ThruHiker
VHF:	Horizon HX350S
Stove:	MSR DragonFly
Camera:	Nikonis IV-A
Film:	30 rolls Kodak Elite
Total Weight:	170 pounds, including boat, equipment, food, and water

A   F E W   L E S S O N S   L E A R N E D

1. Keep everything as simple as possible.
2. There *is* a difference between a Northern and a Southern Hemisphere compass.
3. Don't worry about the things you can't control, and . . .
4. Keep an eye out for drifting apples.

About the Author

Chris Duff has traveled more than 15,000 miles by sea kayak since 1983, when he paddled 8,000 miles around the eastern third of the United States and Canada. In 1996 he became the first person to solo the entire British Isles, and in 2000 he became the second person to complete a solo circumnavigation of New Zealand's South Island. In 2003 he will attempt to paddle around Iceland. He contributed to the book *Seekers of the Horizon* and has written for *Sea Kayaker* magazine and the International Sea Kayaking Association. He is the author of *On Celtic Tides*, the story of his kayaking voyage around Ireland. Duff lectures across the country and lives in Port Angeles, Washington.